Modern Language Association of America

Approaches to Teaching
World Literature

D0181754

Joseph Gibaldi, Series Editor

28. Sidney Gottlieb, ed. *Approaches to Teaching the Metaphysical Poets.* 1990.
29. Richard K. Emmerson, ed. *Approaches to Teaching Medieval English Drama.* 1990.
30. Kathleen Blake, ed. *Approaches to Teaching Eliot's* Middlemarch. 1990.
31. María Elena de Valdés and Mario J. Valdés, eds. *Approaches to Teaching García Márquez's* One Hundred Years of Solitude. 1990.
32. Donald D. Kummings, ed. *Approaches to Teaching Whitman's* Leaves of Grass. 1990.
33. Stephen C. Behrendt, ed. *Approaches to Teaching Shelley's* Frankenstein. 1990.
34. June Schlueter and Enoch Brater, eds. *Approaches to Teaching Beckett's* Waiting for Godot. 1991.
35. Walter H. Evert and Jack W. Rhodes, eds. *Approaches to Teaching Keats's Poetry.* 1991.
36. Frederick W. Shilstone, ed. *Approaches to Teaching Byron's Poetry.* 1991.
37. Bernth Lindfors, ed. *Approaches to Teaching Achebe's* Things Fall Apart. 1991.
38. Richard E. Matlak, ed. *Approaches to Teaching Coleridge's Poetry and Prose.* 1991.
39. Shirley Geok-lin Lim, ed. *Approaches to Teaching Kingston's* The Woman Warrior. 1991.
40. Maureen Fries and Jeanie Watson, eds. *Approaches to Teaching the Arthurian Tradition.* 1992.
41. Maurice Hunt, ed. *Approaches to Teaching Shakespeare's* The Tempest *and Other Late Romances.* 1992.
42. Diane Long Hoeveler and Beth Lau, eds. *Approaches to Teaching Brontë's* Jane Eyre. 1993.
43. Jeffrey B. Berlin, ed. *Approaches to Teaching Mann's* Death in Venice *and Other Short Fiction.* 1992.
44. Kathleen McCormick and Erwin R. Steinberg, eds. *Approaches to Teaching Joyce's* Ulysses. 1993.
45. Marcia McClintock Folsom, ed. *Approaches to Teaching Austen's* Pride and Prejudice. 1993.

Approaches to
Teaching Austen's
Pride and Prejudice

Edited by

Marcia McClintock Folsom

The Modern Language Association of America
New York   1993

Library of Congress Cataloging-in-Publication Data

Approaches to teaching Austen's Pride and prejudice / edited by Marcia
  McClintock Folsom.
     p.   cm. — (Approaches to teaching world literature)
    Includes bibliographical references and index.
    ISBN 0-87352-713-5 (cloth) ISBN 0-87352-714-3 (pbk.)
    1. Austen, Jane, 1775–1817. Pride and prejudice. 2. Austen,
Jane, 1775–1817 — Study and teaching. I. Folsom, Marcia McClintock.
II. Series.
PR4034.P72A65   1993
823'.7 — dc20   92-40642

Cover illustration of the paperback edition: Detail from *Parisian Head-dresses*.
From Ackerman's *Repository of Arts*, January 1817.

Published by The Modern Language Association of America
10 Astor Place, New York, New York 10003-6981

In honor of
Michael Brewster Folsom
1938–1990

CONTENTS

PREFACE TO THE SERIES

In *The Art of Teaching* Gilbert Highet wrote, "Bad teaching wastes a great deal of effort, and spoils many lives which might have been full of energy and happiness." All too many teachers have failed in their work, Highet argued, simply "because they have not thought about it." We hope that the Approaches to Teaching World Literature series, sponsored by the Modern Language Association's Publications Committee, will not only improve the craft — as well as the art — of teaching but also encourage serious and continuing discussion of the aims and methods of teaching literature.

The principal objective of the series is to collect within each volume different points of view on teaching a specific literary work, a literary tradition, or a writer widely taught at the undergraduate level. The preparation of each volume begins with a wide-ranging survey of instructors, thus enabling us to include in the volume the philosophies and approaches, thoughts and methods of scores of experienced teachers. The result is a sourcebook of material, information, and ideas on teaching the subject of the volume to undergraduates.

The series is intended to serve nonspecialists as well as specialists, inexperienced as well as experienced teachers, graduate students who wish to learn effective ways of teaching as well as senior professors who wish to compare their own approaches with the approaches of colleagues in other schools. Of course, no volume in the series can ever substitute for erudition, intelligence, creativity, and sensitivity in teaching. We hope merely that each book will point readers in useful directions; at most each will offer only a first step in the long journey to successful teaching.

Joseph Gibaldi
Series Editor

PREFACE TO THE VOLUME

By almost any standard, Jane Austen's second published novel, *Pride and Prejudice*, stands as one of the most widely read novels ever written. It was first published in 1812 in an edition that promptly sold out, reprinted in the same year, and reprinted again in 1817 (Gilson, "Editions" 135). From 1833 to the present, *Pride and Prejudice*, like all Austen's novels, has been continuously in print. The six novels were frequently reprinted in both cheap and expensive complete editions throughout the second half of the nineteenth century; from 1900 on, separate editions of the novels proliferated.

The number of copies of *Pride and Prejudice* ever printed or the number now in print is probably unknowable. Yet those millions of copies seem curiously possible to imagine — everywhere — in places as various as research libraries and airport bookstands, on dormitory brick-and-board bookshelves or in a short row of books in a bedroom, in English department faculty offices around the world, packed in a box for every move: "Jane Austen is my closest kin," writes one teacher of the novel.

The scholars who compiled *The Jane Austen Companion*, David Grey and his colleagues, pointed out that "Jane Austen remains one of the most popular and admired of classic authors, read and reread by generations of enthusiasts" and that "*Pride and Prejudice* has always been the most popular of Jane Austen's novels" (Litz, "Plot" 335). The novel's enormous popularity persists. *Books in Print* for 1990 lists an amazing twenty editions, competing for the immense market every year of common readers and students who buy the book for courses.

Pride and Prejudice is also widely taught in the college and university curriculum as well as in high school courses. In 1988 the Modern Language Association conducted a survey of instructors who teach *Pride and Prejudice*, and the results confirmed (in case anyone might have doubted it) that the novel is taught at all undergraduate levels, to majors and nonmajors, in high school and advanced placement courses, graduate seminars, and adult continuing education courses. It appears in a wide range of courses: Introduction to Literature, Introduction to Fiction, World Literature, The Eighteenth-Century Novel, The Nineteenth-Century Novel, Women in Literature, British Fiction, undergraduate sophomore survey courses, and in courses like The Novel of Manners, Theories of Narrative Technique, and The Fiction of Adolescence.

Yet despite the novel's permanent place in the curriculum and despite the ample critical attention paid to the novel, there are almost no essays or books published about *teaching* the novel. The exceptions before this volume include an essay by Garrett Stewart in *College English* (1975–76), which uses *Pride and Prejudice* as an example in a discussion about the teaching of fiction; a brief essay by Mary Mathews, in *Social Education* (1978), about the relevance of *Pride and Prejudice* to "today's teenagers"; a whole issue of the *Dolphin* (publication of the English department, University of Aarhus, Denmark) called "On the First Sentence of *Pride and Prejudice*: A Critical Discussion of the Theory and Practice of Literary Interpretation," edited by Per Petersen (1979); an essay by Edward M. White, "Freedom Is Restraint: The Pedagogical Problem of Jane Austen," in *San Jose Studies* (1976), about the difficulty students have in appreciating Austen's novels because of her maturity and their lack of it; and an essay by Barry Roth, "Confessions of a Jane Austen Teacher," in *Focus* (1978), also exploring the challenges in teaching Austen because of her novels' resistance to simplification. Except for Stewart's article, these materials appear in relatively obscure journals, and none but Stewart's offers pedagogical strategies for teaching *Pride and Prejudice*.

Instructors responding to the MLA survey made clear that there is a need for materials to help teachers and that, much as they love the book, they often feel a need both for relevant background materials and for suggestions about approaches to teaching. The sixteen essays in the "Approaches" section, therefore, examine a variety of topics: four offer economic, biographical, historical, and social background to the novel; two connect the novel to Austen's unpublished writing and two set the book in its literary context; four suggest methods of teaching about structure and theme in the novel; and four explore (among other things) ways of appreciating Austen's language. To link the themes and strategies highlighted in the essays, the introduction gives an overview of their contents and concerns. The "Materials" section surveys available editions of the novel, provides a brief review of the criticism and some strategies for opening class discussion, and includes an Austen chronology and a map of places relevant to the novel. The book concludes with a list of survey participants and a list of works cited and consulted by the contributors.

My first thanks are to the students whose questions, fresh readings, excitement, and resistance to the novel continue to teach their teachers — all of us — and to inspire us to read and teach anew. Students' voices came through over and over in the MLA survey respondents' comments on teaching; as I worked on the collection, I found myself remembering the words and insights of many Wheelock students who have read the novel in my courses over the years. To them, again, our thanks. I appreciate the time and thought also of all the teachers who took part in the MLA survey; their responses are reflected in many aspects of this book's design and content. I am especially grateful to the teachers whose essays appear in this volume. Their knowledge of the novel, combined with their enthusiasm for this project, enabled them to frame new essays that reflect a deep understanding of teachers and students who read and talk about the living novel in our classrooms.

At several key moments in working on this book, I have had decisive help from colleagues. At a crucial early stage, Ellen Cronan Rose and Carey Kaplan gave me encouragement and concrete suggestions; at the daunting moment of choosing among many promising proposals, Pamela Bromberg took the time to read all the proposals, evaluate, make notes, and confirm choices; when the table of contents was assembled but not complete, Ruth Perry identified the gaps and suggested scholars who might write essays to fill them; and near the end of the project, when I still needed a chronology and a map, John McAleer volunteered his services and those of the novelist-illustrator Jane Langton. Ruth Perry and Pam Bromberg each devoted an entire day to helping me revise the final manuscript. I acknowledge each of these colleagues with great appreciation for their assistance and friendship. My sister, Carolyn McClintock Peter, my Wheelock colleagues Eleanor H. Chasdi and Theresa Perry, and my friend VèVè A. Clark gave me hope by their enthusiasm. My mother-in-law, Mary Folsom, read many essays at various stages with her attentive editor's eye. Joseph Gibaldi and Alicia Mahaney of the Modern Language Association were patient, encouraging, and generous editors. To Amy Raffety, an unflappable and supremely competent assistant, and Marilyn Day, a craftswoman on the word processor, go my hearty thanks. My husband, Michael, was always the most rigorous and perceptive editor of my writing, and I am grateful for the uncountable times he read my drafts for this book. We both loved the interest, difficulty, and satisfaction of marriage; our twenty-five-year conversation made us value the fulfillment that lies beyond the happy ending—a fulfillment I think Jane Austen suggests will come for Elizabeth and Darcy after the last chapter of *Pride and Prejudice*. To Mike, this book is dedicated with love and thanks.

MMF

Introduction

One day while students in my class were taking turns reading aloud Darcy's letter to Elizabeth Bennet, a student suddenly began to laugh. At the moment when she was struck with amusement, we had already worked our way through Darcy's preliminary remark with its startling use of the adjective *disgusting* — "Be not alarmed, Madam, on receiving this letter, by the apprehension of its containing any repetition of those sentiments, . . . which were last night so disgusting to you." We had noted his intention to answer the "two offences" that she had "last night laid to my charge" (196; all references are to the Chapman edition) and also his failure to answer her even more devastating criticism of his "manners" (193).

We had listened to a student read Darcy's explanation of why he had detached his friend Bingley from Elizabeth's sister Jane, beginning with his account of the Netherfield ball: "while I had the honour of dancing with you, I was first made acquainted . . . that Bingley's attentions to your sister had given rise to a general expectation of their marriage." This comment led him to scrutinize his friend, who he decided was falling in love, and Jane, who appeared so serene that he concluded that her "heart was not likely to be easily touched" (197). We had got as far as his brief though mortifying enumeration of the "causes of repugnance" toward the Bennets: "The situation of your mother's family, though objectionable, was nothing in comparison to that total want of propriety so frequently, so almost uniformly betrayed by herself, by your three younger sisters, and occasionally even by your father" (198).

As each student reader came to a stopping point in the letter, we had turned back to the pages on which the events Darcy was enumerating had first taken place, described and dramatized by the narrator, and witnessed by Elizabeth. From the letter (196–203) we had flipped back to the Netherfield ball and read aloud the passage in which Sir William had interrupted Elizabeth and Darcy as they danced (92–93). We had then turned to Charlotte's comments on the disadvantage of Jane's concealing her affection with such skill (21) and back to the Netherfield ball to read aloud Mrs. Bennet's ecstasies about her daughter's having caught so rich a man as Bingley (99), Mary Bennet's exhibition at the piano (100–01), Mr. Collins's improper introduction of himself to Darcy (101), Darcy's contemptuous attention to all these improprieties (100), and Elizabeth's anguished observation of them all: "had her family made an agreement to expose themselves as much as they could during the evening, it would have been impossible for them to play their parts with more spirit, or finer success" (101).

What made my student suddenly laugh with wonder and awe was the perfect match between what Darcy said he saw and what Elizabeth (and our class) could witness in earlier scenes. "I can just see Jane Austen, working at that little octagonal table, going back and forth in her manuscript, making sure that absolutely every little piece would fit together perfectly," the student said. She went on:

> And yet Jane Austen made it so you don't notice the first time you read it what Mr. Darcy sees or how critical he is, even though she *tells* us that his look changes from "indignant contempt to a composed and steady gravity" (100). When you go back and read it again, you realize that he makes up his mind in this scene to separate Jane and Bingley. And then he *tells* you that in his letter: the very next day he got Bingley to leave Netherfield and go to London. Now we can see that this is when he began talking Bingley out of marrying Jane. It all fits together so perfectly!

As this student laughed and marveled, other members of the class made equally satisfying observations and asked important (if unanswerable) questions about the ways Austen constructed the book. "How did she figure it all out?" "How does she make it so you don't notice how reasonable Darcy is the first time you read it?" "Look how she makes *us* read the letter over and over again, too. First we read the real letter, like we're doing now. Then we see Elizabeth force herself to slow down and try to read it one part at a time. Then we find out that Elizabeth has read it so many times she knows it by heart. In a way, we go through the same thing Elizabeth goes through." "Look how Jane Austen brings the letter back in at the end of the book when Darcy asks Elizabeth what she felt and thought when she read it" (see 368). "It's as if the characters themselves have to reread the book they live in."

One of the joys of teaching *Pride and Prejudice* lies in its inexhaustible structural coherence. The novel, drafted as *First Impressions* in 1795 and 1796, when Austen was twenty and twenty-one years old, was carefully revised, rewritten, "lop't and crop't" (as she said in a letter of 29 Jan. 1818) in 1812 after she had settled with her mother and sister at Chawton Cottage. Before I read Park Honan's biography and Ruth Perry's essay in this volume, I had a notion that the novel's structural perfection was the result of constant tinkering with the manuscript for seventeen years. Seeing its composition as a young writer's draft and a mature writer's revision, however, opens a way to understand and teach about the novel's profound examination of revising, rethinking, reviewing one's past, recognizing one's own errors when the self was in a former incarnation. Elizabeth's startling and resonant statement—"Till this moment, I never knew myself" (208)—is only the most dramatic instance of her conscious self-examination, a pattern that deepens from the middle of the book onward. Other characters contribute to this eminently teachable pattern of reviewing the past. Darcy grows and changes because of his own self-examination and self-criticism (see 367–70), and, to a lesser extent, Mr. Bennet reviews self-critically the consequences of past behavior (see 230–32 and 299).

The book's pattern of reviewing a past that exists within the novel itself necessitates a pattern of reading that is part of the joy of teaching *Pride and Prejudice*. To understand what is happening as the novel unfolds, the reader has to look again at prior chapters. Characters discuss earlier scenes in later ones; earlier conversations are echoed in later dialogue. Telling details about an individual's character are evident when he or she is introduced, but those details are understood fully only after the person is better known to the other characters and to the reader. Even a turn of phrase, echoing across the pages, can accumulate meaning, compound its irony, or lose ironic force in repetition: for example, the phrase "violently in love" or "*violent . . .* love" is spoken three times in a conversation between Elizabeth and her aunt as they try to define it (140–41); their conversation echoes Mr. Collins's allusion to "the violence of my affections" (106); and the phrase is repeated with affectionate humor at the end, when Darcy expresses himself "as warmly as a man violently in love can be supposed to do" (366). These instances of the phrase turn up in essays in this volume (see Langland and McMaster).

To write a good paper about the novel, therefore, a student is almost driven to rereading, moving back and forth across the pages. And because the novel's construction is so completely thought out, all the student's work pays off, for it yields insights that cannot come on first reading.

Four essays in this collection explore ways that thematic patterns in the novel's structure can shape and inform approaches to teaching. My essay suggests how the problem of right interpretation of the social world, what I call the theme of knowing, can be turned into a way of teaching the novel. I see the first proposal scene, Darcy's letter, and Elizabeth's introspection after reading it as the decisive structural moments that make the two halves of the novel different, and I find Austen's treatment of the theme of knowing different before and after those events. In the first half of the book, Austen emphasizes the ambiguity of experience and the fallibility of interpretation; in the second, she examines the patterns of introspection that produce growth in both thinking and feeling.

Bruce Stovel in his essay discovers a remarkably coherent (and teachable) pattern of *fives* in the first and second halves of the novel: five apparent secrets and five real secrets, concealed by different kinds of silence; five surprises to Elizabeth and five surprises to Elizabeth *and* to the reader. Using a hilarious squib that Jane Austen wrote when she was thirteen, Stovel shows how central to her plotting are the concepts of silence, secrets, and surprise. His emphasis on the unexpected gives Stovel a particularly perceptive understanding of first-time readers of the book—most of our students.

Juxtaposing various marriages within *Pride and Prejudice*, Pamela S. Bromberg looks at the contrasting courtships of Elizabeth, Jane, Lydia, and Charlotte Lucas; she considers how the failed Bennet marriage comments on all these matches. She also shows how teachers may construct classroom debate about the dissimilar attitudes toward marriage in the speeches and actions of Elizabeth and Charlotte. In joining this debate, students also can compare this novel with other works built on the marriage plot, such as *Jane Eyre*, *A Doll House*, Kate Chopin's *The Awakening*, or the contemporary novels *The Bluest Eye* (Toni Morrison) and *The Middle Ground* (Margaret Drabble).

Moving from the marriage plot to the family plot, Paula Bennett views *Pride and Prejudice* as a novel about parenting. She argues that the novel is less about marriage than about what comes after marriage — that is, families. Bennett subjects the novel to analysis informed by family systems theory and finds that the structure of the Bennet family corresponds, with startling exactitude, to characteristic patterns of dysfunctional families. Bromberg's essay suggests an approach to teaching the novel that would be suitable in historically organized women's literature or introductory fiction courses, whereas Bennett's approach is particularly appropriate for thematic courses on the literature of adolescence or families in literature.

A second great satisfaction in teaching *Pride and Prejudice* — as teachers who replied to the MLA's survey noted over and over — is the chance to share with students the subtlety, precision, compression, surprise, and wit of its language. Critical works about the language of *Pride and Prejudice* — studies of narrative technique, dialogue and interior monologue, and Austen's diction — have been among the most richly suggestive sources for teachers. Such works have been influential because they enable teachers to help students focus on the finite — on local sentences, phrases, and individual words — and at the same time develop larger patterns of meaning across the novel. Attention to language also encourages students to slow down and thus give the novel the kind of careful reading it deserves.

Many approaches to language in the novel yield consistent patterns — the kinds of repetition that students become adept at tracing, accumulating examples as they read, coincidentally sharpening their sensibilities as readers and as writers. Stovel knew a student who proposed to write a paper on Austen's use of pronouns in *Pride and Prejudice*. "Pronouns?" Stovel thought. But the student's paper demonstrated the subtlety, drama, care of placement, and indeed moral significance in Austen's use of that part of speech. "*You* may ask questions, which *I* shall choose not to answer," Elizabeth asserts to Lady Catherine (354).

Two essays that are not in this collection, one widely known and one obscure, I mention here to suggest how useful critical studies about Austen's language can be to teachers. The first, a commentary on language that was praised by many respondents to the MLA survey on teaching *Pride and Prejudice*, is Joann Morse's brief afterword in the Signet edition (one of the most popular editions in college courses). Morse highlights Austen's creation of an unmistakable speaking voice for each character. "On the one hand," Morse writes, "there is the racy slang of Lydia, 'A little sea bathing would set me up forever'; on the other is the austere priggishness of Darcy, 'I cannot comprehend the neglect of a family library in such days as these'" (328). In contrast to both, she points out, the narrator's language is notable for its polite restraint, as when the narrator says the Bingley sisters "indulge their mirth" rather than that they "sneer." The narrative voice thus sets a standard of politeness that the characters do not meet; the discrepancy measures a character's crudeness, inadequacy, self-importance, unkindness, or hysteria. Against these contrasts, Morse sets Elizabeth's way of talking: "And is this all? I expected at least that the pigs were got into the garden, and here is nothing but Lady Catherine and her daughter!" (158). It is Elizabeth's idiom, "supple and mixed," that demonstrates her intelligence, wit, resistance to pomposity, and realism. Many teachers assign Morse's afterword because it suggests how students may get close to the novel's meaning by attending to dialogue, speech by speech, and by noting the difference between characters' speeches and the narrator's language framing those speeches.

For another example of how attention to details of language can uncover surprising and teachable configurations, consider a brief essay published in *Sydney Studies in English*. In "A Measure of Excellence: Modes of Comparison in *Pride and Prejudice*," J. F. Burrows takes up the apparently simple grammatical matter of how characters and the narrator use comparative and superlative constructions, and he finds patterns that are remarkably consistent and intellectually rigorous. Unthinking characters and the unthinking voice of society frequently use extravagant superlatives: "He was the proudest, most disagreeable man in the world"; Mr. Collins expects to be "the happiest of men"; Jane, Mrs. Bennet says, has "the sweetest temper I ever met with"; Lady Catherine grandly claims, "[N]obody feels the loss of friends so much as I do"; and Lydia gushes that Wickham "did every thing best in the world; and she was sure he would kill more birds on the first of September, than any body else in the country" (11, 122, 42, 210, 318). Burrows notes that although Austen, in the first half of the book, "maintains a degree of restraint over Elizabeth's superlatives" (41), Elizabeth does use them: "You could not make *me* happy, and I am convinced that I am the last woman in the world who could make *you* so" (107). But her growth is marked by her more sparing, sensitive, and discriminating use of both comparatives and superlatives and by her "idiosyncratic line of comparison" (Burrows 55): "I will not be alarmed though your sister *does* play so well" (174). Darcy's comparisons are marked almost from the beginning by intelligent restraint and discrimination: "She is now about Miss Elizabeth Bennet's height, or rather taller" or "it is many months since I have considered her as one of the handsomest women of my acquaintance." Jane Bennet, significantly, eschews all comparisons. Mr. Bennet of course uses comparisons ironically: of his three sons-in-law, he says to

Elizabeth: "Wickham, perhaps, is my favourite; but I think I shall like *your* husband as well as Jane's" (38, 271, 379).

Once a class begins identifying Austen's subtle and flexible use of any language pattern, it yields insights about every character and the narrator's own mode of thinking. Such configurations may be taught in the classroom by having the teacher and students read aloud, by setting up dramatic readings with different speakers taking on the parts of characters and the narrator, and by close reading of specific passages. Students who may at first find Austen's language remote in its formality soon realize how dramatic, brilliant, and funny it is. Reading chapter 1 aloud is a good place to start. This kind of work gives students confidence in their ability to identify tone and to understand the sources of humor. From dramatic readings of dialogue that make the comedy accessible, it is logical to move to close readings of narrated passages, in which complex moral issues are weighed, deep feeling expressed, and subtle discriminations drawn. The essays in this collection on the subject of language suggest how fresh, how resistant to our ever writing the last word, and how perennially analyzable the language of *Pride and Prejudice* remains.

Four essays in this collection focus on teaching about language. Elizabeth Langland's meticulous close readings of three narrative passages that contain no dialogue demonstrate the remarkable responsiveness of Austen's prose to a formalist approach. Her analysis of the novel's celebrated first sentence highlights the tensions in it between money and love, single and married, man and woman, husband and wife, surface and substance; it suggests the apparent impossibility of ever making a definitive statement about the subtleties and complexity of that opening line. Langland next examines the long passage of consonant psychonarration and free indirect discourse when Elizabeth ponders Mrs. Gardiner's letter about Darcy's rescue of Lydia and seeks to understand what that story must mean about his feelings (326–27). Finally, Langland considers, sentence by sentence, the second proposal scene, in which Austen renders the conversation of Darcy and Elizabeth in indirect discourse and from a distanced, omniscient view (366). Langland's scrupulous analysis provides teachers with a vocabulary for discriminating shades of meaning and intention in the narrator's language and for debating with John Halperin's denunciation of the scene as a failure (see Halperin's opinion quoted in Fraiman's essay).

In contrast to Langland, Marylea Meyersohn focuses on dialogue, rather than on the narrator's language, particularly on the exchanges between Darcy and Elizabeth, which she calls "duets": "the speech acts of talkers and listeners who jointly construct social reality." Arguing that this is the Austen work most concerned with conversation, Meyersohn shows that learning to speak the language of love is the subject of the novel. Because her interests are speech and conversation, Meyersohn looks at the direct discourse of Elizabeth and Darcy, their duets, before and after the second proposal, skipping the narrated passage that Langland reads closely.

Susan Kneedler's essay, "The New Romance in *Pride and Prejudice*," examines that whole scene, direct and indirect discourse, in yet another way: it offers, Kneedler suggests, an opportunity for students to participate in the happy ending more fully than if the proposal were dramatized. Because teachers may treat the scene as "a process . . . that must be imagined" rather than overheard, student readers are invited into the ending not just as "would-be heroines, vicarious protagonists lost in Austen's creation, but as readers." In Kneedler's approach to teaching the scene, the student gains a role as imaginative creator.

Kneedler's essay also provides teachers with a way to teach the last nineteen chapters of the book, for she demonstrates that, in those chapters, Austen is not just tying up threads of the plot. Instead, the unfolding events repeatedly surprise Elizabeth, who keeps expecting that Darcy's love "could not in rational expectation survive such a blow" as Lydia's running away with Wickham and its consequences (311). Elizabeth's astonishment reflects what Kneedler calls "the conventional expectation that men cannot be loyal and deeply attached lovers." The plotting of the last nineteen chapters makes Elizabeth often doubt that Darcy could continue to love her despite the damage to her family's respectability; her repeated surprise at discovering that he still loves her measures, in effect, his goodness and generosity. In her essay, Kneedler argues that this careful enlarging of the hero's worth makes him worthy of the maturing Elizabeth and ensures that marriage and erotic attachment are at least equal — in tenderness, mutual sympathy, and disinterested concern for the well-being of the other — to the love between strongly devoted sisters.

Finally, Juliet McMaster discusses another kind of close reading: reading aloud. In her class, students take on the roles of characters in the novel and learn not only to play their parts but to create language and dialogue for characters whom they attempt to know from the inside. In "Talking about Talking," McMaster maps out a geography of conversation and shows how students may understand characters by what they say, the ways they speak, how much they say, what they leave unsaid, and what they say about their own and each other's ways of talking.

A third satisfaction in teaching *Pride and Prejudice* was evident in many teachers' comments on the MLA survey: students love the novel's optimism, joyful spirit, and success in combining personal happiness with responsibility. Julia Prewitt Brown says, "It is interesting to note how frequently the word *happiness* appears in the novel"; Ruth Perry writes of the "sheer happiness of the novel" and describes Elizabeth's happiness. Perry speculates that *Pride and Prejudice* is so joyous and that the word *happiness* appears in it so often because the mood of the book reflects the two periods of greatest joy and optimism in the writer's life, when the novel was drafted at Steventon and when it was rewritten in 1812 at Chawton. Student readers, according to teachers' comments, feel the novel's zest, and teachers sometimes indicated surprise at students' enthusiasm about this aspect of the book: "Overwhelmingly [they like] the characterization, particularly the deftness of it, but also (surprisingly to me) many students are touched by the love story." "It is my most successful novel in class, repeatedly. Students sometimes express wild enthusiasm." "The book is widely enjoyed. They like its psychological texture — its characters come alive." "Students at all levels enjoy it more than any other Jane Austen novel, and I consider it her best work." "Students are enthusiastic about the book. They love the ironical treatment of romance and yet the wish fulfillment of getting one's fondest desire and deserving it to boot." "Most students love Elizabeth Bennet." "Elizabeth and her wit appeal the most." "They appreciate the multiple levels of Elizabeth's appeal."

Pamela Bromberg, a contributor to this volume, comments: "My students almost all enjoy reading *Pride and Prejudice*. A love story with the happy ending of desire fulfilled and legitimized in marriage is, for many of them, the quintessential novel. They would like to tell the same kind of story about their own lives. They recognize their own families and friends in Austen's characters and identify powerfully with Elizabeth Bennet, admiring her wit, independence, self-regard, and capacity for growth. *Pride and Prejudice* supplies an imaginative arena in which students may rehearse their own struggles and strategies for accommodating individual will and romantic dream with social reality."

Jane Austen referred deprecatingly to the buoyant quality of *Pride and Prejudice* in a letter to Cassandra: "The work is rather too light, and bright, and sparkling; it wants shade; it wants to be stretched out here and there with a long chapter of sense, if it could be had; if not, of solemn specious nonsense" (4 Feb. 1813). Her criticism contains its own denial: Austen implies that a "long chapter of sense" would be as welcome in the book as one of "solemn specious nonsense." And despite her comment, there *are* many kinds of "shade" in the book, somber elements that are discussed in several essays in this volume. There is Mr. Bennet's "debilitating weariness" (as Brown terms it), the brutal implications of Charlotte's marriage (see Copeland and Bromberg), Lydia's relation to her family (see Bennett), the limitations placed on female friendship in the novel (see Kaplan), and the glaring unhappiness of the Bennet marriage (see Copeland, Bromberg, and Bennett). Nevertheless, Brown, Perry, Stovel, Kneedler, and McMaster shed light on the celebratory spirit of the novel and suggest that Austen may have been laughing when she said it was *too* "light, and bright, and sparkling." It is, and she thought so too, just sparkling enough.

If its structural coherence, brilliant language, and joyful mood are three of the reasons that *Pride and Prejudice* is a success in the classroom, what are some of the obstacles to teaching it? In an excellent essay written in the early 1960s, Ian Watt identified several kinds of resistance to the novel, and these objections are still expressed in college classrooms. One could be called the "Mark Twain" problem: the resistance of undergraduates to genteel characters who converse in drawing rooms, dance in ballrooms, observe decorum unfamiliar to modern students, and speak with unfamiliar elegance. In an unpublished manuscript that Watt cites, Twain mentions his response to this novel in terms both swaggering and defensive: "Whenever I take up Pride and Prejudice . . . I feel like a barkeeper entering the Kingdom of Heaven" (7). Watt argues that a cultural preference for spontaneity, naturalness, and physical vigor can make Twain or Charlotte Brontë more appealing to American students than Austen. He also observes that there are elements in Austen's novels of a "peculiarly English nature which do not travel well: the class system, the insistence on manners and decorum, the reverence for what is established" (6). Sometimes students sound indignant as well as impatient with the book: "Her characters are stiff; she is concerned with trivia. Why should we waste our time on this?"

At a slightly more sophisticated level, students may resist the book because of what Lionel Trilling called the "work ethic versus leisure" problem, as he noted in "Why We Read Jane Austen," an essay left uncompleted at his death. A recent essay on this topic notes that Austen's novels lack an "emphasis on sustained work as a means of achieving fulfillment" and that students may feel a moral objection to the novels because of this (Nardin, "Jane Austen" 122). Since most American college students feel intense pressure to choose a major and finish their education in preparation for a job, the absence of a work ethic in a novel like Pride and Prejudice makes it seem frivolous to many of them. They sometimes ask, "What did these people do all day? How did they earn a living?" The questions may be particularly pressing for students who seek to change their social class through education and hard work or who identify with the nearly invisible servants in the book. Students of mine have noticed with amazement the tone of "asperity" with which Mrs. Bennet assures Mr. Collins "that they were very well able to keep a good cook, and that her daughters had nothing to do in the kitchen" (65). To most students, such ignorance is nothing to boast about.

These two problems in teaching Pride and Prejudice — students' resistance to a genteel society and to a world without a work ethic — are obviously related. Teachers can help students overcome these objections by placing the novel accurately in its historical context, by explaining social class in late-eighteenth-century England, and by providing students with economic and literary backgrounds to the novel. Yet this context is exactly what many teachers find difficult to explain, and for which reliable, up-to-date, and pertinent background materials seem hard to locate. In fact, in their responses to the question "What sort of information would you like to see included in a volume on teaching this book?" teachers repeatedly cited a need for historical, economic, literary, and biographical background materials. "We need cultural history, especially on marriage, class, and gender roles." "I need an account of the distinctions between social classes and a discussion of the roles of women — and the choices open to genteel women without money. We also need something about all the social ranks and an explanation of money, income, servants, 'trade,' land ownership, inheritance — all kinds of economic and social history that my students (and I) know practically nothing about." "Neither my students nor I have read the novels Jane Austen read, so it's very hard for me to set the novel in literary context. I would appreciate something about the eighteenth-century novel and Austen's reworking of its traditions." "It would be useful to have a brief biography relevant to the novel and suggestions about using the juvenilia, letters, or other novels in teaching the book."

The first half of the "Approaches" section includes eight essays that offer relevant and accessible background materials about the social and economic history of Austen's day, biographical sources that illuminate the novel's relevance to the author's life, and information about the relation between *Pride and Prejudice* and late-eighteenth-century literary history.

The first essay in the group, Edward Copeland's foray into the thicket of economic comparisons, provides us with exact, amusing, and appalling terms for comparing pounds in Austen's day with dollars in our own. Copeland has a keen understanding of what students really want to know, what they mean when they ask questions like "But how rich is he really?" Although he admirably resists the temptation to simplify issues, his essay makes startlingly clear how "dizzying the economic stakes" are in the novel. Copeland's essay comes first because the underlying economic plot is essential to the novel's meaning and because grasping the economic realities of Austen's day is such a struggle for students and teachers.

In the second essay, "Home at Last," Ruth Perry uses the biographical resources of Austen's letters, the new Deirdre Le Faye *Family Record*, and the recent biography by Park Honan to uncover the relations between the novel and Austen's life. Tracing a patchwork of biographical details that reflect the novelist's own experience, Perry goes beyond those resemblances to explain the more profound ways that the mood and spirit of the book reflect the times of its composition. She accepts (as Fraiman does) the essential argument in Q. D. Leavis's important *Scrutiny* essays about Austen's development as a writer. According to Leavis, it is impossible that Austen wrote only in two bursts, one from 1795 to 1798 and the other from 1810 to 1817. Instead, Leavis thinks, even during the years when the family had no settled residence, Austen must have been writing "unceasingly." Perry believes, however, that *Pride and Prejudice* was probably set aside after it was first composed and taken up again at Chawton, for, as noted earlier, the tone and texture of the novel suggest that it was drafted and revised at the two periods of greatest hope and self-confidence in Austen's life.

In "The 'Social History' of *Pride and Prejudice*," Julia Prewitt Brown takes on the ambitious project of answering the question, In what sense *would* being mistress of Pemberley "be something"? The essay explains the central public position that family and marriage occupied in Austen's day, in contrast to their relatively private and diminished significance in our own. Brown places *Pride and Prejudice* in the Austen canon by considering the changing ways that the novels represent the concept of a "private domain." She measures with a steady eye and deep sympathy the limited options open to genteel women who did not marry. Together, Brown's essay and Copeland's make Elizabeth's spirit, courage, and independence seem impressive indeed, shadowed as they are by the Charlotte Lucas Collins story, which can be fully comprehended only in the light of that background.

Johanna M. Smith, taking on the task of exploring the British social ranks and class hierarchy that are so opaque to American readers, suggests how teachers can use such information to illuminate *Pride and Prejudice*. Smith realizes that students resist understanding or even hearing about British class distinctions because they consider them petty, pretentious, externally imposed, or not significant for the truly independent individual. She works through that resistance by diagraming the British class structure for her students and then having them map out the locations of characters from *Pride and Prejudice* on the diagram. In her essay, "'I Am a Gentleman's Daughter': A Marxist-Feminist Reading of *Pride and Prejudice*," Smith provides a template for understanding the rigid and flexible aspects of class rank in British society, a scheme that illuminates all the Austen novels as well as later British fiction. Smith is exceptionally adroit in playing off against each other the implications of class and gender politics. For example, she points out that, in Elizabeth's triumph over Lady Catherine, Austen is criticizing the arrogance of the landed aristocracy; in giving such class pride to the aristocratic *woman*, the novelist is, at the same time, diminishing the power of such a view. Smith's political approach to these issues helps students comprehend how our own ideologies inform our responses to novels.

Two feminist essays make connections between *Pride and Prejudice* and other writing by Austen. In "Peevish Accents in the Juvenilia: A Feminist Key to *Pride and Prejudice*," Susan Fraiman discovers some of the novel's thematic material and narrative concerns in the much earlier juvenilia and also finds prototypes of such characters as the haughty aristocrat, the three sisters, and the undiscriminating suitor. More important, in *Love and Freindship* (sic), Fraiman finds in cruder, bolder form some of the political concerns of the mature novel. She suggests that when selections from the juvenilia are taught with the novel, students gain access to a "bedrock" of Austen's opinions from the rebellious climate of the 1790s, including Austen's critique of marriage, male authority, and proper femininity.

Deborah Kaplan's essay, "*Pride and Prejudice* and Jane Austen's Female Friendships," makes two important arguments. First, Kaplan notes, students can demonstrate that, despite the loving empathy between the oldest Bennet sisters, their close bonds do not supersede their dependence on men. She then explains what students can learn from Austen's letters, beginning with one or two of them read cold in class. Of the 154 or so surviving letters, according to Kaplan, "almost any will do." After leading a classroom conversation about the difficulty in understanding the letters, which of course were not intended for publication and "do not reach out, with extended narratives, intermittent explanations, or even appositives, to strangers," Kaplan goes on to show what the letters suggest about Austen's attitudes toward love and friendship — her old pair of opposites. Comparing female friendship in the letters with its representation in the novel reveals its superior importance in Austen's life. Kaplan's essay implicitly engages a question posed by the critic Carolyn Heilbrun about the fiction of George Eliot: Why is it that women writers do not create heroines who are as outspoken, creative, and successful in combining rich private and public lives as the writers are themselves (Heilbrun 37, 89, 97)? Why does Austen limit the depth and freedom of female friendship in the novel, in contrast to the significance of such friendship in her life? To answer the question, Kaplan reminds her students of the other context within which Austen wrote — the context not just of her life, family, and friends but of literary history and the genre of the courtship-and-marriage novel.

This volume contains two essays by teachers who are also scholars of the literary tradition Austen inherited. The first, Kenneth L. Moler's "Literary Allusion in *Pride and Prejudice*," argues that all the Austen novels "present their vision of life in relation to literature." Moler comments on the relation between this novel and those of Samuel Richardson and Frances Burney, as well as on the reflections in it of such eighteenth-century writers as Berkeley, Hume, and Adam Smith. His essay provides instructors with ways to identify verbal echoes in the narrative voice and to teach about Austen's use of literary allusion as a characterizing device. Highlighting Austen's iconoclastic reworking of the stock eighteenth-century motif of the "patrician hero," he suggests how to introduce such information into different kinds of courses at different levels.

Like Moler, Jocelyn Harris enables us to see that Austen was "not primarily a realist, for imagined worlds were clearly as vivid to her as life itself." In her essay, "The Influence of Richardson on *Pride and Prejudice*," Harris illuminates Austen's intertextual brilliance — her flexibility, wit, and relish of incongruity — by showing how she splits, combines, and recombines Richardson's characters in *Sir Charles Grandison* (whom Austen called her "living friends") to create the cast of *Pride and Prejudice*. Harris's essay also points out the variations, inversions, ironic reversals, absurd replays, and poignant echoes in *Pride and Prejudice* of scenes from *Grandison*. In so doing, Harris catches Austen "in the act of creation."

These two essays, which consider the literary materials Austen used to create *Pride and Prejudice*, both suggest ways to begin responding to that unanswerable question "How did she figure it all out?" — or at least to discuss it more knowledgeably. Together with the essays by Perry, Fraiman, and Kaplan, these two pieces suggest how rich a problem it might be for students and teacher to sort out the elements in the novel from literary tradition and those from Austen's own life. Not an imitator but a writer engaged in "affectionate rivalry" with her literary forebears (as Harris puts it), Austen must be read in literary context to be understood fully; otherwise, students may not see how the conventions of the courtship plot, the cross-class romance, and the relations between men and women and among women mediate what Austen might attempt in her own book. Knowing these literary conventions well enough to identify Austen's reworking of them gives us — teachers and students — a glimpse into the mystery of creation, the process by which an artist brings together and transforms the fragments of reading and living, and writes a novel.

MMF

Part One

MATERIALS

Editions

The standard edition of all Jane Austen's novels is the R. W. Chapman edition, first published by the Clarendon Press, Oxford, in 1923. The Chapman edition was based on a collation of the first and second 1813 editions, the 1817 edition, and relevant information from the letters, which Chapman also edited. Reliable subsequent editions of the novel are all based on Chapman's text. The third edition of Chapman is in print in a six-volume set (the sixth, containing the *Minor Works*, was published in 1954), and *Pride and Prejudice* is volume 2. The Chapman *Pride and Prejudice* provides textual information, a comprehensive chronology of the novel, a brief comment on *Pride and Prejudice* and *Cecilia*, an interesting and useful short essay "Modes of Address," an index of characters (including every servant), and a list of "feigned places." Plainly, the Chapman third is *the* edition for scholars, is useful for teachers, and is the one to which page references in this volume are made.

Teachers replying to the MLA survey mentioned five paperback editions as the ones they assign to students. In order of popularity they are Penguin, Norton Critical, Signet, Oxford, and Riverside. The choice of edition does not determine the teaching process, but it does have significance. First, in some editions the three-volume division is apparent to students (with each volume starting at chapter 1), whereas in others the chapters are numbered sequentially throughout. And, obviously, the introduction available for students to read depends on which edition they purchase.

Those teachers selecting the most frequently used edition, the Penguin, mention its attractive format, the outstanding introduction by Tony Tanner, and the low cost. In this edition, chapters are numbered sequentially. The Norton Critical Edition is preferred for its introduction, notes, facsimile title pages, cover, and useful critical apparatus at the end, including contemporary reviews of the novel. However, many instructors noted that the edition needs to be updated and that some of the modern essays are poorly written. Teachers who use the Signet edition cite its low cost and the afterword by Joann Morse. The Oxford paperback contains Chapman's text and is sturdily bound. The Riverside edition, finally, retains the three-volume format, has clear print and wide margins, and has an excellent introduction by Mark Schorer.

A predictable problem for instructors of *Pride and Prejudice* is that students frequently obtain copies other than the chosen edition (out of those millions already in the world); as for many classic works that exist in multiple editions, classroom reference to consistent page numbers is then impossible. The issue is compounded in the case of *Pride and Prejudice*; giving chapter numbers does not work either, because the retention or elimination of the volume divisions results in totally different numbers after chapter 23 of volume 1. My own solution has been to order the Riverside edition, which I prefer because of the three-volume format and readable print; I have written in my own copy sequential chapter numbers after volume 1 so that I can direct students with other editions to passages discussed in class.

Criticism

There are several fine recent reviews of Jane Austen criticism. Kenneth L. Moler, a contributor to this volume, is author of an excellent short book on the novel, Pride and Prejudice: A Study in Artistic Economy; he provides a brief review of criticism at the end of his book. Park Honan also offers an excellent annotated bibliography of studies relating to Austen, including criticism, in his recent biography.

The editors of The Jane Austen Companion include three essays on the history of criticism. J. David Grey, A. Walton Litz, and Brian Southam divided Austen criticism into three phases and assigned discussion of each phase to a different scholar. I follow this three-part division in commenting on criticism of Pride and Prejudice. The first phase, 1813–70, which encompasses the period from the publication of Pride and Prejudice to the issuance of A Memoir of Jane Austen, by James Edward Austen-Leigh, is discussed in the Companion by Joseph Duffy. The second period extends from 1870 to 1940, the year after the publication of Mary Lascelles's Jane Austen and Her Art, and is reviewed by Southam. The third period, from 1940 to the present, is surveyed by Litz (through 1983).

In the first phase, commentary was scanty, but the few published reviews of Austen's work perceptively identified "most of the important questions raised by modern critics" (Litz, "Criticism" 110). Although some thoughtful criticism continued to be written in the second phase, there was a decline in quality from the standard of the early analysis. Commentary on all the novels was dominated by "genteel appreciations and antiquarian interest" (Litz 111). Lascelles's book of 1939 marks the beginning of modern, methodical literary analysis applied to Austen's novels.

Commentary on Pride and Prejudice in the three phases generally bears out these generalizations about all Austen criticism. For example, Sir Walter Scott remarked in his journal in 1827:

> Also read again, and for the third time at least, Miss Austen's very finely written novel of Pride and Prejudice. That young lady had a talent for describing the involvements, and feelings, and characters of ordinary life, which is to me the most wonderful I ever met with. The Big Bow-wow strain I can do like any now going; but the exquisite

touch, which renders ordinary commonplace things and characters interesting, from the truth of the description and the sentiment, is denied to me.   (Gilson, *Bibliography* 475)

From this suggestive early insight, we go, in the second period, to gushing: A. C. Bradley, the Shakespearean scholar, said about Elizabeth Bennet: "I was meant to fall in love with her and I do" (Southam, "Janeites" 240). The analytic commentary of the third span is exemplified by Reuben Brower's thoughtful observation: "The judicial process by which Elizabeth earlier 'determined possibilities' in judging Darcy's past conduct is matched by the orderly way in which she now 'determines her feelings' toward him" ("Light" 73). Perhaps, as Southam observes, the change is to the loss of "comedy in criticism," but certainly it is to the gain of writing that is of use to the teacher.

Starting with Lascelles's book, which contains an excellent chapter on *Pride and Prejudice*, modern criticism of the novel represents all the significant trends in Austen studies. D. W. Harding's famous iconoclastic essay "Regulated Hatred: An Aspect of the Work of Jane Austen" (first published in 1940) argues that Austen's irony is directed at the very kinds of people who admire her novels. The passage he selects from *Pride and Prejudice* contains the powerfully unironic condemnation: "Their table was superlatively stupid." Harding's view of Austen as socially subversive follows the argument of Reginald Farrer's essay (1917) and anticipates the opinions of Marvin Mudrick (1952), Mark Schorer, in his introduction (1956), and Nina Auerbach, in "Jane Austen and Romantic Imprisonment" (1981), about *Pride and Prejudice*. Commentary on Austen as socially subversive offers teachers a potent corrective to the "Mark Twain" problem, discussed in the introduction to this volume, and Harding's essay, at least, seems almost to be written for that purpose. He begins with a denunciation of the "gentle Jane" school of thought: "I gathered she was a delicate satirist, revealing with inimitable lightness of touch the comic foibles and amiable weaknesses of the people whom she lived amongst and liked. . . . I didn't want to read her" (166–67).

Brower's "The Controlling Hand: Jane Austen's *Pride and Prejudice*" (1945–46), later revised as "'Light and Bright and Sparkling': Irony and Fiction in *Pride and Prejudice*" (1951), looks at the novel's play of ironic wit in the light of Austen's own comment, in the letter to Cassandra, that the "work is rather too light, and bright, and sparkling." His essay, though somewhat bogged down by the working out of an analogy between Austen's prose and the poetry of Alexander Pope, is exceptionally perceptive about the sources of misunderstanding in the first half of the book, and it offers teachable observations about the characters' language.

Dorothy Van Ghent devotes a chapter to *Pride and Prejudice* in *The English Novel: Form and Function* (1953), exploring oppositions in the novel between the individual and society and between feeling and reason. This chapter provides a framework for interpretation that lends itself to development in the classroom. Schorer's introduction to the Riverside edition emphasizes the novel's attention to economic matters — class, money, commerce, and property — both in the design of the plot and in details of diction and phrasing.

The scene in which Darcy and Elizabeth converse by the pianoforte at Rosings (173–74) led the critic Howard Babb to the conception of his book on Austen's use of dialogue. In *Jane Austen's Novels: The Fabric of Dialogue* (1962), he examines the subtleties of intention and understanding in the conversation of the two romantic protagonists. Insights from both Schorer's essay and Babb's chapter can give clear structure to class discussions of particular passages and scenes.

Alistair M. Duckworth's *The Improvement of the Estate: A Study of Jane Austen's Novels* (1971), which focuses on the implications of Austen's use of the "estate" metaphor, has an excellent chapter on *Pride and Prejudice*, exploring epistemological issues as well as commenting astutely on the motifs of books and libraries, letters, and laughter. Teachers can develop such motifs into manageable and rewarding topics for student writing. *Jane Austen and the War of Ideas* (1975), by Marilyn Butler, examines Austen's eighteenth-century literary and philosophical forebears; it too contains a chapter on *Pride and Prejudice*. Duckworth and Butler both provide richly documented arguments against the view of Austen's novels as socially subversive: their analyses of *Pride and Prejudice* are based on a view of her values as essentially conservative.

Since the early 1970s, feminist literary criticism has become an important force in Austen studies, and Litz remarks that "some of the best criticism of Jane Austen in the 1970s and 1980s has been written from a feminist perspective" ("Criticism" 117). In many books of feminist literary criticism published primarily in the 1980s, *Pride and Prejudice* remains a key work considered in itself or as a standard for other works, as, for example, in Janet Todd's *Women's Friendship in Literature*.

Judith Lowder Newton, in *Women, Power, and Subversion*, and Rachel M. Brownstein, in *Becoming a Heroine*, each devote their second chapter to *Pride and Prejudice*, while Patricia Meyer Spacks, in *The Female Imagination*, gives the novel a major place in her argument. In feminist works of literary criticism in which *Pride and Prejudice* is not treated at length, knowledge of the book is taken as a given, and it serves as a touchstone for broader generalizations about women as writers and characters.

Auerbach compares *Pride and Prejudice* with Louisa May Alcott's *Little Women* in *Communities of Women*, and in *The Madwoman in the Attic*, Sandra M. Gilbert and Susan Gubar discuss all the Austen novels in a long chapter, "Jane Austen's Cover Story." In their comments on *Pride and Prejudice*, they explore Austen's disparagement of the powerful woman in

Lady Catherine and her quelling of those qualities of Elizabeth that make her resemble Lady Catherine.

Julia Prewitt Brown's excellent book *Jane Austen's Novels: Social Change and Literary Form* is informed by social history. In a full chapter on *Pride and Prejudice*, Brown analyzes the interconnectedness of cooperative, social forces and anarchic, individual ones in the decisions leading to marriage. Margaret Kirkham's *Jane Austen, Feminism, and Fiction* places the novels in relation to late-eighteenth-century women's writing, and her essay "Jane Austen and Contemporary Feminism" gives a succinct summary of Austen's relation to the feminist-antifeminist controversy of the 1790s. Mary Poovey's *The Proper Lady and the Woman Writer: Ideology as Style in the Works of Mary Wollstonecraft, Mary Shelley, and Jane Austen* is a rigorous historical study based in the 1790s, when Austen was in her twenties, Wollstonecraft died, and Mary Shelley was born. Her analysis of *Pride and Prejudice* emphasizes Austen's conservatism in the novel's celebration of marriage. For a historicist study placing Austen's work in the context of popular fiction written by her contemporary woman writers and showing how Austen participated in the 1790s debate about marriage, female duties, patriarchy, and the family, readers are referred to Claudia L. Johnson's *Jane Austen: Women, Politics, and the Novel*.

In an important essay, "The Feminist Depreciation of Jane Austen: A Polemical Reading," Brown surveys feminist literary criticism of all Austen's novels, especially the writing of Auerbach, Gilbert and Gubar, Poovey, and Johnson. "Jane Austen's stature," she observes, "has declined with the rise of feminist literary criticism" (303). She begins by reviewing appraisals of Austen by major male critics since the 1950s, including F. R. Leavis, Ian Watt, Lionel Trilling, Tony Tanner, and Alasdair MacIntyre. These critics, in Brown's view, emphasized Austen's moral seriousness, her pivotal role in the history of the novel, her place in the moral and intellectual origins of modernism, her relation to Shakespeare, her position in the history of ethical thought, and her achievement beyond fiction and in the worlds of philosophy and linguistics. The feminist depreciation of Austen, however, Brown argues, "hinges on the question of marriage." "To the feminist critic, marriage is too simple and restricted a resolution . . . an inadequate symbol with which to conclude a great novel" (305). To refute this criticism, Brown grounds her argument on the social history of marriage and the family and locates Austen's feminism in a philosophical stance like that of Wollstonecraft, "who derives from Plato in centering her social philosophy outside the self and on the ideal of education, not [in] John Stuart Mill whose feminism (like Charlotte Brontë's) leaves unquestioned the tenets of individualism and self-interest." In Wollstonecraft, Austen, and George Eliot, Brown asserts, we find a "feminist tradition that looks at society as integral rather than aggregate, in which the interest of women does not compete against other groups or men but is seen as part of a contiguous whole" (313). Feminist criticism must itself be considered in context, for the questions that are central to such commentary have naturally changed over time. One of these issues has been feminists' valuation of marriage as an institution and as a device for narrative closure. From the beginning, feminist criticism struggled to make sense of Austen's novels, which have been essential texts in the whole project. Brown's essay suggests how far the enterprise has come, for a radical revision of early feminist criticism of the novel is already under way.

Six intriguing essays on *Pride and Prejudice* published in the 1980s demonstrate, individually and collectively, the apparently inexhaustible responsiveness of this novel to close reading and careful analysis. J. F. Burrows's essay "A Measure of Excellence," mentioned in the introduction, examines the characters' and the narrator's use of superlative and comparative language. Robert K. Wallace, in a chapter of his book, takes the familiar analogy between the formal symmetry and structural perfection of *Pride and Prejudice* and the music of Mozart to an unexpected extreme with fascinating results: he compares the novel to Mozart's Piano Concerto no. 9 (K. 271). Three essays in Todd's collection *Jane Austen: New Perspectives* provide examples of how *Pride and Prejudice* rewards close reading. "*Pride and Prejudice*: The Eyes Have It," by Mark M. Hennelly, locates and analyzes references in the novel to eyes, seeing, and perception. Katrin R. Burlin sensitively traces the theme of painting, portraits, and speaking pictures in the essay " 'Pictures of Perfection' at Pemberley." And Martha Satz's contribution, the brilliant "Epistemological Understanding of *Pride and Prejudice*: Humility and Objectivity," offers a new duality as interpretive framework of the novel — the duality between perception and interpretation (earlier critics identified the dichotomies of the individual and society, feeling and reason, economic conservatism and liberalism, and so forth). Tony Tanner also examines this duality in his essay "Knowledge and Opinion: *Pride and Prejudice*," a chapter in his excellent book *Jane Austen*. Tanner places the novel's examination of epistemology in a context that includes the eighteenth-century philosophers Locke and Hume and the thinkers of the early Romantic movement. His chapter and the Satz essay represent a particularly appealing approach to teaching the novel, and both are discussed more fully in the appendix to my essay in this volume.

The essays in this collection will, I hope, join in this continuing conversation about *Pride and Prejudice*. Most of the writers of the sixteen essays do not make explicit the relation between their approaches to teaching the novel and current debates in literary criticism and theory, nor do they employ a theoretical vocabulary. These essays in pedagogy and practical criticism are written by teachers who love the novel and see their students as human beings with lives outside the classroom. Nonetheless, while the essays do not focus on theoretical concerns, individual essays and the volume as a whole address these issues both implicitly and explicitly; they are informed by current theoretical dialogue and suggest how these debates may serve as the basis for classroom discussion.

For example, although questions of race and ethnicity are not represented in *Pride and Prejudice* or examined in this collection, problems of social class certainly are. The essays of Copeland, Brown, and, especially, Smith provide both information about and analysis of the way British class structure maps itself onto the novel, and Smith's essay shows how knowledge of social class can affect students' interpretations of the novel. For another example, the central issues of feminist literary criticism likewise are engaged by teachers whose essays appear in this collection. Whether *Pride and Prejudice* should be read as subtly conciliatory to the patriarchal society Austen knew or as a subversive, feminist, progressive critique is debated in this volume. The essays of Perry, Fraiman, Kaplan, Bromberg, and Bennett suggest, as much recent feminist criticism of Austen has done, that the book is "profoundly conciliatory" (as Perry characterizes the view of such critics as Marilyn Butler and Claudia Johnson). According to the essays of Brown, Folsom, Kneedler, and McMaster, however, Austen's position in the politics of gender was progressive. Smith's Marxist-feminist essay neatly balances the two positions taken by the other writers.

Another theoretical question in recent literary criticism debated here concerns historical context: Within what context should a reader engage with this text? The essays on backgrounds, especially those of Copeland, Perry, Brown, Smith, Fraiman, and Kaplan, argue that understanding the economic, biographical, social, and political contexts of the novel is essential to interpreting it accurately. The essays of Moler and Harris rest on the assumption that print culture — literary culture — is at least as essential a context for the novel as material culture. All the background essays, in fact, assume that specialized knowledge illuminates the text, that consciousness is partly created by society, and that a text must be located within a cultural context.

Nevertheless, some of the essays devoted to teaching about the novel's structure or language imply that its values and insights have a timelessness that the writers find demonstrated in the success of their approaches in the classroom. In particular, the essays of Folsom, Stovel, Bennett, Langland, Kneedler, and McMaster tend to decontextualize the novel and celebrate its ability to speak directly to late-twentieth-century students.

Strategies for Discussion

Many teachers have favorite materials for generating class discussions, brief readings or remarks intended to start the conversation or to supply a fresh vantage point for talking about the novel. I offer several ideas that have worked in my classes.

Jane Austen's letters are particularly useful for opening class discussions. (The two-volume complete edition of Jane Austen's letters edited by R. W.

Chapman has been out of print for several years. Because this resource is therefore relatively inaccessible, references to Jane Austen's letters in this volume are given parenthetically by date within the text.) The hilarious exchange (in Dec. 1815) with the Reverend James Stanier Clarke, librarian to the Prince Regent, in which Austen politely but firmly rejects his suggestions for a character in her next novel, is wonderful in class. So are all the letters to Cassandra Austen that mention *Pride and Prejudice*, including the one in which she calls it "my own darling child" and says about Elizabeth "how I shall be able to tolerate those who do not like *her* at least I do not know" (29 Jan. 1813); the one in which she says it is "rather too light, and bright, and sparkling" (4 Feb. 1813); and the one in which she jokes about not finding any portrait of Elizabeth ("Mrs. D") in a London exhibition (May 1814). The two famous comments from the letters about novel writing can also stimulate class discussion — the one to Anna Austen that concludes, "You are now collecting your people delightfully . . . 3 or 4 families in a country village is the very thing to work on" (9 Sept. 1814), and the one to Edward Austen about his "Manly, spirited Sketches" as compared with her own "little bit (two inches wide) of Ivory on which I work with so fine a brush" (16 Dec. 1816). Kaplan's essay in this volume is particularly helpful in providing generic strategies for teaching any of Austen's letters.

The comment of Sir Walter Scott about social class in Austen can also serve to promote discussion: "Smoked my segar with Lockhart after dinner, and then whiled away the evening over one of Miss Austen's novels. There is a truth of painting in her writing which always delights me. They do not, it is true, get above the middle classes of society, but there she is inimitable" (Gilson, *Bibliography* 475). "Middle classes?" my students exclaim. "I thought these people were upper class!" The essays of Copeland and Smith help teachers clarify where the characters fit in Scott's "classes of society." And Scott's remark about Austen's "truth of painting" as well as his contrast of her "exquisite touch, which renders ordinary commonplace things and characters interesting" with his own "Big Bow-wow strain" of writing can also get a class into conversation.

Finally, a teacher might bring to class Austen's complaint in *Northanger Abbey* that "there seems almost a general wish of decrying the capacity and undervaluing the labour of the novelist, and of slighting the performances which have only genius, wit, and taste to recommend them." She calls to her sister novelists not to depreciate one another's work in their fictions: "let us not desert one another; we are an injured body" (37). In the famous passage that follows, she turns directly to the reader:

> Such is the common cant. — "And what are you reading, Miss —— ?" "Oh! it is only a novel!" replies the young lady; while she lays down her book with affected indifference, or momentary shame. — "It is only Cecilia, or Camilla, or Belinda;" or in short, only some work in which

the greatest powers of the mind are displayed, in which the most thorough knowledge of human nature, the happiest delineation of its varieties, the liveliest effusions of wit and humour are conveyed to the world in the best chosen language.   (38)

For teachers and for students, here is Austen's resounding statement of joyful pride in her fiction. In the irony and warmth of her heroic superlatives, the twenty-two-year-old Austen seems to say: I know you may think I am exaggerating, but I am not. You may call this "only a novel," but I say that novels are humanity's best source of wisdom, knowledge of human nature, wit, comedy, and thought. This statement can inspire a class to consider the value of reading a novel like *Pride and Prejudice*, and, certainly, it challenges the notion that Austen considered herself a modest miniaturist, limiting herself to a scope "two inches wide." In this ringing assertion from an earlier novel, Austen declares that her intention as a novelist is no less ambitious than to teach us, her readers—students and teachers alike—about ourselves, our choices, and our lives.

A Jane Austen Chronology

1764   26 April. The Reverend George Austen (b. 1731), fellow of St. John's College, Oxford, marries Cassandra Leigh (b. 1739).

1773   9 January. Cassandra Elizabeth, Jane Austen's only sister and closest friend, is born.

1775   16 December. Jane Austen born at Steventon Rectory, North Hampshire, seventh child and second daughter of George and Cassandra Austen.

1782–85   With Cassandra, Jane Austen attends Mrs. Cawley's school, first at Oxford and then at Southampton.

1785–86   Cassandra and Jane Austen at Abbey School, Reading.

1787–93   Jane Austen pens her juvenilia, twenty-seven separate pieces, totaling ninety thousand words, which later she copies into three slim quarto notebooks—*Volume the First*, *Volume the Second*, and *Volume the Third*.

1791   27 December. Edward, third son of George and Cassandra Austen, the designated heir of his rich cousin Thomas Knight, marries Elizabeth Bridges.

1792   27 March. The Reverend James Austen, Jane's oldest brother, marries Anne Mathew, granddaughter of the duke of Ancaster.

1793   23 January. Fanny Austen, later Lady Knatchbull, the niece whom Jane Austen came to regard as a second sister, born to Edward and Elizabeth.

   15 April. Anna Austen, the niece whom Jane Austen encouraged in her aspirations to be a novelist, born to James and Anne.

1794   Jean-François Capot de Feuillide, captain in the Queen's Regiment of Dragoons and husband of George Austen's niece Eliza Hancock, guillotined in France.

1794–95   Jane Austen writes *Lady Susan*, an epistolary novel, and the first version of *Sense and Sensibility*, the epistolary *Elinor and Marianne*.

1796   August to early October. Jane Austen, at twenty, visits Kent and immediately, on her return to Steventon, begins *First Impressions*, in which her heroine, Elizabeth Bennet, likewise "not yet one-and-twenty," visits Kent.

1797   February. Cassandra's fiancé, the Reverend Thomas Fowler, dies in the West Indies.

   August. *First Impressions* finished.

   1 November. *First Impressions* offered by George Austen to the publisher Thomas Cadell, who, to quote his own notation, "declined by Return of Post."

1797–98   *Northanger Abbey* (then entitled *Susan*) written.

1798   The first of Jane Austen's several visits to Godmersham, her brother Edward's imposing estate in Kent.

1799   8 August. Jane Leigh Perrot, Jane Austen's aunt, is arrested at Bath, charged with shoplifting; she is acquitted the following March.

1800   Margaret Holdford publishes a novel called *First Impressions*, the circumstance that led Jane Austen to retitle her book *Pride and Prejudice*.

1801   May. The Austens move to Bath on George Austen's retirement. Summer holiday at Sidmoth.

1802   2 December. Jane Austen becomes briefly engaged to Harris Bigg-Wither. Summer holiday at fashionable Dawlish and Teignemouth.

1803   *Northanger Abbey* sold to Crosby & Co. for £10.

1804   *The Watsons* begun. Autumn holiday at Lyme Regis, a setting, later, for *Persuasion*.

1805   21 January. George Austen dies suddenly at 27 Green Park Buildings, Bath. Jane Austen lays aside *The Watsons* after completing ten chapters.

1806   July. The Austens visit the Leigh ancestral estate, Stoneleigh Abbey, Warwickshire, prototype of Sotherton in *Mansfield Park*.

1806–09   Jane Austen, her mother, and Cassandra for a time share lodgings with her fifth brother, Captain Francis Austen, and his wife, at Southampton, then locate at Castle Square, in that town.

1809   March. Visit to the Frank Austens in Portsmouth. After visits to Warwickshire and, possibly, Derbyshire, the Austens, in July, move to Chawton Cottage, Hampshire, at the behest of Edward Austen, heir to the Hampshire, as well as Kentish, estates, of Thomas Knight.

1811   February. Planning of *Mansfield Park* begun.
Spring. Revision of *First Impressions*, as *Pride and Prejudice*, begun.
November. Egerton publishes *Sense and Sensibility* at Jane Austen's own expense, as "By a Lady," the author otherwise unidentified.

1812   Autumn. *Pride and Prejudice* sold to Egerton for £110.

1813   28 January. *Pride and Prejudice* published anonymously.
November. Second editions of both *Sense and Sensibility* and *Pride and Prejudice* appear.

1814   21 January. *Emma* begun.
May. *Mansfield Park* published.

1815   The year of Waterloo.
August. *Persuasion* begun.
December. *Emma*, dedicated to the Prince Regent, at his expressed wish, published by Murray.

1816   August. *Persuasion* completed. Murray publishes second edition of *Mansfield Park*.

1817   27 January. *Sanditon* begun.
18 March. *Sanditon* broken off for reasons of Austen's ill health.
24 May. Jane Austen relocates in Winchester for medical care.
18 July. Jane Austen dies at Winchester, at 8 College Street.
24 July. She is buried in the north aisle, Winchester Cathedral.
December. *Northanger Abbey* and *Persuasion* published.

1827   Death of Cassandra Leigh Austen, at eighty-eight.

1833   Publication of Bentley's collected edition of Jane Austen's novels, with "Biographical Notice" by Henry Austen.

1845   Death of Cassandra Elizabeth Austen.

1852   Death of Jane Austen's youngest brother, Admiral Charles Austen, commander in chief on the East India station.

1865   Death of Sir Francis Austen, admiral of the fleet and last of Jane Austen's siblings.

1870   Memoir of Jane Austen published by her nephew James Edward Austen-Leigh.

John McAleer

A *Map for* **Pride and Prejudice**

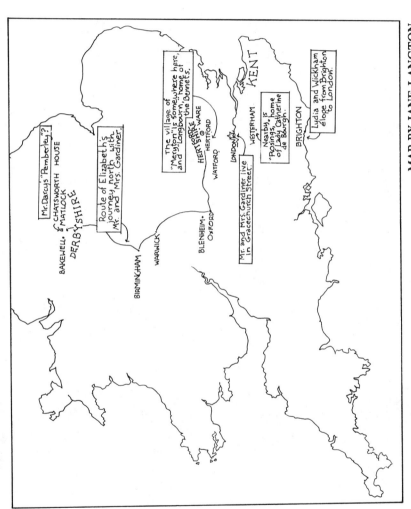

MAP BY JANE LANGTON

Mr. Darcy's "Pemberley"?

BAKEWELL ❦ CHATSWORTH HOUSE
MATLOCK
DERBYSHIRE

Route of Elizabeth's journey north with Mr. and Mrs. Gardiner.

BIRMINGHAM

WARWICK

BLENHEIM ◦ OXFORD

The village of "Meryton" is somewhere here, and Longbourn, home of the Bennets.

HERTSHIRE ◦ WARE
HERTFORD

WATFORD

LONDON

Mr. and Mrs. Gardiner live in Gracechurch Street.

WESTERHAM
KENT

Nearby, is "Rosings," home of Lady Catherine de Bourgh.

BRIGHTON

Lydia and Wickham elope from Brighton to London.

Part Two

APPROACHES

SOCIAL HISTORY AND AUSTEN'S LIFE

The Economic Realities of Jane Austen's Day

Edward Copeland

In teaching *Pride and Prejudice* there is always the temptation, and not a bad one, to let the money in the novel explain itself. After all, Jane Austen takes scrupulous care to keep the reader aware of the relative values of the pounds she assigns to individual characters: Bingley is rich, Darcy is richer still; the Bingley sisters have excellent inheritances, Elizabeth Bennet does not; and the Bennet family, while not nearly so rich as Darcy or Bingley, is well fixed, although saddled with an entail, a legal puzzle for Mrs. Bennet. Austen does not allow it to impede the plot in any way, however—"Mr. Collins," explains Mr. Bennet with supreme clarity, "when I am dead, may turn you all out of this house as soon as he pleases" (61; Treitel 45–51).

Nevertheless, students inevitably want to know more: Just how rich *is* Bingley? How much richer *is* Darcy? What does it mean to have all those servants? How much money, "real money," they say, are we talking about? And they are right to be suspicious: there is a plot, an economic one, running underneath the story in *Pride and Prejudice*, one that contemporaries understood automatically but that the years have made a mystery to us. The shorthand of a one-to-one currency exchange, something students love, can be useful, of course, but a simple conversion from past to present confuses the cultures, and, with today's inflation running as it does, the conversion is out of date almost as soon as it is calculated. My own efforts, in 1979, and David Holbrook's, in 1984, prove the assertion. Moreover, readers who are meeting Austen's work for the first time need to be reminded that the Austen pound is a fictional one. This is a difficult concept. First of all,

Austen's realism is so seductive that it screens the obvious fact that money in novels is always fictional. Because her sums always match the costs and prices of contemporary record, it is easy for students to forget that the pound in *Pride and Prejudice* spends just the way Austen designs it to spend, and not by any means as an unmediated reflection of contemporary economic reality. Second, Austen's culture is the first genuine consumer culture in history, and, since our own society is a consumer culture as well—though vastly different from Austen's—the analogies are close enough to make us more confident than we should be about identifications between the two (McKendrick et al.). The question then becomes what to tell students that will help them understand the economic figures in Austen's novels, without at the same time giving them the unwarranted confidence that Austen's novelistic economy either is like ours or expresses the whole of Regency England. In spite of every caution to the contrary, enthusiastic students will respond to Jane Austen with the inevitable recipes for white soup, "Whip't Syllabub," and plans for a Regency costume ball. Nevertheless, it is worth showing them that there are paths within *Pride and Prejudice* that provide far more interesting views of the money and the consumer pleasures of the novel.

The initial puzzle for first-time readers lies in the manner in which Austen reports her money. Sums arrive in two guises: first, in announcements of yearly income; second, in statements of block sums of capital. For example, Darcy has an annual income of £10,000; Mr. Bennet has an annual income of £2,000, including, in addition to the yearly sum, an estate with the requisite farmlands to produce the annual income, and the built-in consumer delights of a furnished house with its attached pleasure grounds of park and garden. Block sums of capital, however, occur more frequently than annual incomes in the novel and must be explained. Austen assumes that block capital comes to its possessor as inherited money or, particularly for women, as money that devolves upon them through their parents' prearranged marriage settlements. These sums are free capital—that is, money available for immediate investment, and divorced from any attachment to land. In *Pride and Prejudice*, Mr. Bingley has £100,000; Miss Bingley as an heiress has £20,000; Miss Darcy has £30,000; Miss King, also an heiress, has £10,000; and Elizabeth, through her parents' marriage settlements, has only £1,000, as Mr. Collins reminds her when he proposes to her. The significant point to remember is that these one-off, block sums are simply shorthand ways for Austen to report yearly incomes: each has a standard potential as a stable investment income. Yearly income is the bottom line in women's fiction, and that is the figure for which the anxious heroine scans the horizon.

Sums of capital in *Pride and Prejudice* are understood "universally" as invested in the government funds with returns at either 4 percent per annum or 5 percent per annum. In most contemporary women's novels, and in all of Austen's except *Pride and Prejudice*, these sums are assumed to be invested in the 5-percent government funds. In *Pride and Prejudice*, however, Mr. Collins uses the more conservative 4-percent rule of thumb: "I am well aware," he tells Elizabeth, "that one thousand pounds in the 4 per cents. which will not be yours till after your mother's decease, is all that you may ever be entitled to" (106). Mrs. Bennet herself is uncertain about the investment of Mr. Bingley's £100,000 inheritance: it could be in the 4 percents or it could be in the 5 percents, although she reports his income with as much accuracy as might be reasonably expected: "A single man of large fortune; four or five thousand a year" (3–4) — precisely what students will find when they multiply Mr. Bingley's £100,000 by 4 percent and by 5 percent.

Yearly income in the novel is the bouncing ball that must be attended to with the closest attention. It makes sense. In Austen's time women ordinarily could not earn money in any significant amounts, and heroines, as gentlewomen by definition, have only the most limited access to genteel employment (Poovey 3–15, 35–47). A capital sum that produces a comfortable, spendable yearly income is much to be desired, much to be sought.

Within the marriage market, however, the sums that Austen reports in block capital in *Pride and Prejudice* have an additional and particular significance. The amount of ready capital that a woman possesses as her marriage portion is the motor that runs the economic plot of the novel. At the end of the eighteenth and beginning of the nineteenth century, an industrial revolution and a consumer revolution were together moving full steam ahead, both badly hampered by credit and banking laws inadequate to meet the urgent demands for investment capital. Any substantial amount of ready capital that a woman could bring to a marriage had an exaggerated contemporary importance and, in practice, often decided whether a woman was marriageable or not. Elizabeth jokingly refers to the situation in a conversation with Darcy's cousin Colonel Fitzwilliam: "And pray," she says to Fitzwilliam, who obviously admires her, but as obviously has no intention of proposing marriage to a young woman as poor as herself, "what is the usual price of an Earl's younger son? Unless the elder brother is very sickly, I suppose you would not ask above fifty thousand pounds" (183–84). The harsh economic condition surfaces in a joke, but Austen's contemporary Jean Marishall treats it with unsmiling gravity: "People in a middle station, with perhaps a genteel income but a small capital," she writes in *A Series of Letters* (1789), "wish ardently to have their daughters disposed of in marriage." Unfortunately, Marishall concludes, their chances are poor, and, more likely than not, an unportioned girl will be left "to live on the scanty interest of a few hundreds, which in her parents' lifetime would scarcely defray the expence of her chair-hire" (1: 113–14).

Miss Bingley, with her £20,000, is, in this light, a highly attractive marriage candidate. Her inheritance will produce for a future husband at least £800 a year invested in the 4 percents, or £1,000 a year in the 5 percents. Miss King, whom Wickham aims at and misses, may have freckles and red hair, but she also has an attractive £10,000 inheritance, which will yield a "mediocre" income, as Elizabeth reflects, of £400 a year invested in the 4 percents, or £500 in the 5 percents. Miss Darcy, whom Wickham also misses, is the most desirable catch of all for a fortune hunter: her £30,000 inheritance will garner a yearly income of £1,200 or £1,500 — little short of the Bennet family's entire yearly income. In numbers alone, students can appreciate Elizabeth's dangerous situation. She possesses as capital a potential inheritance of only £1,000, which invested in the percents would be a mere £40 a year to offer a husband, and even that small amount available only at the uncertain future date of her mother's death.

Figures by themselves, however, fall short of explaining the context of these incomes, obscure to us but clear enough to contemporary readers. Consumer comforts do a better job, as James Thompson explains in his essay "Jane Austen's Clothing: Things, Property, and Materialism in Her Novels." Such budget guides as John Trusler's *The Economist* (1774), Samuel Adams and Sarah Adams's *The Complete Servant* (1825), and James Luckcock's *Hints for Practical Economy* (1834) present a consistent picture of the buying power of each of the incomes in Austen's works. These guides to household budgets, designed primarily for families in the middling way of life, deal in the most commonly desired consumer comforts: the costs of employing servants, for example, or the price of maintaining a carriage. Mrs. Bennet shows a keen awareness of status consumption and "positional goods" when she tells Mr. Collins with "some asperity" that "they were very well able to keep a cook, and that her daughters had nothing to do in the kitchen" (65). She is convinced also that Mr. Darcy does not speak to Mrs. Long at the Meryton ball because "Mrs. Long does not keep a carriage, and had come to the ball in a hack chaise" (19). She greets Mr. Bingley's arrival in the neighborhood joyously with the specific news that the rich young man comes in "a chaise and four" (3).

Carriages provide the significant index of wealth for the upper ranges of income. Trusler suggests that an income of £800 per annum will provide a carriage, but the Adamses, much more conservative, recommend such a convenience only for incomes between £1,000 and £1,500 a year. The Bennets, on £2,000, have a carriage, but, as Elizabeth and Jane find, it is not always available for visits to Netherfield, since Mr. Bennet's horses must do field work as well as pull the family carriage. Jane Austen's parents tried to maintain a carriage on an income of around £600, but gave it up after a year's trial when it proved too expensive (Le Faye 102). Mrs. Bennet's friend Mrs. Long lacks a carriage, a circumstance that puts her in the same middling, but still respectable, range of Meryton families that must do without such a luxury. Georgiana Darcy's fortune, producing £1,200 to £1,500 a year, would easily bring a carriage, regardless of the income of her husband-to-be. Miss Bingley's invested income could do the same, though not so generously. Finally, Mrs. Gardiner evokes the image of carriages to tease Elizabeth when she is convinced of the seriousness of Darcy's attachment to her niece: "A low phaeton, with a nice pair of ponies, would be the very thing" (325), she writes Elizabeth. Elizabeth confirms the engagement in the same coin: "Your idea of the ponies is delightful. We will go round the Park every day" (382).

The number of servants in a household furnishes the budget writers with their scale for the consumer comforts of less generous but still respectable incomes that are above and below £400 to £500 a year — the income of Miss King's inheritance, for example. For today's students, most of whom know as much about Martians as they do about servants, the servant scale needs explanation.

Domestic help may be thought of as substitutes for the labor-saving conveniences of a modern household. A no-servant establishment of the late eighteenth and early nineteenth century is like a house today bereft of all conveniences, a miserable living standard to contemplate indeed: "It would appear a very ungracious task to attempt to exhibit a lower scale," writes Luckcock (9). Mary D. George quotes a tract entitled "Considerations of the Expedience of Raising, at This Time of Dearth the Wages of . . . Clerks in Public Office" (1767) that paints a horrific picture of life on a no-servant income:

> I have driven him to the dirtiest and meanest parts of town to seek for a cheap lodging; I have cloathed him in the plainest and coarsest manner; I have scarcely allowed him to be clean enough for the place of his stated appearance . . . and yet, with all his economy and penury the wretch, at the year's end, has no more than twelve shillings and ninepence to lay by for sickness and old age. (77–78)

In *Persuasion* (1818) Austen produces just such an income for the heroine's friend Mrs. Smith, who lives with "a noisy parlour, and a dark bed-room behind . . . the absolute necessity of having a regular nurse, and finances at that moment particularly unfit to meet any extraordinary expense" (154). As a modern equivalent, a student might consider life on a no-servant income as bringing only the meager comforts of a fourth-floor studio flat, walk-up of course, with no hot water and a shared bath down the hall. To aspire to a one-servant income, according to the Adamses, would take at least £100 per annum. On this, write the Adamses, "A *Widow* or other *unmarried Lady*, may keep a *Young Maid Servant*, at a low salary; say from 5 to 10 Guineas a year" (5). Students may now add hot running water and a one-burner hotplate to the fourth-floor walk-up.

In assessing Elizabeth's economic plight, contemporary readers must have clasped their hands in horror. Elizabeth's income will be *only £40 a year!* Her only hope for even tolerable domestic comfort, should marriage not come her way — if hope it be — is that all five sisters remain single as well and live together to pool their inheritances, of £40 each, for a meager total of £200 a year. Their father's tardy regret for having allowed this grim situation to develop hardly begins to touch the misery of its implications: "Mr. Bennet had very often wished, before this period of his life, that, instead of spending his whole income, he had laid by an annual sum, for the better provision of his children, and of his wife, if she survived him" (308). No question about it — Mr. Bennet has been grossly irresponsible. He has left his five daughters and his wife exposed to a calamitous fall in fortune. The Adamses suggest that the pooled income of the Bennet women might bring its possessor a rather better servant maid, "*a professed Servant-Maid of All-Work*, at from 12 to 14 Guineas," which might replace the hotplate in the fourth-floor walk-up with a small stove and bring an economy-size vacuum cleaner.

An increase in annual income to £400 or £500, Miss King's potential fortune, produces a confirming sigh of relief in almost every contemporary novel. It also brings three very welcome female servants, "a Cook, House-Maid, and a Nursery-Maid," and perhaps a boy to help with the garden (Adams and Adams 5). Such was the income of Austen's parents and the servant household, slightly more extravagant, that Austen and her mother fantasized for their future home in Bath: "a steady Cook, & a young giddy Housemaid, with a sedate, middle aged Man, who is to undertake the double office of Husband to the former & sweetheart to the latter. — No Children of course to be allowed on either side" (3 Jan. 1801). As one of the characters in Eliza Parsons's novel *The Castle of Wolfenbach* confidently explains as he presents such a yearly sum to the heroine: "Four hundred a year, English money, paid her quarterly, will enable her to live genteelly" (97). In modern creature comforts, this is perhaps the equivalent of a small but pleasant house in rural West Virginia, a useful vegetable garden, a decent cooking range, central heating, and some limited free time to see friends. No car, no travel, no entertaining, and no holidays, of course, except to visit relatives — but not so bad as it might be. Austen explains unforgettably the living standard on such an income in *Sense and Sensibility* (1811): "Altogether they will have five hundred a-year amongst them," the wealthy Mrs. John Dashwood says of her less fortunate mother-in-law and three unmarried sisters-in-law, "and what on earth can four women want for more than that? — They will live so cheap! Their housekeeping will be nothing at all. They will have no carriage, no horses, and hardly any servants; they will keep no company, and can have no expences of any kind! Only conceive how comfortable they will be!" (12).

The living conditions of the Bennet family at Longbourn, while Mr. Bennet remains alive, match the Adamses' recommendations for their income, £1,500 to £2,000 a year — six women servants and five men servants: "A Cook, Housekeeper, two House-Maids, a Nursery Maid, or other Female Servant; with a Coachman, Groom, Footman, Gardener, and an assistant in the Garden and Stable" (6). In *Pride and Prejudice*, we hear of a cook (65), a housekeeper (301), two housemaids (317), at least one footman (30), and a butler (301). We must assume additional female help in the kitchen, at least a scullery maid (perhaps in place of the nursery maid); for the other men servants, a groom and a coachman to manage the carriage, along with unnoted men and boys about the stable, and a gardener and perhaps a boy to take care of the "small park" and "prettyish kind of a little wilderness" that Lady Catherine de Bourgh remarks on her visit to Longbourn (352). The prospective fall of the Bennet women from these comparatively grand consumer comforts should give any reader pause for thought. Even Charlotte Lucas, single, twenty-seven years old, and unportioned, is better off. At least Charlotte, if Mr. Collins had not swum into her range, had brothers to shoulder the financial burden of an old-maid sister. There is no one to perform that function for the Bennet women.

Elizabeth could, of course, seek employment — and students always ask about it. However, to keep her social station intact, her choice of employment would be severely limited and most unpleasant. She could become a governess in a wealthy family or could take on the related position of genteel companion to a more wealthy woman. Mrs. Jenkinson, the lady who accompanies Miss De Bourgh in her phaeton and screens her eyes from the fire in the drawing room at Rosings, is a little of both. Mrs. Annesley, the "genteel, agreeable-looking woman" (267) who is Georgiana Darcy's companion, occupies a position of the same sort, though with more personal dignity and with the happy benefit of a better employer. Lady Catherine de Bourgh, in her usual officious way, prides herself in having found governess positions among her wealthy acquaintance for numerous young women: "It is wonderful how many families I have been the means of supplying in that way," she tells Elizabeth: "I am always glad to get a young person well placed out. Four nieces of Mrs. Jenkinson are most delightfully situated through my means; and it was but the other day, that I recommended another young person, who was merely accidentally mentioned to me, and the family are quite delighted with her. Mrs. Collins, did I tell you of Lady Metcalfe's calling yesterday to thank me? She finds Miss Pope a treasure. 'Lady Catherine,' said she, 'you have given me a treasure'" (165).

The other side of such delight was no mystery to Austen's contemporaries. The position of genteel companion had a dreadful reputation that was firmly established in the woman's novel. "What a terrible life is that of an humble dependent upon upstart insignificance," cries a character in Maria Elizabeth Robinson's *The Shrine of Bertha* (1:5). The alternate genteel employment, going out as a governess, also had its place in the novelists' gallery of horrors. A governess in Mary Charlton's novel *The Wife and the Mistress* complains bitterly of the work she is expected to do in addition to her teaching duties: "I have been mantua-maker, milliner, sempstress, clear-starcher, nursery maid, and lady's maid, though at the same time for talents and accomplishments I was expected to be a female Crichton" (4: 302–03). "Slaves to torture," says the heroine of Elizabeth Bennet's *Beauty and Ugliness* (4: 132). The advantage was, of course, that the employment came with food, a roof over one's head, and a genteel seat in the parlor, but the delicate situation of the governess's lessened economic condition and her consequently shaken social status could make life thoroughly miserable. Moreover, the expensive wardrobe necessary for taking her seat in the parlor could keep a governess or companion as essentially penniless as though she had no paid employment at all. Mary Wollstonecraft reports to her sister, who was at the time desperate for employment, an appalling newspaper advertisement: "A Nobleman's family in the country wants a governess for two young Ladies of 16 and 14 years old," she writes: "She ought to be born in England, to understand French grammatically and needlework — is to be treated like a child of the house — and to secure 25 guineas a year and some presents." Wollstonecraft advised her sister against it, no doubt remembering her own unhappy experience as she tried to make ends meet at the Kingsboroughs (*Collected Letters* 193, 195).

Novelists, however, are not united in their stands on employment for heroines. Austen's refusal to countenance it marks the choice as a strong ideological preference. When the heroine of Austen's unfinished novel *The Watsons* (c. 1803–04) says with a flourish, "I would rather be Teacher at a school (and I can think of nothing worse) than marry a Man I did not like," her more seasoned older sister replies without hesitation: "I would rather do any thing than be a Teacher at a school. . . . *I* have been at school, Emma, & know what a Life they lead" (*Minor Works* 318). Bennet has her heroine in *Beauty and Ugliness* give teaching a try: "She could not be quite indifferent to the success which attended her exertions; with a feeling of pleasure she beheld the school daily more crowded. . . . She was now in the receipt of seven shillings a-week, her board and lodging found here, and she comparatively rich; she had few anxieties, few wishes for the future." Although she laments her loss of the comforts of wealth, she bears it philosophically: "I am alone, but I have strength and health, and the power of still being serviceable to my fellow-creatures: let this be my consolation" (4: 184–85). Mary Brunton, in her novel *Self-Control*, hails the same female accomplishments that Elizabeth, Darcy, and Miss Bingley rehearse in *Pride and Prejudice* (39), but for Brunton they are also a possible source of income for the heroine: "Oh call it not hard my dear father," the heroine consoles him after he loses the family fortune: "Thanks, a thousand thanks to your kind foresight, which, in teaching me this blessed art [painting], secured to me the only real independence, by making me independent of all but my own exertions" (1: 211–12). Austen read the book and reported to her sister that *Self-Control* was "an excellently-meant, elegantly-written Work, without anything of Nature or Probability in it" (11 Oct. 1813). In short, Austen addresses her novels to the standards of her own class, one in which its women, under its semifeudal ideological standards, must be "protected" from the ravaging hardships of a competitive economy. Charlotte Lucas's predicament, however, throws a shadow of anxiety widely felt elsewhere in women's literature onto the bright comic stage of *Pride and Prejudice*. Wish as they might, Austen's heroines do not have such semi-feudal protection; they do indeed live in the harsh, competitive world of early modern capitalism. The world *the way it should be* governs the concluding vision of *Pride and Prejudice*, not the world to which Charlotte Lucas bears witness.

Craven materialism in *Pride and Prejudice* becomes the mark of the fool. Mr. Bennet's congratulations to Elizabeth on refusing Mr. Collins's offer of marriage, however, beg an important question: "it gratified him, he said, to discover that Charlotte Lucas, whom he had been used to think tolerably sensible, was as foolish as his wife, and more foolish than his daughter!" (127). In fact, Elizabeth's marriage to Mr. Collins could have saved all the women in the family from a possible future of poverty, not a negligible consideration. Without question, however, Mrs. Bennet's ecstasies of greed are richly those of the comic fool: "Oh! my sweetest Lizzy!" she cries to the child she loves least, "how rich and how great you will be! What pin-money, what jewels, what carriages you will have! Jane's is nothing to it — nothing at all. . . . A house in town! Every thing that is charming! . . . Ten thousand a year! Oh, Lord! What will become of me. I shall go distracted" (378). Neither can Mr. Collins find words adequate to express his veneration for Lady Catherine's wealth, or to let Elizabeth know what a good thing she missed in declining his proposal: "she could not help fancying that in displaying the good proportion of the room, its aspect and its furniture, he addressed himself particularly to her, as if wishing to make her feel what she had lost in refusing him" (156). Lady Catherine, no less a materialist than Mrs. Bennet, asks Elizabeth point blank "what carriage her father kept" (164). Paradoxically, all the more flaming materialists, except Charlotte, are poor at domestic economy: "Mrs. Bennet had no turn for economy," we are told (308); the Bingley sisters "were in the habit of spending more than they ought" (15); Lady Catherine descends upon the local villagers to "scold them into harmony and plenty" (169); and the predatory Wickham has debts that become a byword for his profligacy (294). Lydia and Wickham, the most destructive materialists of the lot, are eternally short of money: "I do not think we shall have quite money enough to live upon without some help," Lydia writes Elizabeth (386).

The material possessions of Austen's favored, and richest, characters in *Pride and Prejudice* are, however, carefully diverted from any charge of "materialism" that might be levied on their owners. "If it were merely a fine house richly furnished," says Elizabeth's aunt Mrs. Gardiner of their proposed visit to Pemberley, "I should not care about it myself; but," she adds, "the grounds are delightful. They have some of the finest woods in the country" (240). When Elizabeth actually enters Darcy's dining parlor, guided by the housekeeper, Mrs. Reynolds, she turns aside from the vaguely but "handsomely fitted up" room after only "slightly surveying it" to go "to a window to enjoy its prospect" (246). When she tells Jane of her engagement, she teasingly refers to Darcy's great estate: "I hardly know when it began. But I believe I must date it from my first seeing his beautiful grounds at Pemberley," a joking recognition of Austen's own naturalizing program to legitimate the wealth of his class (373). In effect, Darcy's great consumer luxuries are disinfected from materialism by views, prospects, grounds, a rustic bridge, a coppice. His expansive and, moreover, *expensive* landscape appears before the reader "without any artificial appearance . . . neither formal, nor falsely adorned" (245). In addition, Austen has Elizabeth, Darcy, and the Gardiners show themselves as excellent domestic economists, in pointed contrast to the fecklessness of vulgar materialists. Darcy pays Wickham's debts; he is "affable" to the poor; he and Mr. Gardiner together patch up Lydia's honor with financial persuasions for Wickham; Elizabeth and Jane pay for Lydia and Kitty's meal at the inn when the two girls have spent all their money at a milliner's across the street (219). Yet for all that, it is still the pound we are talking of: spent wisely at Darcy's estate, as Austen insists, but spent, nevertheless, in the same nexus of exchange as Wickham's, Mrs. Bennet's, and Charlotte Lucas's.

Austen's fictional world takes shape from her economic ideology, but its structure is not a closed system. Contradiction lies at the heart of any ideology, as Fredric Jameson reminds us in *The Political Unconscious* (49). As Austen's economic plot strives for closure at the end of *Pride and Prejudice* in the happy union between Elizabeth and Darcy, it inevitably reveals cracks in its underside through the compensations and displacements it seeks to repress. One way for students to account for the problem is to explore Austen's separate loyalties in her economic plotting, two loyalties that are not necessarily, or even usually, congruent: gender and class.

Most important to recognize, Austen's own class is *not* the gentry, as is so often assumed, but is a quite separate class that David Spring, in his essay "Interpreters of Jane Austen's Social World," calls the "pseudogentry": that is, they are rural, nonlanded professionals—including the Anglican clergy (like her father), or lawyers, preferably barristers living in the country, officers in the fighting services, retired rentier families, people in respectable lines of great trade—who have strong country connections with the gentry through kinship and personal loyalties. In *Pride and Prejudice* the Gardiners are outstanding examples of highly successful members of the pseudogentry. These people, Spring suggests, are often taken for gentry precisely because they intended to be. They strive to give the impression of gentry life by taking on the same consumer products, manners, accent, and schools for their children as their landowning gentry neighbors. In truth, however, their economic interests are not always the same as those of the landed gentry whom they admire, emulate, and wish to be connected with. Estate consolidation by marriage, for example, which in *Pride and Prejudice* Lady Catherine insists is natural for Darcy and her daughter, has no place in pseudogentry economics for the simple reason that it would exclude them automatically from making highly prized matches into the landowning gentry.

Pride and Prejudice, of course, is set among the landed gentry, or soon-to-be landowning gentry, as in the case of Bingley, with none of the marrying principals out of that economic class. There is, however, significant displacement of rank in the novel. First of all, we find it as Darcy lays aside his aristocratic pride to assume the traditional virtues of the professionally oriented pseudogentry: he is prudent with money, reflective in all his consumer spending (he buys a pianoforte to surprise his sister; he stays away from expensive display at St. James's in London), and devoted to the service of the poor — a rich, secular arm of rural charity.

The second great displacement of money and rank reckons with Elizabeth's social and economic situation. Elizabeth Bennet belongs by birth to the landed gentry (her father has inherited Longbourn), but she is shorn by Austen of her genteel birthright by the entail. Elizabeth is placed in exactly the same economic condition as a daughter of the pseudogentry, Austen's own rank: that is, Elizabeth is in the perilous situation of the daughter of a professional man whose income, like that of Austen's clergyman father, will cease with his death. In this sense, the marriage of Elizabeth and Darcy does not display simply a movement between gentry families, upper and lower ("He is a gentleman; I am a gentleman's daughter; so far we are equal"), but a more startling union altogether, a Cinderella match of great wealth and comparative poverty across significant social lines (356). In another important displacement, Elizabeth and her sister, Jane, unlike all the other women of their family, are given the presumed virtues of cultured, established gentry families: "*You* cannot have been always at Longbourn," Darcy exclaims to Elizabeth (179). One might call it the dream stuff of every pseudogentry girl without a marriage portion. In Austen, however, the trade-ups and trade-downs must be made in "values" that put to the side, or mitigate, the harsh economic system, which, for all that's said and done, still runs ninety percent of the novel's action.

The importunate student's question, however, arises again: "OK, but just how rich *is* Mr. Darcy?" After all the explaining, the student may remain as ignorant as the young Lucas who boasts, "If I were as rich as Mr. Darcy, . . . I would keep a pack of foxhounds, and drink a bottle of wine every day," or as Mrs. Bennet, whose imagination runs in the same line of consumption: "I suppose he has two or three French cooks at least" (20, 342). Moreover, it probably does not help many students to know that the Adamses suggest twenty-six servants for someone of Darcy's wealth, not including land stewards, bailiffs, woodwards, gamekeepers, park keepers, huntsmen, whippers-in, and other contemporary indulgences of luxury. Perhaps it is time for the students, having paid their dues by learning the comfort scales (carriages and servants) of late-eighteenth-century consumerism, to try a simple currency exchange.

General consensus among the scholars with whom I have discussed the matter in informal conversation, and who would hang me if I cited them, is that a multiplier of 70 or 80 might bring the Austen pound into something like a current American dollar equivalency in 1989. If we take 80 as the multiplier — a conservative estimate, in my opinion — we can join the five Bennet women eking out a genteel life in whatever cramped, dismal quarters they might find on $16,000 a year (£200). Darcy, however, has an income of $800,000 a year for Elizabeth to spend on consumer pleasures, with, in addition, a splendid country house, furniture, valuable library, garden, enormous estate lands, and, in London, a house in a fashionable part of town. Another way of thinking of Darcy's wealth is to consider that, over every two-year period, he and Elizabeth have over $1.5 million at their disposal for consumer pleasures. The Bennet family, if Mr. Bennet stays in health, will have their furnished house, their estate, and $160,000 a year (£2,000) for consumer spending. Jane and Bingley, depending on whether his money is in the 4 percents or 5 percents, will live well enough on the interest of Bingley's fortune at $320,000 or $400,000 a year. Miss Darcy can live at Pemberley with her brother and Elizabeth and keep her $96,000 to $120,000 a year for pocket money. Miss Bingley can continue traveling the country-house circuit in her search for a husband with $64,000 to $80,000 a year to spend on clothes and bracelets.

Lydia's little slip from virtue comes into startling perspective for today's youth when they compute the dollar cost of retrieving it. In a flurry of financial arrangements, Darcy arranges for Wickham's commission as an ensign in the regulars at a cost of around £450, or $36,000, probably much more, according to the military historian Anthony Bruce (5). Mr. Bennet commits himself to give Wickham and Lydia £100 a year as long as he lives — a tribute to virtue, or the appearance of it, amounting to $8,000 a year. Darcy pays Wickham's debts in Brighton, £1,000, or $80,000, and Mr. Gardiner and Mr. Bennet unite to pay his debts in Meryton amounting to very little less than that. It is probable that Darcy also comes up with another large capital sum for Wickham as part of the blackmail package, since Wickham will need an independent income as an officer. His ensign's pay will not cover living expenses (Glover 42–43). If Darcy puts up the £10,000 that Mr. Bennet imagines ("Wickham's a fool, if he takes her with a farthing less than ten thousand pounds" [304]), that would be a staggering sacrifice for love at the capital sum of $800,000.

If it does nothing better, the conversion to today's American currency shows how dizzying the economic stakes are in *Pride and Prejudice*. The metaphor of a game of chance is not a bad one. Lydia's favorite game is lottery (76–77); Jane and Bingley prefer Vingt-un to Commerce (23); Wickham is, as Jane exclaims, "A gamester!" (298); but Darcy and Elizabeth avoid cards (37, 47). The chances of gain and loss in *Pride and Prejudice* are enormous, certainly more precipitous than in any of her later works. Among all Austen's fictional heroes, Darcy is the wealthiest, and among the heroines, Elizabeth is potentially one of the most impoverished. Both the exuberance and the terror of women's confrontation with the new consumer economy emerges from the financial abyss that yawns between them. Just as in the Gothic fiction of her contemporary Mrs. Radcliffe, there is little a heroine can do to turn aside her economic fate, whatever it might be (Lovell, *Consuming Fiction* 71). An unlucky card in the great lottery of life could easily leave an Elizabeth Bennet just as closely imprisoned in the confines of her £1,000 inheritance as Mrs. Radcliffe's heroine who is confined in far more comfortable quarters in *The Mysteries of Udolpho*. The subtleties of income gradation that Austen was later to describe in *Mansfield Park* (1814) and in *Emma* (1816) are missing from *Pride and Prejudice*. Here we find a winner-take-all economy, with, hovering in the background, the troubled shadow of Charlotte Lucas reminding us of the real stakes in the game.

Home at Last: Biographical Background to *Pride and Prejudice*

Ruth Perry

It is easy to find biographical parallels to details of plot and character in *Pride and Prejudice* — elements that Jane Austen transformed from the straw of her life into the gold of her art. A survey of her letters yields many examples of identifiable persons and situations that appear to be the "real life" counterparts of the actions and attitudes of the immortal people in her famous novel. Lydia's infatuation with the regiment quartered at Meryton was imagined by a woman who loved balls and openly enjoyed flirting. At twenty-one she wrote gaily to her sister that "the day is come on which I am to flirt my last with Tom Lefroy" (17 Jan. 1796). At the same time she playfully satirized other young women who lived for the pleasures of male attention. When a Miss Fletcher of Canterbury explained that she had not written because "everybody" they knew had left town, Austen interpreted: "By *Everybody*, I suppose Miss Fletcher means that a new set of Officers have arrived there" (15 Sep. 1796). The haughty Lady Catherine de Bourgh may owe her existence to a distant relative, Lady Saye and Sele, whom the Austen women met in 1806 at Stoneleigh Abbey in Adelstrop, where her opinionated, officious manners afforded the author "many a good laugh" (Austen-Leigh and Austen 196–97).[1]

Several critics have pointed out that the title of *Pride and Prejudice*, as well as Darcy's first, snobbish proposal, derive from Frances Burney's *Cecilia* (1782), a novel Austen admired very much (Southam, *Literary Manuscripts* 60).[2] Park Honan conjectures in his astute biography of Austen that the psychological economy of the Bennets' marriage, hilariously rendered in that first, indelible chapter of *Pride and Prejudice*, had its parallel in the teasing relationship between Austen's eldest brother, James, and his second, less verbal wife, Mary Lloyd (232–34). The brilliant opening sentence of the novel — a reminder of the way society appropriates individuals — shares its affectionate ironic tone with this sentence in one of Austen's letters, as she laughs at the way people made plans for her: "I am very much obliged to Mrs. Knight for such a proof of the interest she takes in me," she wrote in response to a conversation Cassandra reported having with that worthy woman about their new neighbors in Chawton. "She may depend upon it that I *will* marry Mr. Papillon [the bachelor rector of Chawton], whatever may be his reluctance or my own. I owe her much more than such a trifling sacrifice" (Austen-Leigh and Austen 221).

And yet, how much should one make of the biographical contribution to a work of art? Isn't what matters how a writer makes use of the materials of his or her life? How do the deeper structures of *Pride and Prejudice* reflect the central experiences of Austen's life? How can we see Austen working through these experiences—fictionalizing them, meditating on them, confronting them, externalizing them—in the pages of *Pride and Prejudice*? Jane Bennet's resolute but strained efforts at a wan sociability after Bingley's defection is probably modeled on Cassandra's strength of will in suffering when her fiancé, Thomas Fowle, died unexpectedly of yellow fever on what turned out to be his ultimate voyage, to the West Indies. He was to have married Cassandra when he returned. The long-term effects of his death—Cassandra never married out of the family, never went to live in Shropshire, but remained devoted to Jane all her life—may have been essential to Austen's evolution as an artist. To the extent that Cassandra's assistance—both her emotional support and, more materially, her supervision of the household, which left Jane free to write—enabled Austen to emerge as an author, the death of Fowle may have made possible Austen's subsequent career. This family crisis and Cassandra's suffering were also memorialized in *Sense and Sensibility*, in Elinor Dashwood's mute agony, her stoicism, her determined efforts not to visit her grief on others. Echoing Harriet Byron's controlled grief in Richardson's *Sir Charles Grandison*—Austen's favorite novel—the silent mourning of Elinor in *Sense and Sensibility* and of Jane Bennet in *Pride and Prejudice*, when they are forsaken by what had appeared to be professed lovers, must be read as Austen's tribute to Cassandra's trial and exemplary resignation after Fowle disappeared from her life.

The importance of male relatives to the maintenance of women—epitomized in the novel by the dreaded entail—was also a fact of Austen's life. Because there were no close male relatives, Elizabeth Bennet's home, Longbourn, was to be forfeited on Mr. Bennet's death, to revert to another branch of the family—in this case, Mr. Collins, who, as Mr. Bennet baldly states, "may turn you all out of this house as soon as he pleases" (61). As the Bennet women depended on Mr. Bennet for their support—and sorely lacked brothers to supply his place when he died—so the Austen women depended on George Austen and his sons (Jane and Cassandra's brothers) for their maintenance. George Austen's death, in 1805, meant that they lost his annual income of £600 and would have been reduced to the £210 that Mrs. Austen and Cassandra between them could command, were it not for the male offspring in the family (3 Jan. 1801).[3] (Cassandra had a small income from the interest on the £1,000 legacy that Fowle left her in his will.) The monetary contributions of the Austen brothers were essential to keep afloat the household of Mrs. Austen, Cassandra, and Jane after George Austen died. Henry, James, and Frank each contributed £50 a year, and Edward added £100, which brought up the Austen women's income to between £450 and £460 a year—just what the fictional Dashwood women lived on in *Sense and Sensibility* (Le Faye 130–31).[4] Deirdre Le Faye remarks that the presence in the neighborhood of the sad figure of Miss Benn, a poor spinster without wealthy brothers, must have been "an uncomfortable reminder to Jane and Cassandra that, but for their own brothers' financial support, such an existence could all too easily have been theirs" (156). Without sons, Mrs. Austen would have been in the same predicament as Mrs. Bennet and her brood of girls in *Pride and Prejudice*: threatened by penury and homelessness on the death of her husband. The urgency, for an unmarried woman, of finding an establishment is calibrated rather precisely in *Pride and Prejudice*, in the extent to which we pity or blame Charlotte Lucas for marrying Mr. Collins.

But these are superficial resemblances, visible reflections in the mirror Austen held up to nature. There is a more profound way in which *Pride and Prejudice* is expressive of Austen's state of being when she wrote it. The sheer happiness of that novel, the way it skips and dances, the fairy-tale perfection of the romance, the exaggerated but harmless foibles of the "villains" — these betray a heart finally at ease after many years of dislocation and interruption, a writer embarked at last on a literary career after the disappointments of her youth. *Pride and Prejudice* is a contented book, and, as I argue here, its deep satisfaction derives from Austen's new confidence in herself as a writer and from the fact that she had launched her career and become a serious breadwinner for her family.

Austen's joy of vocation, her writerly pleasure, brightens the pages of *Pride and Prejudice* — her delight when she found herself at last in a situation that permitted her to write, in full possession of her literary powers, and encouraged in her labors by the ever-supportive Cassandra. In the three years since she, her mother, and her sister had come to Chawton, she had finally published a novel, started another one, and was revising a third. She had resurrected her earlier, epistolary *Elinor and Marianne*, reworked sometime in 1797 as *Sense and Sensibility*, written in the third person but with a less well-defined narrator than she was to develop for *Pride and Prejudice* — and had published it "on commission." It was a modest success from the start and was praised in the February 1812 *Critical Review* (Le Faye 168). She was planning similarly to take apart and restitch *First Impressions*, which she hoped would fetch a good price, and had begun work on an entirely new novel, *Mansfield Park*, the first new writing she had undertaken in five years. At last she was doing what she was meant to do.

To understand the significance of 1812 for Jane Austen — the year in which she rewrote *Pride and Prejudice* for publication from the earlier, possibly epistolary *First Impressions*[5] at the same time as she was working on a draft of *Mansfield Park* — we need to take a retrospective glance at her life. Until July 1809, when she and her mother and Cassandra finally relocated in a six-bedroom cottage on her brother Edward's Hampshire estate, they had been moving uncomfortably among suites of rented rooms and shared lodgings in Bath and Southampton for a number of years. Their life had been especially difficult for Jane, who had been deeply attached to the place in which she had grown up, the parsonage at Steventon. She is supposed to have fainted dead away when her mother first told her of the intention to leave that house and live in Bath (Austen-Leigh and Austen 155–56). George Austen wanted to retire and, without discussing the matter with his daughters, had decided to resign his living to James, his eldest son, along with the Steventon parsonage, and to move his remaining family to the resort town. So the Austens sold their furniture — including Jane's library — and left those beloved surroundings for rented lodgings in Bath. Following that profound shock, the peripatetic life they led in Bath, changing dwellings three times in four years, and her father's death in January 1805 — after which they moved again, first to Gay Street in Bath and then to Southampton — were only corollary sorrows.[6]

Leaving Steventon was the most traumatic event in Jane Austen's life. The extreme shock of this crisis for the twenty-five-year old author can be gauged by the obsessiveness with which she wrote about displacement in her novels: the Dashwoods forced out of their home by relatives, the threat of disinheritance by entail hanging over the Bennet women in *Pride and Prejudice*, Fanny Price alone and vulnerable at the estate of her wealthy cousins in *Mansfield Park*, and Anne Elliot displaced at Kellynch Hall by renters in *Persuasion*. Indeed, part of the configuration that makes of Mr. Woodhouse, in *Emma*, the perfect wish-fulfillment father is that he cannot be pried loose from his own hearth.[7] All the novels (with the exception of *Emma*) are arranged to recoup this particular loss — the loss resulting from dislocation — to resettle their heroines and try out different solutions for being in the world. And the novel most optimistic about the possibility of successful relocation, of settling permanently and happily in an establishment of one's own (for the fates of Jane and Elizabeth Bennet far outweigh that of Charlotte Lucas) is *Pride and Prejudice*.

The move to Chawton Cottage, after eight homeless and unsettled years, was, for Austen, something like returning to the home of her childhood. Hampshire had always been special to her, and Steventon, where her brother James and his family now lived, was just a morning's ride away. As plans for the move proceeded, she decided that as soon as she was settled, she would buy a pianoforte, "as good a one as can be got for thirty guineas," the first instrument of her own since Steventon days (27 Dec. 1808). The sprightly poem she wrote to their brother Frank a few months after taking up residence in Chawton Cottage, to congratulate him on the birth of a son, expresses in its last verse her satisfaction at once again having a home of her own.

> As for ourselves, we're very well;
> As unaffected prose will tell. —
> Cassandra's pen will paint our state,
> The many comforts that await

Our Chawton home, how much we find
Already in it, to our mind;
And how convinced, that when complete
It will all other Houses beat
That ever have been made or mended,
With rooms concise, or room distended.
You'll find us very snug next year,
Perhaps with Charles and Fanny near,[8]
For now it often does delight me
To fancy them just over-right-us. —
                    J.A. — (26 July 1809)

Thus, by 1812 Austen had been settled in Chawton long enough to see the successful issue of her first published novel, to be in the midst of revising another work from the Steventon period, and to have a new novel under way. Her new literary career was in full swing. Cassandra ran the household capably and left to Jane only the light duties of morning breakfast. According to family tradition, "*that* was *her* part of the household work — The tea and sugar stores were under *her* charge — *and* the wine — Aunt Cassandra did all the rest" (Le Faye 158). After breakfast, her time was her own.

In the years at Steventon before the peripatetic Bath-Southampton period, Jane Austen had been active and productive as a writer, with the full support of her family. Both *Sense and Sensibility* and *Pride and Prejudice* had been first drafted at Steventon and read aloud to Cassandra in their shared bedroom. James's daughter Anna, then a precocious two-year-old, sometimes sat in on these sessions and had to be prevented from giving away in company the names and details of the characters whose adventures were being related nightly upstairs by Jane (Austen-Leigh and Austen 73).

It is to this early draft, no doubt, that we owe the youthful gaiety of *Pride and Prejudice*, for the "light, and bright, and sparkling" tone of the novel is there in Austen's letters of 1796–97 (4 Feb. 1813). Park Honan suggests that her flirtation with Tom Lefroy late in the year of 1795–96 supplied the erotic energy of the attraction between Elizabeth Bennet and Darcy. "Ten months after Tom left she began with zeal her Elizabeth Bennet and Darcy story," he observes (113). As for Elizabeth Bennet herself, Austen thought her "as delightful a creature as ever appeared in print," when she received her advance copy of the novel; "how I shall be able to tolerate those who do not like *her* at least I do not know," she added (29 Jan. 1813).

What makes Elizabeth so wonderful is her happiness. She is more happily circumstanced than any other of Austen's heroines, and her happiness is more unalloyed. She has at least one parent who appreciates her and in whose wit and intelligence she can take pleasure. Her relationship with her sister Jane is closer and more reciprocal than any of the sister relationships in the other novels are.[9] Darcy is richer and more highly born than any of her other heroes; Pemberley is a fairy-tale estate. And Elizabeth is brimming with youthful enthusiasm, not having had to endure disappointment, like Anne Elliot, the only other sexually passionate exogamous heroine Austen ever created.

It seems clear that Austen first drafted this novel in a younger state of mind, when she still believed that all things were possible. The original version, *First Impressions*, was apparently meant to mock a sentimental trust in impulse and spontaneous feeling (as does her juvenile *Love and Freindship* [sic]) — a common enough theme of novels of the 1790s. One feels that the author herself was under the influence of just such stirrings while writing the first version of this novel. And later, at Chawton, when revising this manuscript into its present form, she reconnected with that earlier self through Anna, now a heroine-aged niece, who often stayed with her grandmother and aunts in Chawton Cottage. She reminded Jane Austen of her own pleasure in youthful gaities at that age, regaling them with stories of her balls and suppers and flirtations. Indeed, Anna remembered the summer of 1812 as the period of her "greatest share of intimacy" with her aunt Jane, when "the original 17 years between us seemed to shrink to 7 — or to nothing — " as they giggled together over the absurdities in the latest novels from the circulating library (Le Faye 170).

Austen's family, her first audience, thought well of *First Impressions*, that earlier draft of *Pride and Prejudice*. In 1797, while they were still living at Steventon, George Austen had tried to find a publisher for it. "Sir," he wrote to Thomas Cadell, the London publisher, in November:

> I have in my possession a manuscript novel, comprising 3 vols. about the length of Miss Burney's *Evelina*. As I am well aware of what consequence it is that a work of this sort shd. make its first appearance under a respectable name, I apply to you. I shall be much obliged, therefore, if you will inform me whether you choose to be concerned in it, what will be the expense of publishing it at the author's risk, and what you will venture to advance for the property of it, if on perusal it is approved of.   (Austen-Leigh and Austen 97–98)

We know that Austen was working on the manuscript again in 1799, having redrafted *Elinor and Marianne* in the meantime, from a sentence in one of her letters to her sister (8 Jan. 1799). Cassandra must have mentioned it to their good friend Martha Lloyd, who asked to read through the manuscript again. To this request Jane Austen replied:

> I would not let Martha read "First Impressions" again upon any account, and am very glad that I did not leave it in your power. She

is very cunning, but I saw through her design; she means to publish
it from memory, and one more perusal must enable her to do it.

(11 June 1799)

But whatever progress was made at that stage was interrupted by the abrupt
and wrenching move to Bath.

The period in which the novel was drafted and the period in which it
was redrafted, then, were times of great optimism in Austen's life: the first,
when she believed naively that everything would work out for the best, and
the second, when she had learned again to hope for a life for herself as a
writer. Of all her novels, *Pride and Prejudice* represents the best possible
accommodation for women in a patriarchal world. Originally written in
the high spirits of youth, this novel projects a rosier view of life than any
of her other novels. The good women all marry up in class; the villains all
are thwarted. Even the elopement of Lydia and Wickham — the acting out
of sexual impulse — turns out "better" than the shocking and adulterous elopement of Henry Crawford and Maria Rushworth in *Mansfield Park*.

Critics from Marilyn Butler to Claudia Johnson have recognized the
inherent conservatism of this profoundly conciliatory novel, the one that
finds the least fault with the world, the one in which moral gradations map
most unproblematically onto the hierarchy of the social universe (Butler,
Jane Austen 197–218; Johnson 73). Elizabeth accepts without question
Darcy's prescription for accomplished womanhood, delivered in the drawing
room at Netherfield. And he becomes an increasingly idealized figure of
authority in Elizabeth's eyes, when his qualities as a just patriarch are dis-
closed to her by his housekeeper at Pemberley: "As a brother, a landlord,
a master, she considered how many people's happiness were in his guardian-
ship" (250). As for Elizabeth, she learns not to place too much reliance in
her own powers of discernment and is rewarded for her pains by the husband
with the greatest fortune and most vaunted lineage in all Austen's novels.

In her brilliant series of articles on Austen's fragmentary and less finished
writings, Q. D. Leavis demonstrates that Austen never stopped working
as a writer, never stopped thinking of herself as an author, in the years
between Steventon and Chawton.[10] Although she produced nothing of
lasting reputation during that time, it was her apprenticeship period, during
which she tried out various narrative techniques, plot arrangements, and
character sketches later turned to account in her finished novels. Between
1800 and 1805, Austen at least copied over *Lady Susan* and probably gave
it an ending (Fergus, *Literary Life* 74). She composed the fragment *The
Watsons* and revised another work from the Steventon years, *Susan*, to be
published in the end as *Northanger Abbey* (Austen-Leigh and Austen 175).
In 1803 she sold the copyright of this last novel, *Susan*, to Richard Crosby
& Co. for £10, expecting it to be published soon after (Honan 199). Jan
Fergus conjectures that Austen revised this manuscript quite thoroughly in
1802–03 before selling it (*Literary Life* 96–98, 104).

Six years later, in April 1809, just before moving to Chawton, she wrote to Crosby and Co. and asked if the firm had lost the manuscript copy of *Susan* it had bought — and whether the company expected to publish it. She told the publisher that if he was not going to print it, she would try to place the work elsewhere (5 Apr. 1809). From the start, then, she thought of her life at Chawton as a chance to consolidate her literary production and to begin to market her novels. A secure home made writing possible, just as writing made wherever she was living into home. This association between writing and being "at home" is there in the metaphor she used to condole with her nephew Edward, when he lost two and a half chapters of a novel he was writing. "It is well that I have not been at Steventon lately, & therefore cannot be suspected of purloining them," she wrote to him; "two strong twigs & a half towards a Nest of my own, would have been something" (Le Faye 218).

As it happens, Crosby and Co. refused to release *Susan*, and she apparently decided instead to make over *Elinor and Marianne/Sense and Sensibility*, thrifty reworker of materials that she was. Just as she turned her old gowns into petticoats (24 Dec. 1798) or used a shabby cloak to line a newly refurbished pelisse (15 Oct. 1808), so she did not waste the perfectly good material she had written a dozen years before. As we have seen, she published this manuscript "on commission," probably borrowing money from Henry to cover initial costs (Honan 284–86). Happily, it was a moderate success; favorably reviewed, it sold steadily. When the first edition sold out in the first two years, netting her £140, Austen was delighted.

The money that Austen was earning from *Sense and Sensibility* certainly contributed to her confident and joyful mood in 1812 while she was revising *Pride and Prejudice*. The additional income must have been very welcome to the household at Chawton, for the letters between the sisters testify to their pinched circumstances and enforced frugality. "I am determined to spend no more money," wrote Jane from London in 1811 (30 Apr.). The sisters were probably worried about losing a significant portion of their yearly income when the time came for their semi-invalided mother to die, for then her South Sea stock (and its income) was to be divided among all her children. As the profits from *Sense and Sensibility* began to add up, then, surely Jane Austen was gratified to see that she might be able to sustain herself and Cassandra with her writing in the event of Mrs. Austen's death. Indeed, by the end of her eight years as a published author, she had earned the considerable sum of £684 13s. The interest on this nest egg, which she put into the "Navy 5 per cents," added a significant increment to the Chawton Cottage coffers (Honan 393).

I have been arguing that Austen undertook the rewriting of *Pride and Prejudice* in an optimistic mood, as a published author, with a real career opening up before her. She told Martha Lloyd that she was hoping Egerton would give her £150 for this second novel, although she took with alacrity the £110 that he offered (29 Nov. 1812). The success of *Sense and Sensibility* encouraged her as she worked on cutting and revising *First Impressions*. Park Honan conjectures that she took out a quarter of the prose from the original, toned down her burlesque of romantic fiction, and added a more elaborate psychological dimension to Elizabeth's character (308). She may also have deepened the theme of revision in the final draft—Elizabeth's clearer second sight into the characters of Wickham and Darcy—as she revised and sharpened her manuscript. None of her later books is quite so unambivalent about life's possibilities: *Mansfield Park* is too painfully aware of the vulnerability of women's lives; *Emma* is too concerned with socializing one of the lucky ones to think beyond her own pleasure and to look out for others; and *Persuasion* is wistful about being offered a second chance. None have *Pride and Prejudice*'s optimism and trust in an almost limitless future.

Austen was elated when that first bound copy arrived from the publisher. Cassandra was at Steventon at the time, and so we have Jane's excited letter to her: "I hope . . . that you will be ready to hear from me again . . . for I feel that I must write to you to-day," she said. "I have got my own darling child from London." She was surprised by how short the second volume of her triple-decker printed up, so successfully had she "lop't and crop't" that it was shorter than she had anticipated. (In most modern editions volume 2 consists of chapters 24–42, in which the Bingleys decamp for London, Elizabeth visits Charlotte Lucas Collins at Hunsford, is proposed to and then written to by Darcy, and begins her Derbyshire tour.) Nevertheless, she was pleased with the overall effect. That night the unsuspecting Miss Benn dined at Chawton, and Jane and her mother read aloud half the first volume, without telling their visitor who had written it. "She was amused, poor soul!" reported Austen. "*That* she could not help, you know, with two such people to lead the way, but she really does seem to admire Elizabeth" (29 Jan. 1813). Our author, too, enjoyed hearing the book despite her mother's shortcomings as a dramatic reader. There was nothing she wished changed or amended. "I am quite vain enough and well satisfied enough," she wrote happily to Cassandra (4 Feb. 1813). Besides, she was already preoccupied with her next novel.

The story I have told here, about the authorial consciousness informing this novel, is only one of many stories one could tell about how the text works out the issues of Jane Austen's life. Biographical details are layered through *Pride and Prejudice* in vertical structures of meaning almost as interesting to the biographically minded critic as the horizontal narrative structure of character and incident. Susan Kneedler's and Deborah Kaplan's essays in this volume suggest readings other than the one I have offered, readings that shed further light on Austen's feelings about the choices of her life. The availability of Austen's letters and other excellent biographical sources—Deirdre Le Faye's revised *Family Record*, for example—makes possible the excavation of these layers of biographical meaning that refract the novel ever more variously. Courses on Jane Austen, women's fiction, biography, and narrative structure (among others) could profit from class discussions or paper topics that pair *Pride and Prejudice* with its biographical sources in order to examine how authors make use of their materials, how fictional narrative and literary biography illuminate each other, and how, in this particular instance, the experiences of a life are transformed into art.[11]

NOTES

[1]For a description of Lady Saye and Sele, see also Honan 224–26.

[2]Southam also refers the reader to the appendix of Chapman's edition of *Pride and Prejudice* for discussion of "other possible connexions" between *Pride and Prejudice* and *Cecilia*. See also Honan 307 and Doody, "Jane Austen's Reading" 358.

[3]George Austen's income derived from his livings at Steventon and Deane and his small annuity in the Hand-in-Hand Society (Le Faye 130).

[4]Discreet Cassandra wanted Jane to alter the figures, in her fictional narrative, of the shamefully reduced income of Mrs. Dashwood and her daughters. I think she found the similarity to their own financial situation embarrassing and wanted Jane to change the amounts so that the novel's opening could not be construed as a criticism of their brothers James and Edward (25 Apr. 1811).

[5]Although there is no evidence that *First Impressions* was epistolary — of the solid sort that we have for the nature of the first draft of *Elinor and Marianne* (Caroline Austen noted that *Sense and Sensibility* was "*first* written in letters and *so* read to her family") — Southam sets out a number of grounds for considering that it might have been written, initially, entirely in letters. Its original bulk and the degree of its recasting suggest an originally epistolary construction as well as the number of letters "mentioned, quoted, or given verbatim" in the text as it now stands. Forty-four letters help to tell the story, as compared with the twenty-one remaining letters in *Sense and Sensibility*, and there is an epistolary armature still visible in the correspondence between Elizabeth and Charlotte Lucas, or Elizabeth and Jane and Mrs. Gardiner, adequate to carry a narration managed entirely in letters (Southam, *Literary Manuscripts* 68–72). For Caroline Austen's remark on *Sense and Sensibility*, see Southam 54.

[6]For the Austens' movements within Bath and their relocation to Southampton, see Le Faye 119, 125, 126, 131, 136, 142, 154.

[7]Mr. Woodhouse is paradigmatic in a strictly Freudian sense: he provides his name and his authority to protect Emma, but he lets her do exactly as she wishes. Emma says of her doting father and her relation to him: "I believe few married women are half as much mistress of their husband's house, as I am of Hartfield; and never, never could I expect to be so truly beloved and important; so always first and always right in any man's eyes as I am in my father's" (84).

[8]She probably means her brother Charles and his wife, Fanny.

[9]In *Sense and Sensibility* the sisters love each other, but Elinor has to take emotional responsibility for immature Marianne. In *Mansfield Park* the Bertram sisters compete for Henry Crawford (as Fanny Price and Mary Crawford compete for Edmund). In *Persuasion* the heroine's sisters seem to belong to another species.

[10]Although Southam challenges Leavis's premise that Austen took her materials from life and emphasizes, throughout his criticism, the *literary* origins of her characters, he never questions Leavis's assertion that Austen worked continually as a writer. Southam insists, for example, that Austen's character Lady Susan, the eponymous heroine of that unpublished novel (first printed in the second edition of Austen-Leigh's *Memoir*, in 1871), derived from the literary stereotype of the "merry widow" rather than from the qualities — however rearranged — of her sister-in-law Eliza de Feuillide (*Literary Manuscripts* 136–48).

[11]Jan Fergus generously read and corrected an earlier draft of this essay.

The "Social History" of *Pride and Prejudice*
Julia Prewitt Brown

In what sense are Jane Austen's novels historical? This is often the first question students ask when they read Austen. It may be posed in the form of the familiar question, Where are the Napoleonic Wars, the decisive historical event of her time? Or, more frankly, Why did Austen choose such limited subject matter? Why did she focus exclusively on personal relations? A reminder that "ordinary life" constitutes the blood and bone of the novel genre usually does not satisfy the eighteen-year-old who seeks in works of literature some grandeur of human purpose — and why should it? "Don't *begin* with proportion," urges a wise character in E. M. Forster's *Howards End*. "Only prigs do that. Let proportion come in as a last resource, when the better things have failed" (73). The student who begins by hating Jane Austen, I have discovered, usually ends by learning more from her than does the budding Janeite.

As for the historical content of the novels, students may not see it because they think of social history as "history with the politics left out," as G. M. Trevelyan once described it, rather than what it is: the essential foundation that gives shape to everything else. For the cultural historian Raymond Williams, for example, Austen's novels provide an accurate record of that moment in English history in which high bourgeois society most evidently interlocked with an agrarian capitalism. "An openly acquisitive society," writes Williams, "which is concerned also with the transmission of wealth, is trying to judge itself at once by an inherited code and by the morality of improvement" (*Country* 115). What is at stake here is not personal relations but personal *conduct*: "a testing and discovery of the standards which govern human behaviour in certain real situations" (113). Those situations arise from the unsettled world Austen portrays, with its continual changes of fortune and social mobility that were affecting the landed families of her time. Thus, although Darcy is a landowner established for "many generations," his friend Bingley has no estate and has inherited £100,000 from his father, who made money in trade; and although Mr. Bennet has an estate, he has married the daughter of an attorney who has a brother in trade, and his estate will not pass to his own children; and so on.

Readers may glimpse the "openly acquisitive society" in the heroine's first sight of Pemberley, Darcy's beautiful estate. Deeply impressed, even awestruck, by its elegance and grandeur, Elizabeth cannot but admit to herself that "to be mistress of Pemberley might be something!" (245). Later Elizabeth satirizes her own response when her sister asks her to explain when she first fell in love with Darcy: "It has been coming on so gradually," Elizabeth replies, "that I hardly know when it began. But I believe I must date it from my first seeing his beautiful grounds at Pemberley" (373). Elizabeth's wit distances her from herself, from the woman with the conventional response to Pemberley, just as the narrator's irony distances the reader from conventional responses. But before entering into a discussion of Austen's narrative irony, we may as well ask the conventional question, In what sense *would* being mistress of Pemberley "be something"?

In Austen's day England was still to a large extent an "aristocracy," or hierarchy based on property and patronage in which people took their places in a pyramidlike structure extending down from a minority of the rich and powerful at the top to ever wider and larger layers of lesser wealth to the great mass of the poor and powerless at the bottom. Together, the aristocracy and gentry owned more than two-thirds of all the land in England. In this largely agrarian society, government was conceived of as the authority of the locality, the government of parish, county, and town, whose officials were members of the gentry appointed by the Crown. In the course of the century, this system of local government was replaced by a modern bureaucracy of trained and elected administrators, but at the time Austen was writing, the gentry were the real governors of the countryside. Not until the commercial and political revolutions, accumulating full force in the eighteenth century, disrupted the solidarity of families founded on landed wealth did these ancient families, and the women who belonged to them, lose much of the power they had so long exercised. Only then did the state pass to the control of parliaments composed of men and elected by men.

Lady Catherine de Bourgh and her nephew Darcy are members of one such ancient family, and they are highly conscious of the power they possess. Both control the lives and incomes of scores of people on their estates, many of whom had no voting power until the Reform Bill of 1832. Even after that, until the secret ballot was passed in 1872, landlords could have a decisive effect on votes, since they were taken orally. Traditionally, the steward of an estate such as Darcy's would round up the tenants who could vote, take them to the polling place, and remain there while they called out their preference. A man such as Darcy, were he to run for a seat in the House of Commons, could then be sure of this built-in constituency of tenants. Wickham's chronic resentment, Austen implies, is a function of his having grown up as the son of the elder Darcy's steward, daily observing so many more advantages accrue to Darcy than to himself.

Although women in the gentry had less authority than men, a matter I take up later, some had considerable power. The tradition of primogeniture established that, under the law, property was passed to the eldest son; and English matrimonial law stipulated that, through marriage, the husband became the owner of all his wife's property. But there were ways in which the gentry could and did protect its women. Mr. Bennet cannot alter the entail requiring that his estate go to the nearest male relation, but he can settle money on his daughters that, if proper legal measures are taken, will remain their own after marriage. Because Lady Catherine's estate is not entailed from the female line, she enjoys most of the advantages of her nephew. She is patroness of the living of Mr. Collins, for example, and he is only one of many people who are dependent on her and therefore must pay court to her. Elizabeth is right when she recognizes that to join Darcy's family and become mistress of Pemberley would indeed "be something." Family and marriage occupied a far more public and central position in the social government and economic arrangements of English society than they would later. In the novels of Austen, marriage is then accurately seen as an institution that both determines and is determined by history.

By the early nineteenth century, England was in the full swing of the first phase of the industrial revolution, which created the new class society of the Victorians. Vertical economic conflicts arose to challenge the horizontal layers formerly joined in agrarian dependency. Wide-scale competition among groups or classes with differing economic interests produced the vertical antagonism known as "class feeling." In *Pride and Prejudice* such tension is evident in the snobbery of the Bingley sisters, which disguises their sense of inferiority in having a parent who made money in trade, and in the way Lady Catherine looks down her nose at the Gardiners, who live in an unfashionably industrial section of London. (It is interesting to note how much more tolerant Austen is of the class of new merchants, revealed in her sympathetic portrait of the Gardiners, than some later novelists— Thackeray, for instance, in *Vanity Fair*.)

The common complaint against Austen then—that the novels are too narrow in their exclusive attention to the private marriage decisions of a single class—is based on a present-day conception of social organization, with its sharp division of the public and private domains. The word *private* is itself applied anachronistically to her world. What is its opposite? Is it perhaps *public*? Yet for much of the nineteenth century, the public authority of the state was only emerging; the public domain was in the process of extending its territory to include all that it would encompass in this century. For most people living in Austen's society, it could be argued that all of life was private, because it was centered in the private estate. In *Emma* Mr. Knightley talks about his responsibilities as a magistrate in the same breath as his deliberations about the plan of a drain. In *Pride and Prejudice* Darcy's virtues as a landlord are established by a dependent living within his own house, his housekeeper (248–49).

Perhaps we should define the opposite of *private* as *social* or *communal* and then see if we can locate this nonsocial, noncommunal presence in Austen's novels, especially within the institution that she places at the center of society: marriage. Austen permits us to overhear "private" conversations between husband and wife in several novels. The opening chapter of *Pride and Prejudice* is one such conversation, and there we notice that even when they are alone, Mr. and Mrs. Bennet address each other as "Mrs. Bennet" and "Mr. Bennet," suggesting a social and formal dimension within the "private" experience of marriage that has all but disappeared today. At the same time, the fact that Austen makes us privy to the conversation points to one of her greatest overriding themes: the growing privatization of marriage. In Austen's early novel, *Northanger Abbey*, marriage is linked to the general functioning of society and to the land; in her last, *Persuasion*, it is separated from the land and from stable community. In *Persuasion* particularly we see the origins of modern marriage, with its intense focus on the private "relationship" that a secular society imposes and its anticipation of the egalitarian marriage of companionship, represented by Admiral and Mrs. Croft (who, as the heroine notes, share the reins of their carriage — that is to say, marriage). This shift from marriage as a public, social institution to a private relationship is apparent in all the novels. That two of Austen's most famous scenes, in the opening chapters of *Sense and Sensibility* and *Pride and Prejudice*, point to the private hell she saw marriage could become suggests such a shift as well, and there is a telling difference between the scenes. In the earlier novel, Austen shows the public and formal structure of marriage determining a loathsome alliance: Mr. and Mrs. John Dashwood conspire to cheat their relations of their patrimony. In *Pride and Prejudice* we see more of the truly private misery of Mr. Bennet beneath the comedy. Actors who have played Mr. Bennet in film and theater have often failed to portray the darker side of his character — his debilitating weariness and boredom, his cynical inattention to his family — and in so doing have made the world of the novel seem weightless and insipid. The novel's "lightness," which Austen remarked on in her letters, cannot be appreciated if we do not feel its weight, and much of this substance is located in Austen's ever-increasing attention to the private self, most particularly in her rendering of the heroine's inner life.

Here again, the historical shift is apparent. In *Sense and Sensibility* the private experience of both Marianne and Elinor is almost always understood by means of a juxtaposition of their characters. When Marianne screams in misery at the center of the novel, her sister is there to hear it; the reader is given to understand the cry in its social context. But when Elizabeth Bennet reads Darcy's letter, she suffers alone: "Till this moment, I never knew myself" (208). When Emma realizes how much she has muddled and mangled her own and Harriet's emotions, "she sat still, she walked about, she tried her own room, she tried the shrubbery," yet no place will accommodate her; she cannot escape herself (323). And the heroine of Austen's last novel is consistently estranged in the way Austen represents her subjective life and role as observer.

The social historian Lawrence Stone calls this change the rise of "affective individualism," suggesting by the term an intrinsic relation between the democratization of society and the inner life. Austen shows her awareness and perhaps endorsement of this shift in culture by having Elizabeth Bennet declare her right to be happy; and it is interesting to note how frequently the word *happiness* appears in the novel. Elizabeth refuses Mr. Collins because he could not make her happy (107), although their marriage would secure her entire family economic protection for life. Later in the novel, when Lady Catherine attempts to appeal to Elizabeth's sense of social duty by insisting she agree not to marry her nephew, Elizabeth replies, "I am only resolved to act in that manner, which will, in my own opinion, constitute my happiness, without reference to *you*, or to any person so wholly unconnected with me" (358).

Stone's theory of social history suggests that only in a highly individualist society does happiness arise as an ideal: those who see themselves as living for themselves become interested in happiness. But if they view themselves as living for something beyond the self — say, the community — happiness loses its central place in human concern. That Austen reveals in almost every novel how difficult it is to negotiate a compromise between the drive for happiness and the necessity of a life of service all communities require of its citizens (most commonly in their role as parents) is not surprising. The question of happiness lies at the heart of the English tradition of liberal rationalism, particularly as it expressed itself in the works of Austen's contemporary Jeremy Bentham and later in the formulations of John Stuart Mill. One of Mill's major efforts was to reconcile a Benthamite faith in making happiness the supreme goal of human life with his communitarian belief in service, probably acquired through the classical education he received from his father (as Austen did from hers). In order to do so, Mill eventually insists on the existence of a private domain, set apart and separate from the demands of law and custom. This abstraction, the private domain, which we have difficulty imagining as an abstraction so much do we take Mill's ideas for granted, is the basis of the argument of *On Liberty* (1859). So little did Mill himself take it for granted, however, that a large section of *On Liberty* is devoted to establishing and defining its existence. Another example is that, until the secret ballot was passed, parliamentarians expressed their astonishment over the proposal on the grounds that no honorable person would have any reason to cast a vote in secret; the private domain was imagined only with difficulty.

These same ambiguities concerning the private self and its relation to custom and community make themselves felt in *Pride and Prejudice*. Austen tempers her affirmation of individual happiness as an ideal by means of a deep aesthetic vigilance over its possible excesses. The hero of the novel, for example, is as different in substance and temperament from the heroine as could be; he embodies the traditional self, one whose identity is based on a sense of his own position in the social hierarchy rather than on an evaluation of his inner worth. This is what Darcy means when he says to Elizabeth, after they have been united, that he was a good man in theory but not in practice. He accepted his own merit as given; until Elizabeth forces him to, he has no impulse to look critically inward. A traditional self with a strong sense of duty (as distinct from conscience), Darcy has before him a traditional — that is to say, arranged — marriage when the novel opens. Of course, contact with Elizabeth changes Darcy, but that Elizabeth ends by marrying so traditional a personality is perhaps the largest check on the modern drive for happiness (most intelligently represented by Elizabeth) in the novel.

Not all the self-seekers in the novel are as intelligent and virtuous as Elizabeth, however, which brings us to another way Austen tempers her affirmation of the pursuit of happiness. The novel continually juxtaposes to Elizabeth and Darcy's marriage the completely selfish marriage, such as the unions between Lydia and Wickham and between Charlotte and Mr. Collins, who live only for themselves and their own advancement. In contrast, Darcy and Elizabeth are envisioned at the conclusion of the novel as surrogate parents, moral guardians, and educators to Georgiana and Kitty, and as host and hostess at their ancient estate to members of the rising class of merchants, the Gardiners. The novel ends, then, on a note of affirmation of the power of marriage as an agent of constructive social change.

The last and most intimate qualification of the ideal of personal happiness concerns the way in which Austen treats Elizabeth's first involvement: her brief infatuation with Wickham. Whereas Darcy's presence at this point is a constant irritant to her, Wickham's presence makes her happy and is described as a "refreshment" (90). Today we would say that he makes her feel "comfortable" — that is, narcissistically contented with herself. Later Elizabeth comes to see that the pleasure she derived from his company had only to do with his silky talent for appealing to her vanity. The narcissistic *feeling* of happiness is thus not to be trusted, unless it has been earned, as it later is with Darcy, by means of vigorous criticism directed against oneself and the other. Plato wrote that we must learn to *bear* pleasure as well as pain, and it is this kind of vigorous joy that Elizabeth is experiencing when she writes to her aunt at the conclusion of the novel. "I am the happiest creature in the world. Perhaps other people have said so before, but not one with such justice. I am happier even than Jane; she only smiles, I laugh" (382–83).

With such qualifications and contrasts working off of and against the pursuit of individual happiness, it is easy to see why critics of the novel traditionally draw from it a moral emphasizing the classical value of living not for oneself but for community. The meaning of life in Austen, they would argue, is to be found not by focusing on ourselves, as Lydia and Wickham do, but in service, as Darcy and Elizabeth do at the conclusion of the novel. Some readers of Austen find this moral comforting; others (particularly feminist readers and critics) consider it objectionable because it appears to endorse patriarchal marriage and to be incompatible with the ideals of modern feminism. Insofar as feminism has been linked with the larger political shift toward liberal democracy over the past two centuries and has accepted unquestioningly the subjectivist premises of Mill, with their emphasis on the self and self-interest, such an interpretation may be justified. But Austen's seeming endorsement of the ideal of service is not incompatible with feminism at its roots, in the writings of her contemporary Mary Wollstonecraft. The author of the first major political treatise on behalf of women's rights, Wollstonecraft drew on Plato in centering her social philosophy outside the self and on the ideal of education; in *A Vindication of the Rights of Woman* she writes of women as "citizens" in whom we must expect "the conduct of an accountable being" (189; Oxford ed.) — a phrase that we can imagine encountering in an Austen novel.

We do not encounter it, however, although phrases like it are put into the mouths of characters; the ironic narrator rarely advances such bald moralities. It is all very well to say that, at the conclusion of the novel, Elizabeth and Darcy are living for something beyond themselves — the national community that Pemberley idealistically embodies, the younger persons they influence, eventually their own children — and that responsibility, rather than happiness, lies at the center of their concerns, but the ethos of *Pride and Prejudice* as a whole is one of pleasure. This is especially evident in the celebratory atmosphere of the closing chapters, which understandably have been compared to the conclusion of Mozart's *Marriage of Figaro*. Is Austen having it both ways? Is she endorsing Elizabeth's admittedly selfish drive for happiness while at the same time condemning it in others? Elizabeth's words to Lady Catherine, in which she unabashedly asserts her right to think only of herself, make her no different *in theory* from Lydia. And in marrying the high-spirited individualist Elizabeth to such a traditional, community-minded man, is Austen having her cake and eating it too?

Of course she is. The spirit of *Pride and Prejudice* is one of pleasure, a high-minded joy in mastering contradictions not to be confused with regressive indulgence or romantic wish fulfillment. At no moment in the elegant and intense verbal combat between Elizabeth and Darcy is the moral attention relaxed. When they do come to an understanding, it is truly that, not the starry-eyed romantic business we see going on between Jane and Bingley. That Austen does marry off her heroine to one of the richest men in England, who is also about her age (no father figure), vigorous, attractive, intelligent, and obviously passionate, shows how reluctant Austen was to sacrifice the small independence Elizabeth already enjoyed as the daughter of an indulgent father to anything but the best and freest circumstances for a woman at that time. How free were such circumstances, one may ask? How challenging will life at Pemberley be for Elizabeth? How fulfilling could such a vicarious form of existence be by modern standards? Beyond bearing in mind, as I have already suggested, that family and marriage in the ruling class Austen wrote of occupied a far more decisive position in social organization than they would in a later, more democratic society, it would be a grotesque luxury to judge it by modern standards.

Feminist critics who have condemned Austen for not opening up any new vistas for the female spirit, for merely reaffirming the traditional option of marriage, may as well say to a starving person, "Man cannot live by bread alone." Like all her sisters, Elizabeth has only humiliating dependence on relations before her if she does not marry. No professions to speak of are open to her, and laws on every side are designed to restrict her independence. Within the privilege of the gentry class, wives had far less control over their lives than husbands did, and daughters had virtually none. Charlotte Lucas marries Mr. Collins because she does not wish to remain a daughter all her life; that marriage to Mr. Collins is seen as liberating by comparison with "spinsterhood" tells us all we need to know of the depth of Austen's irony on the subject of women.

What is remarkable about Austen's perspective on this subject is that she does not lapse into sentimental wish fulfillment but renders the crass, survivalist posture required of women with unfailing honesty and irony. The "honesty" and "irony" are interchangeable because of the fundamental contradiction in the gentry woman's situation: that she enjoyed tremendous privileges and relative comfort as a member of that class but that her ability to act independently within it was severely restricted. Elizabeth's refusal to marry Mr. Collins, for example, is not ponderously portrayed as an act of courage; it would take little courage to refuse so ridiculous a person as Mr. Collins. But given the situation of women and her own particular economic circumstances, to refuse him without giving way even for a moment to anxiety concerning the future shows an exceptional spirit. Elizabeth's sangfroid is again apparent when she refuses the far more imposing Darcy; she cannot be frightened by circumstance or intimidated by power. Popular women novelists writing at the same time as Austen often show heroines engaged in far more obvious acts of heroism and have been praised over Austen by feminists for portraying more adventurous women; in one such novel the heroine travels down the Amazon River. But Austen did not have to show Elizabeth traveling down the mighty river; she walks three miles in the mud to visit an ailing sister, and the society around her (including the hero) behaves as if she had (32–33). That Elizabeth remains unfazed by their exaggerated response to this most commonplace act — Darcy's admiration no more turns her head than Miss Bingley's visible contempt ruffles her — is not the least of her virtues. It is in Austen's ironic critique of her society, with its vulgar idolatry of the "lady" combined with its brute legal and economic restriction of her independence, together with her passionate endorsement of women who live within it and still manage to retain their self-possession (*dignity* is too lofty a word) that her feminism lies.

Nowhere is this passionate endorsement more complicated and subtle than in Austen's later work *Emma*. That Elizabeth Bennet must go through so much painful self-scrutiny to "earn" the happiness that is hers at the conclusion suggests perhaps the more youthful Austen's straightforward sense of justice. ("Justice," it will be remembered, is a word Elizabeth herself uses in connection with her own happiness in the letter to her aunt referred to earlier.) Austen was in her early twenties when she first drafted *Pride and Prejudice*. Within the brilliantly eccentric ironies of the more mature novel, Austen is far less concerned with reconciling the drive for happiness with the needs of the community. On the surface, however, Austen does make a deceptively good case for this theme, so good that many critics have read *Emma* as her most conservative novel from the point of view of social history, with the paternalistic landowner Mr. Knightley educating the young heroine in her responsibility to English community (an education most succinctly expressed in his lecture to her at Box Hill). Such a reading ignores the overriding irony of *Emma*. Entertaining the kind of massive reversal of sympathies and values that she had already shown herself capable of in *Mansfield Park*, Austen indulges Emma's caprices, amorality, and mistakes to the full, mourning before the fact the day she becomes Mrs. Knightley and can no longer afford to make mistakes — the way a parent might spoil a terminally ill child. By the time she wrote *Emma*, Austen's sense of "justice" to women had matured; and unless we appreciate her irony, it may seem bitter. In *Emma* Austen is secretly rejoicing over the passage of the old order, perhaps rejoicing all the more in knowing that many of her readers would feel it without knowing it, and that she was alone (or so she thought) in imagining a heroine "whom no one but myself will much like" (Austen-Leigh 157).

That Elizabeth Bennet is so easy to like makes *Pride and Prejudice* the less ironic novel. But Elizabeth's marriage to Darcy, as we have seen, is not without contradiction and irony. After they are united, Elizabeth "remembered that [Darcy] had yet to learn to be laught at" (371). Perhaps a juxtaposition of the two novels suggests more than anything else that no discussion of the social-historical context in which the heroines move can proceed without consideration of Austen's irony. The moral discrimination that forms the basis of that irony is so insistent, writes Raymond Williams, "that it can be taken as an independent value . . . which is in the end separable from its social basis." After making this profound observation, Williams goes on to attach that value to the democratic social agenda: "she provided the emphasis which had only to be taken outside the park walls, into a different social experience, to become not a moral but a social criticism," such as one finds in the Victorian moralists (*Country* 117). But we will leave it to the historical ideologists to determine the political direction Austen's emphasis would take later. Whatever one concludes, one cannot help but feel that Austen wrote more for later generations than for her own. This perception is apparent not only in her steady refusal to court the public attention she could so easily have gained but in the way the novels seem to feel themselves forward into time, articulating our own historical distance from her world by means of their irony. Historians have long been in the habit of claiming, as A. J. P. Taylor has written, that, among novelists, history began with Walter Scott, the historical novelist and contemporary of Jane Austen. But if history is a form of self-consciousness, perhaps history began with Jane Austen as well.

"I Am a Gentleman's Daughter":
A Marxist-Feminist Reading
of *Pride and Prejudice*

Johanna M. Smith

In my experience it can be difficult to teach students about class structures in English novels. In the first place, students often feel that literature exists in a realm apart from and superior to such quotidian concerns. In addition, most American students are unfamiliar with English class structures and so tend to reduce their complexities to the upper-middle-lower model. Furthermore, students often regard class structures as imposed by "society" and thus external to individuals; hence they find it hard to see how an individual might *identify* herself or himself by membership in a class. For this reason they tend to oversimplify the difficulties of a cross-class romance like Elizabeth Bennet's; they often feel that individuals can easily transcend class distinctions and that lovers in particular should be above such petty considerations as class standing. Unaware that they themselves accept certain ideologies — individualism, love conquers all — they may be irritated with what they see as the shallow or pretentious ideologies of class distinction.

I have found these general problems especially troublesome in teaching *Pride and Prejudice*. While Austen is no revolutionary, this novel does challenge her culture's received signs of class status. Unless students understand traditional class structures, however, they tend to see the novel's complex reevaluation of them as a trivial commentary on an essentially trivial subject. This problem is increased because the novel addresses caste in terms of romance. In their belief that romantic love involves only individual feeling, for instance, students often lose the significance of Elizabeth's final upward mobility. And, because they tend to focus on *her* pride and prejudice as barriers to the romance, they often miss the class and feminist undertones of Darcy's change of heart: the fact that he is not allowed to win Elizabeth until his class pride is humbled and his masculine prejudices corrected.

I approach these related issues of class and gender by first diagraming the levels of class structure in early-nineteenth-century England. I begin by writing on the board an outline of class ranks, in descending order (see appendix to this essay). As this diagram shows students the full range of class ranking, it also demonstrates some aspects of *Pride and Prejudice*: they see, for instance, that industrial workers are absent from Austen's world and that servants are generally present only in the *pas devant les domestiques* sense. The diagram's range makes it especially helpful in a course on the nineteenth-century novel to mark how ways of conceiving class status changed between Austen's time and that of, say, Elizabeth Gaskell's *North and South.* In addition, while the chart might at first seem so programmatic as simply to replicate students' tendency to see class structure as fixed, I have found it useful precisely because the structure looks so rigid when diagramed but in fact allows a great deal of mobility.

This complexity becomes clear to students when I ask them to locate the characters of *Pride and Prejudice* on the class scale. As they do so, the students begin to see several aspects of the novel's class rankings that had previously been opaque, if not invisible. In the first place, they learn to read with an eye for information about class. For instance, in a first reading, students tend to pass over the introduction of Sir William Lucas; a second, close reading provides information — he had been in trade; his knighthood was the reward for his mayoral address to the king — that enables students to see that Mr. Lucas of the trading class rose to become Sir William of the gentry class. With this data students not only realize the permeability of class barriers that is one of the novel's subjects but also see how Austen is reevaluating the meaning of rank. For instance, Sir William is described as "inoffensive, friendly and obliging" by nature and "courteous" by virtue of his rank (18); we discuss how these qualities are played off against the better-born Darcy's discourtesy to Elizabeth (12). Students now realize that, for all his fatuity and despite his origins in trade, Sir William has an amiability that Darcy lacks, so that in some ways he is being represented as the truer gentleman.

Of course, from a strictly Marxist perspective this is a distinction without a difference — in fact, the sort of distinction that protected the English aristocracy from the fate of the French in the 1790s. By introducing students to such a Marxist reading at this point, I counter the long-standing critical view of Austen as ignorant of or uninterested in her culture's political concerns. Her reevaluation of class rankings is implicitly if not explicitly a political response to the French Revolution's attack on the aristocracy, and a Marxist reading of her ideology helps to show students that even the novel of manners is not devoid of political content. A Marxist interpretation also indicates that Austen's new class distinctions are not revolutionary but reformist; that is, even as they redefine the qualities that signal true status, they ensure that some form of class distinction remains the measure of individual worth. Finally, I try to show students that even though Austen inserts achieved worth into a structure of status by birth, this does not automatically mean that she endorses individualism, much less class struggle or a rebellion against the caste system. This point prepares students for our later discussions of Lydia's and Charlotte's stories, when we explore the limits that Austen's new class structure imposes on feminine independence.

To further prepare for this interdependence of class and gender status, the students look closely at the Bennet family. Students tend to see the Bennets as just folks until they realize the class significance of the data Austen provides. And as students place the Bennets on my diagram, our discussion of class distinctions gradually opens up to include those of gender. Because the Bennets are "the principal inhabitants" of Longbourn village (12) and Mr. Bennet has the Longbourn estate (although only for life), students place the Bennets in the squirearchy; but as we go on, they also see that it is only Mr. Bennet who belongs there by birth. They realize that, as the daughter of an attorney, Mrs. Bennet married up when she captivated the landed Mr. Bennet and that her continued associations with her own class — her sister married their father's clerk; her brother is in trade — pose problems for Elizabeth's romance with Darcy. We see, for example, that although Elizabeth's father is a careless parent and her cousin Mr. Collins is an egregious ass, these masculine relatives are represented as a less serious threat to her romance than the vulgarity of her mother and younger sisters.

At this point in the discussion, I try to show students why Austen often places conventional — hence in her view incorrect — class distinctions in the mouths of women. As an example we look at how the Bingleys' attitudes toward the Bennets are distinguished along gender lines. While both Bingley and his sisters have trade origins and are therefore lower in the social scale than the Bennets, Bingley reveals himself a true gentleman by loving Jane in spite of her family; in contrast, his sisters display their unworthiness as they try to shore up their own uneasy class status by baiting Elizabeth, snubbing her mother, and dropping Jane. And while Darcy at first shares the sisters' disdain for the Gardiners (Elizabeth's trading-class, or "Cheapside," relatives [36]), he is later distanced from this feminized class contempt when he welcomes the Gardiners to Pemberley; moreover, it is a woman, his titled aunt Lady Catherine, who speaks the most arrogant version of this class pride. Through such examples I try to show students that, because women maintain inappropriate class distinctions while men discard them, those distinctions come to seem insignificant obstacles to romances of upward mobility; in other words, objections that might be insuperable if accepted by suitors are gradually fobbed off onto the heroines' jealous rivals. But I also remind the students that, as in the contrast between Sir William and Darcy, even though Austen is redefining class distinctions, she continues to use them as important markers.

We then go on to discuss other interrelated class and gender distinctions that block Elizabeth's romance until they are reevaluated. When we look at Darcy's first marriage proposal, I point out that his class pride is of a piece with his masculine arrogance. As he insists on Elizabeth's status "inferiority" and then leans against the mantel casually assuming her grateful acceptance of his proposal (189–90), we see that although Darcy may be higher on the class scale than Mr. Collins, as suitors they share a masculine incomprehension of Elizabeth's feelings. When we read Darcy's letter, I note the subtle ways in which it mutes class-based objections to the Bennets and instead plays up a gender-based moral code. Although Darcy finds Mrs. Bennet's relatives "objectionable," his harsher censure is reserved for the "total want of propriety" displayed by her and her younger daughters (198); that is, the letter shows him critical not of the Bennets' class vulgarity but of the Bennet women's feminine impropriety. Moreover, he assures Elizabeth that she and Jane are tarred by neither brush, so that they are set apart from other women and thus made worthy of the upward mobility to come.

As students read the several confrontations between Elizabeth and Lady Catherine, I suggest that these scenes too reformulate the issue of class by making gender distinctions that elevate Elizabeth above other women. When Elizabeth mocks Lady Catherine's class arrogance, students appreciate such scenes as both a contrast to Mr. Collins's toadying and a demonstration of Elizabeth's fitness to join the class that Lady Catherine does not adorn. However, in their enjoyment of what they see as Elizabeth's personal independence, they tend not to recognize the ideologies behind it, and a Marxist-feminist reading illuminates the class and gender distinctions Austen is making through her heroine. In one sense, of course, there is a feminist statement in the fact that a woman (Elizabeth) rather than a man (Mr. Collins) defeats the novel's highest-ranked character, but I also note that Elizabeth challenges a titled *woman*. I ask whether the novel would have allowed her to speak as she does if her antagonist had been Sir Lewis de Bourgh, and I suggest that such a challenge to class *and* gender authority might well have seemed too radical. I also have my students read carefully the final confrontation between Elizabeth and Lady Catherine, for the terms in which Elizabeth asserts her equality with Darcy. When Lady Catherine cites Elizabeth's "inferior birth" (355) and Elizabeth replies, "[Darcy] is a gentleman; I am a gentleman's daughter; so far we are equal" (356), this speech puts Elizabeth and Darcy on the same patrilineal level by sinking the fact that she is not a lady's daughter. Although her defiance of Lady Catherine caps the novel's reevaluation of birth-worth categories, I remind my students that it does so by pitting patrilineage — the gentleman's daughter — against Lady Catherine's matrilineal desire to marry Darcy to her own daughter. Hence, while Elizabeth's victory over Lady Catherine is in some sense a feminist one, the episode also has antifeminist as well as antiaristocracy elements.

As we discuss the ways in which other women in the novel are defeated, students come to see the limits of the two ideologies endorsed by the central Elizabeth-Darcy plot. When Darcy tells Elizabeth that she has "properly humbled" him (369), we are encouraged to believe that love conquers all, but this feminine — even feminist — fantasy of women's power is undercut by the story of Charlotte's marriage to Mr. Collins. Students first tend to accept Elizabeth's judgment against such loveless marriages, until a close Marxist-feminist reading highlights the importance of Charlotte's material conditions of existence; her reasons for accepting Mr. Collins are entirely logical in a culture that provides middle-class women almost no "preservative from want" except marriage (123). And when I ask the students why, even though Charlotte's and Wickham's ambitions are identical, they—like Elizabeth—judge Charlotte's marriage more harshly than Wickham's fortune-hunting, they begin to see that our culture, like the novel's, has a prejudice against *feminine* individualism.

This contradiction, that an ideology of individualism allows opportunity only to men, is made even clearer when we discuss Lydia's story. "Boy-crazy" and "airhead" are among the students' kinder terms for Lydia, and the novel endorses this view of her. Yet Austen has also suggested, through Charlotte's story, that women of slender means—like Lydia—have few alternatives to marriage. More important, I remind the students, Elizabeth and Jane are both rewarded (albeit for very different virtues) with a man; why, then, I ask, does the novel chastise Lydia for wanting the same happy ending the heroines achieve? I suggest too that students think about such parallels between Elizabeth and Lydia as their shared infatuation with Wickham. By raising such questions, I try to help students see that Austen's endorsement of Elizabeth's version of individualism requires a foil and that Lydia fills this role.

By comparing the two sisters, students come to realize that Elizabeth's individualism is given a more acceptably "feminine" form than Lydia's. Just as Darcy sets Elizabeth and Jane apart from their mother's and sisters' follies, for instance, so Elizabeth separates herself from them by advising her father to forbid Lydia's visit to Brighton. This advice, of course, questions her father's judgment, but it does so by making some of Darcy's arguments for feminine propriety; in effect, then, Elizabeth's feminine challenge has masculine backing. In addition, here we see most sharply how the likenesses between Elizabeth and Lydia—especially that both desire a husband—are mystified as a radical difference in propriety: where Lydia pursues, Elizabeth is pursued. We then discuss how the results of the Brighton trip—Lydia's elopement with Wickham and Darcy's engineering of their marriage—finally serve to condemn Lydia's unfeminine forwardness, reward Elizabeth's feminine virtues, and validate the displacement of Mr. Bennet's paternal carelessness by Darcy's trustworthy masculine authority. I conclude, however, by suggesting a feminist reading of this apparently conservative endorsement of feminine propriety: even as *Pride and Prejudice* condemns Lydia's man hunt, it hints that her behavior, like Charlotte's, is a logical extension of her culture's insistence that marriage is middle-class women's only option.

I have found this Marxist-feminist approach to *Pride and Prejudice* useful in several ways. The class-rank diagram, in both its rigid and flexible aspects, introduces students to a structure that they will meet again in English literature courses, and it is especially illuminating for all of Austen's novels. By beginning with the diagram and then showing how class and gender hierarchies reinforce each other, my approach not only locates Austen in her rapidly shifting culture but also demonstrates how she contributed to those changes. Finally and most important, a Marxist-feminist reading of *Pride and Prejudice*'s ideologies helps students to an awareness of how our ideologies —mine as well as theirs—inform our responses to the novel.

Appendix: Diagram of Class Structure for Teaching Pride and Prejudice

Royals	king, queen
	prince, princess
Aristocracy[1] or peerage	duke, duchess
	marquis, marchioness
	earl, countess
	viscount, viscountess
	baron, baroness
. . . .	
Gentry[2]	baronet, lady
	knight, dame
	squire
	gentleman, lady
Yeoman[3]	
. . . .	
Trading class A	exporters, importers
	bankers
	factory owners
Trading class B[4]	small shopkeepers
Working class A	domestic servants
	agricultural laborers
Working class B[5]	industrial workers

[1]These hereditary titles measure birth or ascribed status rather than worth or achieved status. Women, however, may "achieve" these ranks by marriage, as Lady Catherine did.

[2]The gentry are landowners whose income does not derive from manual labor; this rank and the aristocracy constitute the upper classes. "Baronet" is an anomalous rank; although the title is inheritable, it is a late creation (1611) meant to fill the

gap between peers and knights and so lacks the cachet of a peerage title. "Knight" and "dame" are titles awarded for service to the crown; they are not hereditary. A squire is the principal landowner of a district whose holdings are not large but who does not work the land himself (compare "yeoman" below).

In Austen's time the terms *gentleman* and *lady* had a specific (if increasingly indeterminate) class meaning. Gentlemen stand on the lowest and shakiest rung of the status ladder. They are distinguished from the truly lower orders in part by the source of their income: either it is unearned (e.g., revenue from rents or investments) or it is earned but not at a salaried rate (e.g., a clergyman's annual stipend). There are four acceptable professions for a gentleman: the army, the navy, the law, and the church. Each of these professions is conceived not as a job but as service to the realm — military, legal, or spiritual. We should remember, too, that gentlemen do not join the cannon-fodder ranks of the army and navy (like Wickham, they buy an officer's commission), nor do they become law clerks (Mr. Philips is not a gentleman) or unbeneficed curates (Mr. Collins is). Ladies do not work. Should they fall on hard times, however, the allowable occupations of governess and lady's companion do not irretrievably damage their class standing; Emma Woodhouse's governess Miss Taylor, for example, is able to marry up.

[3]The line between yeomen and gentry is indistinct. Roughly speaking, yeomen own land but are not quite gentry because they often work the land themselves; that is, unlike Mr. Bennet, they engage in manual labor.

[4]As Mr. Gardiner and Bingley demonstrate, members of the trading classes may be or become gentlemen; through this permeability of the gentleman class, worth may be rewarded and status achieved.

[5]During Austen's time it was highly unlikely that a working-class man would achieve upward mobility. As with entry to the aristocracy, however, a woman might marry up a rung or two.

AUSTEN'S UNPUBLISHED WRITING AND HER READING

Peevish Accents in the Juvenilia:
A Feminist Key to *Pride and Prejudice*

Susan Fraiman

In a 1942 *Scrutiny* essay, "A Critical Theory of Jane Austen's Writings," Q. D. Leavis makes several points about Austen's mode of production that strike me today as no less fresh or necessary. To begin with, she counters the myth that Austen wrote in two spontaneous bursts — one from 1795 to 1798, resulting in the "first trilogy," another from 1810 to 1817, rounding out the corpus — and that she poured tea for the dozen years in between. Whether or not we agree with every detail of Leavis's alternative chronology, which sees Austen writing "unceasingly" from 1789 until her death, we must, I think, take up her argument that Austen's method of composition involved continual, painstaking revision, that the novels we admire sprang not from some unsought miracle of inspiration but from a routine of dedicated labor. Given the biographer John Halperin's recent, irrelevant lament that Austen wasn't married with children, it seems important to persuade students that she was, above all, a serious and unstinting professional. A discussion of Leavis's essay can also lead into the larger point that readings of Austen's life and work are inevitably shaped by cultural attitudes about women and writing.

But my primary interest here is in Leavis's assertion that Austen's practice of constantly reworking old materials built up her novels like "geological structures, the earliest layer going back to her earliest writings" (296; citations are to the excerpted essay in Norton Critical Edition). To support this, Leavis gives numerous examples of characters and scenes from the mature novels whose origins are recoverable in the juvenilia. Underlying Lady Catherine de Bourgh and her rudeness to Elizabeth Bennet, for example, is Lady Greville of "A Collection of Letters" (Letter the Third), who was hectoring the merchant-class Maria back in 1791. Elizabeth, Jane, and Lydia Bennet can likewise be traced to "The Three Sisters" (1792), and an early Mr. Collins is there as well in the repulsive suitor who doesn't care which sister he marries. Such prefigurations, of which there are many, might not by themselves warrant the inclusion of the juvenilia in a course on Jane Austen. But I want to propose that, beyond the shadowy lineaments of secondary characters, the early writings introduce much of the thematic material and many of the narrative concerns that constitute the later works, and they do so in terms that are grosser, less adorned, and consequently harder to miss than those of a text like *Pride and Prejudice*. The juvenilia are, it seems to me, pedagogically invaluable because they bare what we may provisionally think of as the deep structures of the subsequent novels.

Leavis's speculations about Austen's work habits supply one reason why this should be so, and it makes general sense that a writer-in-training would use cruder machinery and hide it less ably than she will later on. But there may also be a historical reason for the bluntness I value in the juvenilia, which has to do with their composition in the still-rebellious political climate of the early 1790s. Three critics have argued that Austen is political and her politics implicitly feminist by linking her backward to eighteenth-century movements. Margaret Kirkham ties her to the rationalist tradition of Enlightenment feminism originating with Mary Astell (1688–1731); Claudia Johnson places her left of center on a spectrum of politically engaged novelists during the revolutionary era; and Alison Sulloway links her to a group of eighteenth-century female satirists including Frances Burney and Maria Edgeworth. All three see Austen in some relation to Mary Wollstonecraft, and Kirkham and Johnson stress the need to camouflage this relation as the 1790s turn reactionary. Criticism of authority was generally inhibited by the Treasonable Practices and Seditious Meetings Acts of 1795, and association with Wollstonecraft became particularly dangerous after William Godwin (Wollstonecraft's husband) published his scandalizing *Memoirs of the Author of* A Vindication of the Rights of Woman in 1798. Such a historical schema supports my own sense that Austen's critique of marriage, male authority, and proper femininity participated in the feminist discourse of her day and also that this critique is closer to the surface in works written before 1794. This essay considers two of those texts, "The Three Sisters" (1792) and *Love and Freindship* (sic; 1790), in order to suggest how teaching them can help to excavate those feminist paradigms present but more deeply buried in *Pride and Prejudice* (1813) — not that this (or any) novel actually possesses some bedrock level of essential meaning but that the geological metaphor may offer a useful way for us to think about its relation to Austen's earlier work.

Much of the humor of *Love and Freindship* lies in the gap between a language of elevated feeling and actions that are undeniably crass. Stealing money from relatives is described in incongruously high terms: Augustus and Sophia "had been amply supported by a considerable sum of Money which Augustus had gracefully purloined from his Unworthy father's Escritoire, a few days before his union with Sophia" (*Minor Works* 88); likewise, "as Sophia was majestically removing the 5th Bank-note from the Drawer to her own purse, she was suddenly most impertinently interrupted in her employment" (96). The largest point here may be to discredit "sensibility" as a guise for self-indulgence, but Austen also more specifically indicts the lovers' denial of economic realities. They cannot admit to stealing because they will not admit the need for any currency but love. "And did you then never feel the pleasing Pangs of Love?" Edward demands of his insensible sister. "Does it appear impossible to your vile and corrupted Palate, to exist on Love?" (83). More than a spoof of facile and excessive feelings in general, *Love and Freindship* is a send-up of *romantic* feelings, the pangs of love, especially when alleged to transcend all considerations of the palate. Contrary to Edward and Laura's claims, this story observes that lovers need to eat—further, that women may marry less from love than from economic desperation. Thus in Laura's delirious rhapsody on Edward's death, "Cupid's Thunderbolts" rapidly give way to Meat and Vegetables: "I see a Leg of Mutton—They told me Edward was not Dead; but they deceived me— they took him for a Cucumber—" (100). When it comes right down to it, *Love and Freindship* hints, what Edward means to Laura is food on the table. "The Three Sisters" reinforces the implication that, excluded from wage labor and often from inheritance, middle-class women must tie the knot for money. In this short piece, courtship is completely and comically reduced to negotiating Mary Stanhope's price for living with a man she openly despises. The first line's rhetoric of romance—"I am the happiest creature in the World, for I have received an offer of marriage from Mr Watts" (57)—is dramatically exploded by the ensuing haggle over carriages and servants.

In *Pride and Prejudice*, a comparable view of marriage is represented by Mrs. Bennet and by Charlotte Lucas, who marries for the wholly unsentimental reasons that Lillian Robinson elaborates so compellingly in "Why Marry Mr. Collins?" What was shrill in "The Three Sisters" becomes muted in *Pride and Prejudice*, for Charlotte is a secondary character whose anti-romanticism is repudiated by the heroine. Yet the action of this novel derives in large part from that patriarchal legalism, the entail, which functions both to heighten the usual economic vulnerability of girls and to make this an issue from the outset. *Pride and Prejudice* begins like *Sense and Sensibility*, with the disinheritance of daughters. In addition, though Elizabeth is joking when she dates her love for Darcy since "first seeing his beautiful grounds at Pemberley" (373), it *was* in fact while touring Pemberley that her feelings for its owner began to improve. And finally, however much she may reject the pragmatism of her friend, Elizabeth's own marriage to the richest man around is far from reckless. Beginning with *Love and Freindship* may help students see that in *Pride and Prejudice* financial motives to marry are not supplanted by emotional ones but only submerged by them. In the later novel as in the early sketch, a language of feeling covers over actions driven by material need; the story of Elizabeth's sentimental education masks the story of Charlotte's simple exigency — and Elizabeth's own, which is actually more dire. Like Wollstonecraft's *The Wrongs of Woman* (1798) or Burney's *The Wanderer* (1814), Austen's mature as well as juvenile work resents the economic reliance of women on men and mistrusts the ideology casting marriage as an institution exclusively of tenderness.

I am not claiming that Elizabeth and Darcy's betrothal has no emotional integrity, only that its bliss is qualified by Austen's shrewdly complex understanding of marriage. Young women may marry because they are poor and also, Austen intimates, because they are bored. Once again, *Love and Freindship* presents this theme in amusingly exaggerated terms. The population in Laura's neighborhood is not just limited; it consists of one other person. In the quiet Val of Uske, a knock on the door is a shattering occasion, causing endless speculation among a company dying for event. It also represents Laura's only chance to flee the Val of Uske — on seeing the Stranger, she immediately realizes that he is the key to her future (*Minor Works* 78–80). It is precisely such circumstances of female isolation, boredom, and constraint that make Bingley's arrival in town so momentous to the Bennet sisters, or the prospect of Frank Churchill so refreshing to Emma Woodhouse. The tedium of their days is apparent in the Bennets' despair when it rains: "Even Elizabeth might have found some trial of her patience in weather, which totally suspended the improvement of her acquaintance with Mr. Wickham; and nothing less than a dance on Tuesday, could have made such a Friday, Saturday, Sunday and Monday, endurable to Kitty and Lydia" (88). Hinging her plots on a strange man's knock at the door, Austen submits that a woman's escape from lonely monotony is just so precariously hinged.

That women turn to marriage hoping to see more of the world, to gain greater mobility, is implicit in Mary Stanhope's fixation with Mr. Watts's carriage. Though her passion seems to be for blue with silver spots, Mary quarrels with her fiancé not only about what color the coach will be but also about how often she can use it, and Mr. Watts's enthusiasm for "Women's always Staying at home" (59) almost makes her turn him down. That Mary gets brown with a silver border plus a prohibition against going "to Town or any other public place for these three Years" (67) suggests that husbands may not, after all, guarantee the wished-for freedom. *Love and Freindship* is finally skeptical toward husbands as well. While the story promises to be about "the determined Perseverance of disagreeable Lovers" (77), its actual topic — the mysterious disappearance of agreeable lovers — is inversely cruel. Sophia's husband is imprisoned, and Laura's vanishes in pursuit. When Laura accidentally reencounters Edward, her one desire is to know where he has been. Edward's sudden expiration leaves this question hanging in the air and so adds desertion to Austen's list of the hazards of married life. *Pride and Prejudice* includes, of course, disagreeably persevering lovers in Mr. Collins and, at first, Mr. Darcy. In Wickham, Mr. Bennet, and, for a time, Bingley, it also warns of lovers who disappear into indifference.

Austen's demonstration that the meanness of women's estate forces them to wed unsatisfying men may go some way toward explaining her notoriously abbreviated proposals and rushed endings. In "The Three Sisters" and *Love and Freindship* Austen's fun at the expense of proposals, marriage, and the conventions of comic closure is predictably broad. "The Three Sisters" lampoons Mr. Watts's offer to withdraw his proposal from Mary and give it to Sophy instead, laughs darkly at Mary's reluctance to accept him — "Well then (said Mary in a peevish Accent) I *will* have you if I *must*" (64), and leaves the happy couple wrangling their way toward the altar. In *Love and Freindship* Edward meets, propositions, and weds Laura all in an instant — after which, as we have noted, he departs from the scene. This text closes its account of two disastrous marriages with the requisite multiplication of unions, all of them so patently implausible or inappropriate as to render this convention ridiculous. The marriage of Augusta and Graham joins two vaguely unpleasant, entirely minor, and previously unacquainted characters. Sir Edward finally clarifies his greed by taking for himself the lovely heiress he intended for his son. Finally, and particularly defiant of heterosexual last rites, male cousins Philander and Gustavus crown their theatrical collaboration by removing "to Covent Garden, where they still Exhibit under the assumed names of *Lewis and Quick*" (109).

Halperin in his biography accuses Austen's conclusions of being invariably "unsubtle, undramatic, and ineffective," and he finds the end of *Pride and Prejudice* typically botched:

> To be told in cool third-person commentary, without dialogue or any direct access to the minds and thoughts of either character, of the final reconciliation of Elizabeth and Darcy and their agreement to marry . . . is an anticlimax of awful proportions, and it is a mistake Jane Austen makes in all of her books. (*Life* 78)

Yet the calculated irreverence of the endings we have just considered, the frank view of marriage and husbands we have just explored, as well as *Northanger Abbey's* explicit mockery of novels that resolve into "perfect felicity" (250), all argue that the cool haste of these last moments is far from mistaken. It is, in my view, as pointed and dramatically effective as the grimness of Marianne Dashwood's marrying an older man she has never much liked, or the doubtfulness of Edmund Bertram waking up to find he loves Fanny, or the awkwardness of turkey thievery bringing Mr. Knightley to Emma.

Introducing students to Jane Austen through selections from the juvenilia can serve, in short, to bring out this writer's precocious and sustained interrogation of what Adrienne Rich has termed "compulsory heterosexuality." It demonstrates, further, that Austen consistently counters marriage by posing against it, à la Philander and Gustavus, same-sex relationships. As many have observed, rivalry among women in Austen is one visible and logical result of their absolute need to marry at a time when men, drawn off by the Napoleonic Wars, were scarce. But for every Mary Stanhope determined to triumph over the Duttons and her own sisters, there is inevitably a pair of loving women. Georgiana and Sophy Stanhope, for example, are as kind to each other as they are careless of their shallow sister, clearly anticipating Elizabeth and Jane Bennet. In *Love and Freindship*, the adventures of women together actually displace heterosexual romance as the narrative's central concern. Pitting love *versus* friendship, the story ultimately finds female "friendship" more reliable and satisfying. We have only to contrast Laura's oblivious ranting through Edward's death with her grieved attention to Sophia's in order to appreciate this point. Indeed I would argue that Sophia's decline is the only extraparodic moment in *Love and Freindship*, when a character actually has feelings appropriate to circumstances. Laura's emotions are still extreme—"I had wept over [Sophia] every Day—had bathed her sweet face with my tears & had pressed her fair Hands continually in mine" (102)—but for once they are practically and morally apt. Identifying this moment as key to *Love and Freindship* directs our attention to the similar moment in *Pride and Prejudice*, when Elizabeth muddies her reputation along with her skirts in order to nurse her feverish sister (32–33). However submerged, a tension between "love" and "friendship," a profound esteem for ties between women, and a dismay at courtship plots disrupting these ties, persist here and in all the novels, and in *Emma* they come again into prominence.

My final point concerns the epistolary form of many of Austen's juvenile works, including, scholars suspect, *First Impressions*, an early draft of *Pride and Prejudice*. One thing Austen's epistolary pieces do is to stage women in the act of writing, which is to say they reflect on Austen's own position as a woman who has seized control of the pen. Patricia Spacks has noted that Austen's *Lady Susan* (c. 1794) differs from previous epistolary novels in which characters "*feel* rather than *do*" ("Female Resources" 93). Susan, by contrast, uses letters to make things happen: for her, "writing becomes a form of agency" (91). Similarly in *Love and Freindship*, Sophia's letter within Laura's letter is an active intervention (*Minor Works* 94–95). Like Austen's own unsigned manuscripts, this anonymous text deftly orchestrates the demise of one courtship and the triumph of another. Significantly, it is right after her authorial feat that Sophia gets caught "majestically" robbing the paternal desk (95–96). The double episode dramatizes, I believe, Austen's recognition both that writing gives women performative power and that it amounts to an illicit raid on the father's library. This equation of scribbling women with (stolen) authority implies something more ominous about *Pride and Prejudice*, which begins with Elizabeth in league with her father — her critical acumen granting her access to his library — but turns on Darcy's lengthy, masterful letter (196–203). Proving that he is right and Elizabeth wrong, Darcy's missive steals back the heroine's borrowed authority and grants him from then on the novelist's role of passing moral judgment and arranging marriages. But if teaching Austen's epistolary writings as I have proposed casts a shadow over *Pride and Prejudice*, it may also shed a brighter light on *Persuasion*, which Austen revised to include the moment when Wentworth, anxious to hear what a woman has to say, gallantly drops his pen.

Pride and Prejudice and Jane Austen's Female Friendships

Deborah Kaplan

Jane Austen spent much of her adult life in the company of women. In 1806, a year after her father died, the unmarried Austen moved to Southampton with her mother, her sister, her friend Martha Lloyd, her sister-in-law Mary, and her brother Frank. But Frank, in the next few years, was often away at sea. She moved again, in the spring of 1809, this time to Chawton with her mother, sister, and Martha, and resided with them there until her death, in 1817. The relationships she sustained with these female housemates over many years were important to her, as were her enduring attachments to women such as Catherine Knight, Alethea and Catherine Bigg, Anne Lefroy, Anne Sharp, Harriet Bridges, and her nieces Fanny and Anna.[1]

I teach about female friendship in undergraduate courses on Jane Austen not only because such bonds contributed prominently to her experience but also because they provide a sensitive register of her attitudes toward her culture's gender-based inequities. In a world that prescribed marriage as the only acceptable destiny for adult women, female ties could support those heterosexual and hierarchical unions, as friends encouraged one another to find mates and to perfect the roles of wife and mother. But the more egalitarian bond of same-sex friendship could also provide an alternative to marriage, sometimes functioning as a site of resistance to it. Because female friendships expressed a politics of gender, they offer a window onto Austen's view of female subordination.

The topic of female friendship also affords an opportunity to examine with students, albeit in a preliminary way, the still tenaciously adhered to assumption that literature mirrors life. When I teach *Pride and Prejudice*, I show that although the novel offers a sustained treatment of female friendship, it does not "reflect" its author's experience of same-sex bonds. Or, rather, it does not reflect that experience as we encounter it in the most important evidence we have about Austen — her letters.

These interlinked instructional aims are fostered by pairing *Pride and Prejudice* with Austen's letters.[2] Although I generally have to set aside extra time for introducing Austen's letters — for reasons explained below — I think these works merit it. A comparison of the novel with the letters enables students to see that the politics of female bonds, as conveyed by one woman, could vary, depending on her social context and choice of literary form. In the novel female friendships perpetuate a man-centered worldview. But in the letters they sometimes provide opportunities for subtle challenges to the status quo by nurturing the development of a woman-centered consciousness.

Austen's letters are not just important documentary evidence about her experience; they are the form of writing that gave shape to that experience. In class discussions I shift the emphasis away from the duality between art and life to the nonhierarchical duality of public and private *texts*. The pairing of the letters with *Pride and Prejudice* throws features of each type of writing into relief; it also helps to show not only *what* it was possible for a gentlewoman writing at the turn of the nineteenth century to express about female friendship but *where* she could express it.

In classroom discussions my juxtaposition of *Pride and Prejudice* and Austen's letters begins with the novel. I'll summarize briefly my route through it. Those interested in interpretations of same-sex bonds in this novel and Austen's other fictions may wish to consult the rich and diverse treatments by Nina Auerbach (*Communities*), Susan Lanser, Ruth Perry, and Janet Todd (*Women's Friendship*).

It is a truth universally demonstrated in *Pride and Prejudice* that single women without fortunes must be in want of husbands. Young women and their mothers are occupied with the quest for suitable spouses. That the Bennets have no son to inherit their Longbourn estate but rather five unmarried, portionless daughters only makes more desperate and intense the "business" of Mrs. Bennet's life — "to get her daughters married" (5). When I ask students to gather evidence of the effect of this "business" on female characters' relationships, they readily forward as examples the competitive feelings that Miss Bingley and Lady Catherine (representing her daughter's interests) evince toward Elizabeth Bennet. They note as well the instrumental views adopted by Mrs. Bennet and Lady Catherine toward their daughters, and the inability of Mrs. Hurst or Miss Bingley to pay attention to their female friends when men are in the room. The two women, for example, are quite "agreeable" when Jane comes down to the Netherfield drawing room for the first time since she's been ill. But the pleasures of all-female society end immediately when Mr. Bingley, Mr. Darcy, and Mr. Hurst enter the room: "Jane was no longer the first object" (54).

Students persuaded by the narrative's overt dichotomizing of the Bingley sisters and the two oldest Bennet sisters may have more difficulty seeing that the hunt for husbands impinges even on the female bonds formed by lovable Elizabeth and Jane. Women's social and economic dependence on men restrains, if it does not entirely inhibit, the contacts that the heroine and her sister Jane have with each other, with their aunt Mrs. Gardiner, and with Charlotte Lucas. To be sure, these bonds are emotionally supportive. The two sisters, in particular, are quick to empathize with each other (12, 334). Such imaginative identification enables Elizabeth to read Jane's feelings in the subtle play of her manners and expressions even in a crowded ballroom (95, 332). Nevertheless, the many private conversations of Elizabeth and Jane, Elizabeth and Mrs. Gardiner, and Elizabeth and Charlotte are strikingly narrow in their range of subjects, restricted to men and marriages.

I ask students to note the topics of these women's conversations, and we pool them. The lengthy list includes the following concerns: Jane admits to Elizabeth her admiration of Mr. Bingley; Elizabeth and Charlotte consider how a woman who wishes to attract a man should behave; Jane conveys her doubts to Elizabeth that Mr. Bingley loves her and will return to the neighborhood; Charlotte tells Elizabeth that she has accepted Mr. Collins's marriage proposal; Mrs. Gardiner warns Elizabeth not to fall in love with a penniless man; Charlotte and Elizabeth speculate about Mr. Darcy's visits to Mr. Collins's parsonage; Elizabeth confides to Jane Mr. Darcy's marriage proposal and new information she has gained about Wickham's character. These interactions manifest the affection of one woman for another. But that feeling is always put to use in efforts to mediate a female friend's heterosexual relationships. Alone together, female friends incessantly evoke men in their talk. They do not generate interests or values separate from the quest for a spouse; they do not create their own distinct cultural arena, one that might minimize women's subordination.

Do the interactions of female characters in *Pride and Prejudice* mirror Austen's own relationships with women? Did the quest for husbands constrain their same-sex bonds too? And how do we know anything about those bonds? Biographers of the novelist have had access to her life in two ways. A handful of her kin left memoirs or reminiscences of their illustrious relative, and a few of these written testimonies are not only in print but in paperback. Nephew J. E. Austen-Leigh's *A Memoir of Jane Austen*, for example, is currently included in the Penguin edition of *Persuasion*. The *Memoir*, however, is shaped by Victorian assumptions, and many of its "facts" are nostalgic and partial (in both senses of the word) memories by a man writing fifty years after his aunt's death. Other, briefer published accounts—by Henry Austen, Anna Austen Lefroy, and Caroline Austen—while interesting, are just as partial. The other access to Jane Austen's life is through her letters. Although she had several correspondents to whom she wrote regularly, only slightly more than 150 of her letters have survived. Nevertheless, these provide extensive evidence about her relationships with women. Of the total, 94 were addressed to Cassandra, 19 to nieces Fanny and Anna, and another 21 to other female kin and friends. They attest to her intimate ties to the addressees and to other women referred to in the letters.

After calling attention to the letters as texts that necessarily mediate our understanding of Austen's life, I generally introduce one or two in class—almost any will do—asking students to read them cold. We talk about why they are so hard to follow. These difficulties in reading lead us to focus in a preliminary way on the letter writer and letter reader's relationship and the effect of this relationship on the texts themselves. What did Austen assume the recipients of her letters knew that we don't? Students should come to see that the letters remain somewhat opaque to modern readers not just because they were written almost two hundred years ago but also because they are private. Never intended for publication, the letters do not reach out, with extended narratives, intermittent explanations, or even appositives, to strangers.

I follow up this discussion by providing a little of the common stock of social knowledge on which Austen's letters depend. To see more in the letters than a parade of names, students need information on Austen's family, neighbors, and friends as well as on their homes. The indexes to R. W. Chapman's edition of *Jane Austen's Letters to Her Sister Cassandra and Others* are helpful; so are the family trees provided in Park Honan's biography, *Jane Austen: Her Life*. But it is also useful to create social maps of the Hampshire neighborhoods around Steventon and Chawton and the Kent neighborhood around Godmersham. Honan's depictions of Austen's genteel neighbors supply serviceable material for this project (see, for example, 84, 103–06, 118, 266–69).

I also follow up the initial discussion of the difficulty of the letters by urging students to read through them for evidence about their social purposes. I ask them to attend primarily to letters written to Cassandra and Fanny, as these provide particularly rich evidence and, because of their multiple functions, are the most stylistically complex. The letters dated 9 January 1796, 17 November 1798, 25 November 1798, 24 December 1798, 8 January 1799, 1 November 1800, 8 February 1807, 15 June 1808, 30 June 1808, 30 November 1814, 20 February 1817, and 13 March 1817, for example, work well. Why and under what circumstances did Austen write letters? To whom did she write? What did she write about? The letters testify in part to the service a woman's letter writing and reading did her family.

Students generally observe that Austen and her sister wrote to each other frequently when one or the other was away from home, usually on a visit to an Austen brother. They may note as well that the letters to Cassandra and to nieces convey not only news about but sometimes messages from other family members in one Austen household. Because these were in turn transmitted by the letter recipient to her Austen household, correspondents helped create family unity and loyalty among dispersed kin. Students may notice that the letters also offer news about family members' genteel friends and neighbors and that Austen had several correspondences with women who were not her relatives. In both reporting about and writing to people outside the family, Austen helped maintain her family's ties to other elite families. And finally, students may identify in the letters more personal information and opinions offered by Austen to her interlocutor as part of the content of their own particular friendship. Similarly, some of Austen's correspondences with women who were not kin sustained a personal friendship and served as a bridge between genteel families.

These social functions produce textual features of which students will find numerous instances. Family and neighborhood "news" often takes the form of brief descriptions, strung together paratactically into collective portraits.

A letter Austen wrote from Steventon to her sister at Godmersham in 1800, for example, provides this crowded canvas of family and neighbors:

> Miss Harwood is still at Bath, & writes that she never was in better health & never more happy. Jos: Wakeford died last Saturday, & my father buried him on Thursday. A deaf Miss Fonnereau is at Ashe, which has prevented Mrs. Lefroy's going to Worting or Basingstoke, during the absence of Mr. Lefroy. My Mother is very happy in the prospect of dressing a new Doll which Molly has given Anna. My father's feelings are not so enviable, as it appears that the farm cleared £300 last year. James & Mary went to Ibthrop for one night last monday, & found Mrs. Lloyd not in very good looks. Martha has been lately at Kintbury, but is probably at home by this time. Mary's promised maid has jilted her, & hired herself elsewhere. The Debaries persist in being afflicted at the death of their Uncle, of whom they now say they saw a great deal in London. Love to all. I am glad George remembers me.   (1 Nov. 1800)

Representations generated by a more personal voice are also evident in the letters, often intermingled with family and community news. We encounter in these instances the hallmark of female friendship, what Austen calls "unreserved discourse," "comfortable Talk," and "unreserved Conversation" (7 Jan. 1807, 26 June 1808, and 30 June 1808). What did Austen say in these frank and personal communications? Austen's letters to Cassandra and Fanny provide many instances of talk about men and marriage not unlike Jane and Elizabeth Bennet's discussions in *Pride and Prejudice*. Austen describes her flirtation with Tom Lefroy and a Mr. Blackall's interest in her, and shows an ongoing, often playful interest in actual and imagined marriage matches (9 Jan. 1796, 17 Nov. 1798, and 8 Feb. 1807). Her renderings of balls, in the late 1790s in particular, often focus on her own popularity with men: "I do not think I was very much in request," she writes to Cassandra. "People were rather apt not to ask me till they could not help it: one's consequence, you know, varies so much at times without any particular reason" (8 Jan. 1799; see also 24 Dec. 1798 and 1 Nov. 1800). And like the female friends in *Pride and Prejudice*, Austen voices prudential and romantic motives for marrying, especially in letters to her niece Fanny (see 18 Nov. 1814, 30 Nov. 1814, 20 Feb. 1817, and 13 Mar. 1817).

But some of Austen's personal comments challenge her culture's insistence on marriage as the desirable destiny for women. They do so implicitly by representing female friendship itself as a satisfying emotional *alternative* to heterosexual relationships. It is worth looking closely with students at a letter written in 1799 in which Austen sketches for Cassandra her visit to James and Mary Austen. At her brother's parsonage, she also encountered her friend (and Mary Austen's sister) Martha Lloyd. The couple's infant son was still very much the focus of their household: he had just been christened, and Mary, according to her sister-in-law, was only beginning to be "more reasonable about her child's beauty." The two friends' status as bystanders to marriage and childbirth is underscored, in Austen's rendering, by their spatial position in the small parsonage. But though relegated to the small space of the nursery, they manage to turn crowding into snugness:

> Martha kindly made room for me in her bed, which was the shut-up one in the new nursery. Nurse and the child slept upon the floor, and there we all were in some confusion and great comfort. The bed did exceedingly well for us, both to lie awake in and talk till two o'clock, and to sleep in the rest of the night. I love Martha better than ever, and I mean to go and see her, if I can, when she gets home.
>
> (8 Jan. 1799)

Other expressions of pleasure in female friendship and of the desire to be with friends may be found in letters such as those dated 21 January 1799, 20 June 1808, 17 January 1809, 2 December 1815, and 24 January 1817.

In "unreserved discourse" Austen's letters occasionally criticize marriage more directly. When they do, it is hard to imagine the recipient of such letters — her sister or niece Fanny, for example — making the texts available to other members of her household. And, indeed, a few comments in Austen's letters showing how she treated missives sent to her suggest that recipients regularly screened letters from female friends and kin and then read aloud or showed only parts of them (3 Nov. 1813 and 30 Nov. 1814). This tactic explains how it was possible for her to mix collective with more personal and private news in a single letter.

In writing to Fanny about their married niece Anna, Austen notes, for example, the taxing effect of repeated pregnancies on wives. Moreover, she suggests that control over reproduction is not in their power: "Anna has not a chance of escape; her husband called here the other day, & said she was *pretty* well but not *equal* to so long a walk; she *must come in* her *Donkey Carriage.* — Poor Animal, she will be worn out before she is thirty. — I am very sorry for her. — Mrs Clement too is in that way again" (23 Mar. 1817). Another letter subtly compares the subordination of wives to the freedom and pleasures of unmarried women. While staying with Mrs. Knight, she and her widowed friend receive visitors, including her friend Harriet and Harriet's new husband, Mr. Moore. As Austen informs her sister, "we sat quietly working & talking till 10, when he ordered his wife away, & we adjourned to the Dressing room to eat our Tart & Jelly" (26 June 1808).

In passages not meant for consumption by members of the letter recipient's household, Austen sometimes expresses the desire for greater social and economic self-determination. She wants to plan and manage her own travel itineraries; she wants to be able to have control over invitations to relatives and friends; she wants not to be crowded and, sometimes, interrupted (see, for example, 15 June 1808, 26 June 1808, 11 Oct. 1813, 26 Nov. 1815, and 8 Sept. 1816). She implicitly criticizes marriage by longing for something other than that female destiny — indeed, by longing for an independence marriage generally did not provide.

What do we make, then, of the differences between female friendship in *Pride and Prejudice* and in Austen's letters? Sometimes students will volunteer age as a significant cause of difference — the age of the fictional Bennet sisters, and the changing age of Austen and her friends as they are represented in her letters. The Bennets are young women just ready for marriage; over the course of the letters, Austen and many of her friends travel from late adolescence to middle age. A woman well past the mean age of marriage in Austen's society — twenty-three — would have increasingly spent time in all-female society and, perhaps, would have come to place particular value on it. The central characters in *Pride and Prejudice* are young women, but Austen herself was nearing her late thirties when she set about revising *First Impressions* for publication as *Pride and Prejudice*. In that same period of her life she was representing in her letters not only the importance of close female friendships but also values and concerns generated within them other than those associated with marriage. Why didn't she write that representation of female friendship into *Pride and Prejudice?*

At this point I try to shift attention from biographical to literary explanations. I remind the students of what we have just seen — that the letters are not the life but the text of that life and that this autobiographical text is formed by the complex relationship between the writer and her readers. Most of the letters were addressed to two different audiences at once — members of a household and one woman — and they are thus unusually inclusive and multivalent. Of course, the novel too is a product of a relationship between writer and readers, but Austen wrote it for one public audience whose expectations were in part shaped by other courtship novels.

I also ask students to consider the generic conventions of these novels. We turn attention to the impact of not husband hunting but the courtship plot on relations among female characters. What would happen to the novel's plot if female characters did not feel the necessity to marry, if they talked and thought about other things, if they found emotional ties separate from and perhaps equal to heterosexual bonds? We try to imagine as well how the letters would be different if they had been subject to the generic conventions of the courtship plot, to the powerful constraints it places on what may be represented.

The juxtaposition of *Pride and Prejudice* with Austen's letters introduces students to some of the range of and pressures on Austen's self-expressions. It enables students to probe still-pervasive mimetic assumptions and invites them to see the letters as a textual mediation of the life with its own stylistic imperatives. Finally, because it makes available more of the emotional and political diversity of women 's bonds, the pairing renders possible a richer understanding of and appreciation for female friendship in Austen's culture than students can develop from reading *Pride and Prejudice* by itself.

NOTES

[1]The last names of some of these women changed during the time Austen knew them. Catherine Bigg married the Reverend Herbert Hill in 1808; Harriet Bridges married the Reverend George Moore in 1806; Anna Austen married the Reverend Benjamin Lefroy in 1814; and Fanny Austen's last name became Knight in 1812.

[2]Two editions, the collected and the selected letters, were prepared by Chapman. The former is out of print, but the latter, currently available in paperback, includes a useful introduction by Butler. Unfortunately, some of the most relevant letters for a study of female friendship do not appear in this paperback selection. References in my text are to the collected letters, *Jane Austen's Letters to Her Sister Cassandra and Others*, available in many college and university libraries. Teachers also might encourage students to look at *Jane Austen's Manuscript Letters in Facsimile*, edited by Modert. It conveys a sense of the letters as physical objects.

Literary Allusion in *Pride and Prejudice*

Kenneth L. Moler

Jane Austen relies heavily on literary allusion as an artistic strategy: her novels consistently present their vision of life in relation to literature. Austen uses local allusions — verbal echoes of passages, phrases, or terms likely to be known to her contemporary audience — frequently. She also uses larger-scale allusive patterns, manipulating character types and motifs from what Mary Lascelles, perhaps the greatest of Austen scholars, called the "world of illusion" found in eighteenth-century fiction. Her contemporary readers' interpretations of what *Pride and Prejudice* is saying, and their enjoyment of a substantial portion of its superb wit, arose in part from their reactions to such allusions. For me, one of the great challenges in teaching *Pride and Prejudice* lies in bringing twentieth-century students to some approximation of the response to the novel an audience that shared Austen's literary backgrounds would have had.

I like to begin at the beginning — in fact, a little before it — with the novel's title. I note that the phrase "pride and prejudice" is a commonplace in the literature of Austen's day, found in all sorts of works, ranging from Frances Burney's novel *Cecilia* to a volume of sermons published by one of Austen's cousins, and I quote to the class a number of instances of its occurrence. What, we speculate, are the implications of choosing a title for a novel that would immediately echo in the minds of one's readers? Isn't Austen probably cluing her readers to the fact that what is to follow is strongly literature-oriented work — alerting their minds' ears to be prepared for more such reverberations?

By the time a class is ready to start on the topic of literary allusion in *Pride and Prejudice*, we have had a good deal to say about the famous opening sentence and its incisive irony. Returning to "It is a truth universally acknowledged, that a single man in possession of a good fortune, must be in want of a wife," I call attention to the first phrase of the sentence. I show that "it is a truth universally acknowledged," with slight variations, is a formula often used in eighteenth-century philosophical discourse, to introduce the first premise of an argument. I quote passages from Berkeley, Hume, and Adam Smith in which the same or similar forms of words are used. ("When general rules . . . are universally acknowledged . . . we frequently appeal to them as to the standards of judgement," as Smith writes in the *Theory of Moral Sentiments* [378].) It is then possible to see that, amusing as the passage is to us as twentieth-century readers, its effect of ironic deflation would be even funnier to an audience that would associate the first phrase with works like Berkeley's *Principles of Human Knowledge* or Hume's *Treatise of Human Nature*. From "class" to crass in twenty-three words.

We move from verbal allusion as a device for heightening the effects of the narrative voice to Austen's use of it in the speech of her characters. Here, in addition to its humorous effect, the technique serves as a characterizing element. Characters whom Austen wants us to respect — such as Elizabeth and Darcy — may demonstrate intelligence and extensive reading by alluding to familiar eighteenth-century sources in ways that are appropriate and interesting. In contrast, characters whom Austen intends to ridicule may be made even more foolish by being stuck with ponderous, inappropriate "borrowings" or with a tendency to drop allusions too often in their conversations. We turn to the tedious and unnecessary distinction between vanity and pride that Mary Bennet introduces into the discussion of Darcy's pride by the women of the Bennet and Lucas families (19–20), and I demonstrate that it is lifted almost verbatim from the pages of Smith's *Theory of Moral Sentiments*. Thus Mary's "pride-vanity" dichotomy would indicate her pedantry even more sharply to an audience that would hear or sense imitation in it than it does to us. Again, in Mary's speech to Elizabeth on the subject of their sister Lydia's ruin (289), the effect of her frigid moralizing is increased by the fact that she makes two explicit verbal borrowings in two consecutive sentences. Her "we must . . . pour into the wounded bosoms of each other, the balm of sisterly consolation" is lifted from Samuel Richardson's *Sir Charles Grandison* (see Moler, "The Balm of Sisterly Consolation"). Mary's later statement that a woman's "reputation is no less brittle than it is beautiful" is taken from Burney's *Evelina*, where it is said that "nothing is so delicate as the reputation of a woman: it is at once the most brittle and most beautiful of all human things" (150). Another borrower whose allusions enhance the comic contempt in which we hold him is Mr. Collins. The "olive branch" cliché with which he decorates his first letter to Mr. Bennet, for instance (62–63), which is associated with him twice more in the course of the novel (64, 364), is almost certainly designed to echo the rhetoric of one or more novels by Richardson. It is a favorite expression with Elias Brand, the clammy clergyman of *Clarissa*, and appears several times in *Sir Charles Grandison* in connection with attempts to reconcile Lady Clementina della Poretta and the family from whom she has fled to England. Collins is thus found guilty not only of plagiarism but also of hypocrisy, since later, when invited to read to the Bennet women from the novel they are reading together at teatime, he declares that he "never reads novels" and chooses a volume of Fordyce's *Sermons* instead (68). If he never touches the stuff, why does he reek of Richardson?

Austen's most important use of literary allusion in *Pride and Prejudice* involves her manipulation of a character type and situation from eighteenth-century noveldom that I have called the "patrician hero" motif. This motif involves a flawless and irresistible hero, a wealthy and well-born society figure, who unknowingly captures the heart of a young woman who is of lower status and, often, lacking in social savoir faire. The classic examples are Sir Charles Grandison — "A Man of Religion and Virtue; of Liveliness and Spirit; accomplished and agreeable; happy in himself, and a Blessing to others" (1.4) — and Harriet Byron, both from Richardson's novel, and Lord Orville — "a pattern for his fellow creatures . . . a model of perfection" — and Evelina in Burney's novel (241). It is necessary to provide students with the details of this motif, as well as to demonstrate its popularity in eighteenth-century literature and Austen's familiarity with it, and my methods for doing so vary according to the sort of class I am teaching. I teach *Pride and Prejudice* in a graduate seminar on Jane Austen, an under-graduate course devoted exclusively to Austen, surveys of eighteenth-century fiction, and several other courses in which it is one in a series of masterpieces. In the first two classes it is possible to have students read *Evelina*, relevant bits of Austen's juvenilia, and other materials; in the third, *Evelina* is gen-erally part of the reading list. For the purposes of this essay I discuss handling the last category of classes, in which reading of relevant source material must be replaced with description, quotation, and summary.

I begin with a brief (well, as brief as possible) summary of *Grandison*, stressing the often ludicrous references to the perfection of Sir Charles's appearance and manners, his overwhelming appeal to women, and his mentorlike relationship with Harriet Byron. I also describe the little court of admiring friends with which he is surrounded, his tendency to take over the management of their affairs, whether romantic or financial, and the tearful gratitude into which a self-described "undeservedly happy" Harriet dissolves when she finally learns that she is his matrimonial choice (7.463). In synopsizing *Evelina*, I stress that almost all the features mentioned in connection with *Grandison*, from the beauty and beneficence of the hero to the gushing gratitude of the heroine when she learns of his love, are present also in Burney's novel. To emphasize the familiarity of the patrician hero motif to Austen's audience, I note that Richardson and Burney were among the best-known novelists of the day and discuss the frequent occur-rences of the motif in the derivative subliterature of the circulating libraries, quoting such gems as Thomas Hull's *The History of Sir William Harrington* and Anna Maria Porter's *The Lake of Killarney*. I also point out that in the mid–nineteenth century, Thackeray, in *Vanity Fair*, relies on his audience's acquaintance with the motif in his handling of the Becky plot of the novel. To establish Austen's connection with the motif, I describe and quote at length from the juvenile sketch "Jack and Alice," in which the patrician hero is mercilessly ridiculed in the character of Charles Adams, who delivers "peremptory refusals" to lovelorn young ladies seeking his hand and "asks nothing more in my wife than my wife will find in me — Perfection" (*Minor Works* 25–26).

We can now return to *Pride and Prejudice* and a reading of the novel as what I call "the put-down of the patrician hero." Austen's contemporaries, I suggest, could hardly avoid seeing Darcy and Elizabeth and their story in relation to the popular motif. All the basic ingredients are there: wealthy, socially prominent hero, surrounded by his little court of aficionados, meets heroine of lower rank and little or no fortune. Yet what a difference! Darcy's pride in his advantages turns him to an arrogant, conceited near-parody of his prototypes who butts into the weak Bingley's love affairs, superciliously deigns to accept the toadying of Miss Bingley, and fears lest he may have taken too much notice of Elizabeth during her stay at Netherfield and thus "elevate[d] her with the hope of influencing his felicity" (60). The fun continues in two of the novel's ballroom scenes — the original one, in which Darcy sneers at the partnerless Elizabeth (11–12), and the later one, in which Sir William Lucas attempts to join their hands for a dance (92). These are explicit, easily perceived comic parallels to similar ones in Burney's novel, in which Orville speaks gently though rather negatively of, and later behaves gallantly toward, Evelina. And imagine the additional comic resonance that the scene in which Darcy buries his head in a book to avoid eye contact that Elizabeth may find inflammatory (60) would have for an audience coming to it from a background of Grandisons and Harriet Byrons.

We now come to the most amusing part of the novel's allusive pattern, the role that Elizabeth Bennet plays in it — or rather the role that she refuses to play. Throughout the book — or most of it — she behaves in ways exactly opposite to those in which a Burney-Richardson heroine "ought" to behave. Instead of responding to Darcy with hero worship and diffident love, she dislikes, mocks, and argues with him. She is, if anything, unfavorably impressed with his social status, seeing in it a source of snobbery and a means of oppressing the charming Wickham. And when, to her intense surprise, Darcy proposes to her, she turns him down with a tongue-lashing he is never to forget. Can we not almost hear the laughter of an audience — recalling the swooning gratitude of Harriet's and Evelina's receptions of their heroes' proposals — when they read Elizabeth's deliberate refusal to thank Darcy for his love? "In such cases as this, it is, I believe, the established mode to express a sense of obligation for the sentiments avowed. . . . and if I could *feel* gratitude, I would now thank you" (190). *Our* heroine has kicked the Richardsonian pedestal from under her patrician hero.

But she is not allowed to demolish him altogether. Once Elizabeth has properly "kicked" Darcy's pedestal, she herself gets some salutary blows from her author. The postproposal letter from Darcy forces her to admit that she has exaggerated his faults. The trip to Pemberley and Darcy's behavior in the Lydia-Wickham affair make her see the positive side, the sense of noblesse oblige that accompanies his consciousness of social status. And respect and love follow.

So does a change in Austen's handling of the patrician hero motif — for a contemporary of Austen's would almost certainly find in the Pemberley scenes late in the novel a number of straightforward allusions to *Sir Charles Grandison* that link Darcy with Sir Charles in a positive way. I have the class return to the chapter in which Elizabeth tours Pemberley, noting especially the detailed description of the house and grounds — the only such description in this remarkably nonvisual book. I then read from a chapter in *Grandison* in which Harriet visits the country estate of Sir Charles. Pemberley House and its grounds are an almost exact replica of those of Sir Charles — even the artificially but tastefully enlarged trout stream (245) has its counterpart in Richardson. Moreover, both Elizabeth and Harriet speak with elderly, respectable servants, and both visit picture galleries in which they contemplate portraits of their heroes at length. Can this be accidental? Isn't it a sort of in-group joke between Austen and her contemporaries? But it is a serious joke also, for by means of it Austen accepts a modified version of the patrician hero, just as Elizabeth accepts a "properly humbled" Darcy (369).

When I teach *Pride and Prejudice*, my most important goal is to help students respond to the beautiful economy of the novel — to the way in which technique and theme so perfectly blend. I am happy to conclude a study on *Pride and Prejudice* as literary allusion by suggesting that Austen's complex manipulation of the patrician hero motif exactly parallels the novel's thematic patterns of opposition but ultimate reconciliation between differing value systems. It works thematically, just as everything else in Austen's masterpiece does.[1]

NOTE

[1]There are many more examples documenting the allusions discussed here than the length of this article allows me to cite. For more examples and for information regarding the scholars who have made them known, see Moler, Pride and Prejudice: *A Study in Artistic Economy*, sec. 9.

The Influence of Richardson on *Pride and Prejudice*

Jocelyn Harris

To set Jane Austen's books against other books is to catch her in the act of creation. She is not primarily a realist, for imagined worlds were clearly as vivid to her as life itself. Rather, she was an imitator in the old sense of affectionate rivalry of her predecessors. The differences, however, make her novels hers.

In *Pride and Prejudice* Austen especially recalls Samuel Richardson's *Sir Charles Grandison*, whose characters, as we know from James Edward Austen-Leigh's *Memoir*, were her "living friends" (89). Details plundered from Richardson make up a cast, who by acting in character precipitate a plot. Wickham she reveals to be a compound of four of Richardson's villains and so resolves her tale; she incongruously combines Richardson's rake, his pedant, and his worthy hero to create Mr. Collins; she transforms Darcy from his rake to his hero and thereby tells a tale; she turns Elizabeth from his witty woman to his humbled mistress to mark a growth of self-knowledge. These changes bring about causation, compression, and complication.

Wickham is proved to be a military fortune hunter like Captain Anderson, agreeable in person and air. Charlotte Grandison was trapped by her own vanity, "since, to doubt his veracity, would be to question her own merit" (407); even Jane Bennet cannot "question the veracity of a young man of such amiable appearances as Wickham" (85). Elizabeth, though equally deceived, learns to love Darcy, of whom first impressions were disagreeable. Richardson lets his fortune hunter go, but Austen employs hers to the very end.

Duty made Sir Charles clear the debts of his gamester cousin Everard (2.512), but when Darcy clears Wickham's, his dealings with a man he loathes suggest love (321–22). Richardson's Lorimer sets out to harm his boyhood friend Sir Charles, attempts revenge on good Dr. Bartlett, and dies in horror not to be described (1.456–62). Wickham is equally said to show "vicious propensities," "extravagance and general profligacy," and his revenge is on his own friend's sister, Georgiana Darcy (200–05). Instead of dying, he is realistically punished by marriage to a silly wife. And where Sir Hargrave Pollexfen "ruined . . . three young creatures" (1.63), Wickham is prevented from ruining three young creatures, Georgiana, Miss King, and Lydia, only by the most active interventions of other people.

Mr. Collins also derives from several characters, but this time they are farcically mixed. His proposal to Elizabeth (105–09) is essentially the same as Sir Hargrave's to Harriet Byron: inquiry as to preengagement, compliment by common report, voluble laying out of the advantages to the heroine (which include his wealth and her poverty), perseverance in self-deception when the heroine promptly and frankly refuses with thanks and good wishes, demands that she should love him out of gratitude, accusations of willful suspense turning to accusations of pride, determination and cruelty in the face of the heroine's withdrawal, hurt pride, and the seeking of approval from relatives. But how differently, how absurdly, it is replayed!

When Mr. Collins finds *all* the Bennet sisters "as handsome and amiable as they were represented by common report" (70), he enlarges ridiculously on Sir Hargrave's "running over with the praises he had heard given [Harriet] at last Northampton races" (1.57). Where Sir Hargrave boasts of wealth in possession, Mr. Collins boasts of wealth in anticipation, when Mr. Bennet dies. Where Sir Hargrave points to his rank, Mr. Collins claims rank by association with Lady Catherine. Where Sir Hargrave believes that Harriet's relations will approve, he says, "if I may have the honour of your consent for applying to them" (1.85), the joke in Mr. Collins's being "persuaded that when sanctioned by the express authority of both your excellent parents, my proposals will not fail of being acceptable" (109) almost defeats analysis. Typically for Austen, Elizabeth's parents respond in character. Her mother will never see her daughter again if she does *not* marry Mr. Collins, and her father will never see her again if she *does* (112).

Sir Hargrave's complaint of being refused by a woman of inferior fortune (1.98) becomes Mr. Collins's reproach:

> To fortune I am perfectly indifferent, and shall make no demand of that nature on your father, since I am well aware that it could not be complied with; and that one thousand pounds in the 4 per cents. which will not be yours till after your mother's decease, is all that you may ever be entitled to.   (106)

To these unforgivable particularities Austen adds one more: "Your portion is unhappily so small that it will in all likelihood undo the effects of your loveliness and amiable qualifications" (108). But where Harriet merely resents the fop's address, it is insulting to Elizabeth when Mr. Collins turns promptly to Charlotte Lucas, and Charlotte as promptly accepts.

Richardson's pedantic would-be gallant Walden provokes Harriet's sharp comment, "every scholar, I presume, is not, necessarily, a man of sense" (1.53); Mr. Collins is not "a sensible man, and the deficiency of nature had been but little assisted by education or society" (70). Sir Hargrave laughs at Walden's "parcel of disastrous faces" (1.82), just as Mr. Bennet draws out Mr. Collins to be "as absurd as he had hoped" (68). Austen also reworks an opinion that Sir Charles might be "a grave formal young man" (2.274) for her "young man" with a "grave" air and "very formal" manners (64). The delectable mismatch of rake, pedant, and hero makes up the verbosely vain, the awkwardly amorous, the immortal Mr. Collins.

Mr. Collins's marriage to Charlotte Lucas mirrors Charlotte Grandison's to a man she calls a fool. Charlotte Grandison asks:

> What can a woman do, who is addressed by a man of talents inferior
> to her own? . . . Must she hide her light under a bushel? . . . But what
> will [women] do, if their lot be cast only among Foplings? If the Men
> of Sense do not offer themselves?   (1.230)

No man of sense offers himself for Charlotte Lucas. She marries a man
neither sensible nor agreeable, whose society is irksome and attachment to
her imaginary. "But still he would be her husband . . . [her] pleasantest
preservative from want" (122–23). Elizabeth, however, refuses to hide her
light under a bushel for such an absurdity as him.

Charlotte Grandison learns to love and respect her husband, as Charlotte
Collins never can. Elizabeth admits that comfort — a Richardsonian word
(2.264) — must do for Charlotte so long as there are not enough men of sense
to go round (157). Austen reserves happiness, a word that rings through
the last volumes of *Grandison* as it does through the closing pages of *Pride
and Prejudice*, for others. Charlotte Lucas gets the comfort she sought, but
Elizabeth and Jane are granted comfort and happiness, both.

Elizabeth begins as a Charlotte Grandison, who practices her wit on stuffy
Lord G., saying, "I love to jest, to play, to make him look about him"
(2.506). How like this is to Elizabeth, who "dearly loves a laugh" and sets
out to tease Darcy, a man as lordly, stiff, and solemn as Lord G. himself.
Darcy, however, is less vulnerable than Lord G.: "Teaze calmness of temper
and presence of mind! No, no — I feel he may defy us there. . . . Mr. Darcy
may hug himself" (57). Reverence for her brother reins in Charlotte Grandison's vivacity (1.237), while in a nonsensical variation Mr. Collins knows
that Elizabeth's wit and vivacity must be acceptable to Lady Catherine,
"especially when tempered with the silence and respect which her rank will
inevitably excite" (106). Charlotte Grandison's sweetness and "archness"
make "one both love and fear her" (1.179–80); "there was a mixture of sweetness and archness in [Elizabeth's] manner which made it difficult for her
to affront anybody; and Darcy had never been so bewitched by any woman
as he was by her" (52). In Richardson's novel, Charlotte will teach her
husband to jest (2.399); Darcy, says Mrs. Gardiner, wants "nothing but
a little more liveliness, and *that* . . . his wife may teach him" (325).

To complete Elizabeth, Austen adds Richardson's heroine to his witty
woman. Harriet imagines it might be said of her that her "features, taking
them either in whole or part, [are not] *much* amiss" (1.69), but when Darcy
"at first scarcely allowed [Elizabeth] to be pretty . . . hardly a good feature
in her face" (23), he insults her. Harriet is distinguished by the "*Expression*"
of her eyes (1.12); Elizabeth's face too is "rendered uncommonly intelligent
by the beautiful expression of her dark eyes" (23). Richardson has Uncle
Selby conclude, "give me the beauty that grows upon us every time we
see it" (1.29); although the Bingley women had been amazed to find Elizabeth reputed a beauty, that, says Darcy, "was only when I first knew her,

for it is many months since I have considered her as one of the handsomest women of my acquaintance" (271).

Harriet and Elizabeth both come to repent the impulses of their satiric tongues. But where nothing follows from Harriet's complaint of Sir Charles's "*intolerable* superiority!" and her wish that he would show resentment (2.89), Elizabeth's taunt that "Mr. Darcy has no defect. He owns it himself without disguise" provokes Darcy's admission of a resentful temper, which she then to her cost believes (57–58). Harriet plans briefly to be "captious" and to "study to be affronted" (2.13), but Elizabeth "exasperate[s] herself" into a hatred of Darcy that thwarts his first proposal (188). Harriet acknowledges the vanity and pride of her censoriousness (1.34), just as Elizabeth admits, "I . . . have prided myself on my discernment! . . . and gratified my vanity, in useless or blameable distrust" (208). But where Harriet's "squibs" (1.412) have no important result, Elizabeth's vanity and rapid, wrong decisions make up her plot.

Finally, Elizabeth, like Harriet, rationalizes her love as gratitude (*Grandison* 414–15; *Pride and Prejudice* 265). But both Richardson and Austen know that gratitude can oppress, especially for what Harriet calls "*pecuniary* surprizes!" (2.284). When Darcy bribes Wickham into marrying Lydia, "it was painful, exceedingly painful, to know that they were under obligations to a person who could never receive a return," thinks Elizabeth (326). But for the obligation they thought never to repay, their hearts turn out to be sufficient fee.

Darcy himself seems at first a parody of Richardson's hero. For instance, if Sir Charles, an avid dancer, leaves "the numerous assembly at Enfield, while they were in the height of their admiration for him" (2.348), Darcy refuses to dance at the Meryton ball, and "every body hoped that he would never come there again" (11). Yet Richardson's "*good man,*" who makes "the judgment or approbation of the world matter but of second consideration" (1.182), contains all the elements of Austen's. Darcy similarly admits that his temper is "too little yielding—certainly too little for the convenience of the world" (58), but in a novel in which the judgments of the world are often proved wrong, Elizabeth will learn to appreciate that unyieldingness. Harriet guesses, "[S]uch sweetness of manners; such gentleness of voice—Love has certainly done all this for him" (2.82); at Pemberley, Elizabeth finds Darcy's manner "altered" and "softened" by love (255).

Grandison Hall and Pemberley are alike in figuring forth their owners. Sir Charles is there "proved to be the best of brothers, friends, landlords, masters, and the bravest and best of men" (1.303), just as Elizabeth at Pemberley learns to appreciate Darcy as "a brother, a landlord, a master" (250). He will act heroically to rescue Lydia. Elizabeth would surely acknowledge the truth of Harriet's advice to be "cautious . . . in passing judgment," especially on good men (1.443), for Darcy is a true Grandison after all.

He starts out, though, as Sir Hargrave Pollexfen. Darcy's passion, volubility, sense of stooping to an inferior, and anger at Elizabeth's refusal all derive, like Mr. Collins's, from Sir Hargrave; but where the rake's fury that he must beg "only for a *wife*" has little effect (1.158), Darcy's sneer at Elizabeth's relations wounds her to the heart. And how much more dreadful than rakish faults seems Darcy's separation of Jane and Bingley, or his unkindness to his childhood friend Wickham! The misunderstandings created in this one scene — Darcy's first proposal — need a whole novel for their untangling.

Darcy proves to be a Sir Charles, indeed, and a Grandison in love. Sir Charles is honor-bound to Clementina but returns to Harriet. Richardson's hero may resent the snubs of the highborn Italians, but when Darcy speaks of Elizabeth's "inferiority," the "degradation," the "family obstacles which judgment had always opposed to inclination" (189), he tells a brutal truth about female powerlessness. These ideas reappear in Lady Catherine's finest scene. Where Richardson's arrogant Porrettas dwell on "their rank, their degree, their alliances" (2.218), Lady Catherine emphasizes her own family's noble line, adding, "Your alliance will be a disgrace" (355). But Elizabeth makes the same proud claim to equality as Sir Charles (2.458). "He is a gentleman; I am a gentleman's daughter; so far we are equal," she says (356).

Inversion as well as likeness controls Austen's scene. Where the Porrettas complain that Sir Charles rejects their daughter, Lady Catherine is enraged that Elizabeth will not reject her nephew. In the most characteristic difference of all, Sir Charles's resentment affects his fate not at all, but Elizabeth's democratic sturdiness precipitates a second and very welcome proposal from Darcy.

Austen's finale takes several stages: the interesting encounter at Pemberley, the puzzling visit without declaration, the explanatory proposal, and the informing of the Bennets, all of which have parallels in *Grandison*. But whereas Harriet is already married when she arrives at Grandison Hall, Elizabeth is not, at Pemberley, which makes her plight much more complex and consequential. Sir Charles's proposal is long, in direct speech, and defensive; Darcy's is short, reported, and all the better for it. "All your friends encourage [my] hope," says Sir Charles smugly (3.98), but it is a splendid reversal that Lady Catherine "taught [Darcy] to hope" (367). Harriet accepts a man called always "the best of men"; Elizabeth accepts a man "condemned as the worst of men" by the world at large (138).

Austen begins with her living friends, the characters of *Grandison*. One or two traits suffice to animate her simple characters, but her "deep, intricate," and "amusing" characters (42) are made up of several elements that the book can then unfold. Elizabeth seems to be a witty Charlotte Grandison but becomes a humbled Harriet. Darcy appears to be a Sir Hargrave but is really the Sir Charles that his appearance, house, and garden have already proclaimed him to be. By such splitting and recombining, Austen gives her creatures life.

Direct copying is rare. Austen employs her early literary-critical mode on *Grandison* or changes contexts to throw up absurdity by incongruity. Most notably, though, where Richardson is characterized by story, Jane Austen is characterized by plot. She makes everything connect, so that incidents illustrate character and character determines incident in the sparkling, kaleidoscopic *Pride and Prejudice.*[1]

NOTE

[1]This essay appeared in extended form in *Jane Austen's Art of Memory* (Cambridge: Cambridge UP, 1989). It is printed here by the generous permission of the Syndics of the University Press.

TEACHING ABOUT STRUCTURE AND THEME

"Taking Different Positions":
Knowing and Feeling in *Pride and Prejudice*
Marcia McClintock Folsom

"It's just like a soap opera," some students say when they begin reading *Pride and Prejudice*. Student readers notice immediately that the novel focuses on the feelings of young women who are trying to find romance and marriage within a confining social world, and they are right that this struggle is a staple of popular culture. I have learned to expect someone in class to say, "It's all so predictable. I just know that Elizabeth will end up with Darcy, and Jane will marry Bingley." These first impressions are offered with pride at recognizing a genre and with prejudice against its trivializing of women's lives. Such comments also suggest students' impatience with having to read a novel that tells the same old story.

However, when student readers shift their attention from predicting the outcome of the romance plots to examining the novel's analysis of how a person comes to know herself and other people, the novel becomes more subtle, challenging, rewarding. Students who begin by comparing the book to a soap opera may end up seeing in it a paradigm of their own intellectual and emotional growth. Their engagement as readers who are trying to know the novel, and their struggles as writers of essays about it, are dignified by Jane Austen's patient, respectful chronicle of her main character's growth in understanding. By the end of our work on the novel, students can talk about how Austen does celebrate romance, after all, not as an impulsive surrender to first impressions but as passion that becomes possible because of growth in thinking. In this novel, deep love is associated with intellectual depth; the heroine really loves only after she really knows herself and her lover.

The images Austen uses when Elizabeth looks out the windows at Pemberley at Darcy's estate illuminate my approach to teaching the novel. I discuss this passage in class only when we get to the last third of the novel, but I mention it early in this essay because it provides a dramatized moment when a character compares first impressions with later ones, if only implicitly:

> Elizabeth . . . went to a window to enjoy its prospect. The hill, crowned with wood, from which they had descended, receiving increased abrutpness from the distance, was a beautiful object. Every disposition of the ground was good; and she looked on the whole scene, the river, the trees scattered on its banks, and the winding of the valley, as far as she could trace it, with delight. As they passed into other rooms, these objects were taking different positions; but from every window there were beauties to be seen.   (246)

In this intense, reflective moment late in the novel, Elizabeth has the openness of a traveler to new sights and the insights they can inspire. Looking out through windows in different rooms of Darcy's house, Elizabeth sees objects in the landscape arrange themselves in varied combinations. Of course, the objects do not move; it is Elizabeth who is "taking different positions." The grounds of Pemberley are analogous to their owner in presenting a viewer with "increased abruptness" from a distance and surprising beauty when seen from a new vantage point. At this moment, Elizabeth is experiencing one of the novel's central insights: that perceptions from fixed vantage points must be corrected by movement through space, as first impressions must be corrected by movement through time. (See appendix to this essay.)

My way of shifting students' attention away from predicting who will end up with whom is to spend time in class exploring this insight, particularly in the first twenty chapters. On page after page, Austen shows that objects, events, and people's behavior look different when they are viewed from different vantage points. Frequently, those differing vantage points are the distinctive interpretive modes of the various characters, for Austen consistently characterizes people in this novel by their modes of interpreting events and other people. In dialogue, Austen often contrasts side by side the views of two or more characters about the same event or person (as when members of the Bennet family comment one after other on Mr. Collins's letter). For this reason, the whole book is remarkably responsive to epistemological inquiry. By "epistemological inquiry" I mean asking questions about how the mind constructs the world.

For example, student readers can compare the ways Elizabeth and her sister Jane make sense of such people as Miss Bingley and her brother. Each sister perceives certain actions and hears certain spoken words; each attempts to fit these perceptions into a coherent account that satisfies her sense of what is probable. Insisting that no malice, thoughtlessness, or want of resolution could be present in either Miss Bingley or her brother, Jane defends her view of those two characters with poignant intensity: "Let me take it in the best light, in the light in which it may be understood" (137). Elizabeth's view that Miss Bingley is malicious and that Mr. Bingley lacks resolution does not "explain" their departure from Netherfield to Jane; Elizabeth's interpretation makes the Bingleys' behavior impossible for Jane to understand (118–19, 136–37).

It is not just because different characters see things differently that the novel is susceptible to epistemological inquiry, however. Austen also demonstrates that one person may see the same thing differently at different times and places, as when Elizabeth realizes at Pemberley that the hill she has just descended looks steeper from a distance than when she was riding down it. Some characters are more perceptive than others, but all of them (even the perceptive ones) make errors in judgment. Although Elizabeth often seems better able than her older sister to draw the right inferences from evidence (as she does in the case of Miss Bingley), Elizabeth makes serious mistakes in judging other characters, mistakes that Jane pointedly warns Elizabeth may *be* mistakes because of her lack of knowledge of other characters or her impulse to leap to a conclusion (85–86). The most important misjudgments in the novel, in fact, are Elizabeth's: her faulty reading of Darcy's character and her counterpoised misreading of Wickham's. These two errors represent the pivotal plot problem of epistemology.

The novel's optimistic lesson, however, is that a person who is willing to undertake the struggle can come to know what is true. I think that this hope is a highly appropriate one to extend to college students, whose cognitive struggle is to become intellectually flexible, aware of their *own* interpretive modes and prejudices and willing to admit new information into their thinking so they can mature as thinkers and responsible adults. For students to take a different position, to abandon the soap opera analogy and to begin experiencing this novel seriously from a new vantage point, means that they too are making a small step in the kind of intellectual change that the novel dramatizes in the growth of the main character.

My task in teaching *Pride and Prejudice* is to help student readers slow down enough to attend to subtleties of dialogue and narrator's language, to become skilled at the kind of close reading the novel demands, and to move away from simple generalizations about the plot. Paying attention in class to epistemological issues, like the difficulty characters have in understanding each other, inevitably requires students to engage in just this kind of reading. The misunderstandings between Darcy and Elizabeth provide the chief illustration of the difficulty of knowing another person. I lead the class through Elizabeth and Darcy's first meeting and the narrator's explicit disclosure of their unlike early opinions of each other: "But no sooner had he made it clear to himself and his friends that she had hardly a good feature in her face, than he began to find it was rendered uncommonly intelligent by the beautiful expression of her dark eyes." The glamour and gravity of this romantic diction are available to us but not to Elizabeth: "Of this she was perfectly unaware; — to her he was only the man who made himself agreeable no where, and who had not thought her handsome enough to dance with" (23).

I then divide students into groups of three and ask them to consider the sources of misunderstanding in a series of conversations between Elizabeth and Darcy: at the Lucas's ball, where Elizabeth says, "Mr. Darcy is all politeness" (26); during the Netherfield visit when Elizabeth joins the conversation about "accomplished" young ladies (39); when Darcy asks Elizabeth if she feels a "great inclination" "to seize" the "opportunity of dancing a reel" (52); when Elizabeth discovers that "Mr. Darcy has no defect" (57); and at the Netherfield ball when Darcy asks, "What think you of books?" (93). I put the following set of questions on the board and ask each trio of students to respond to all of them. These questions require students to ponder the specific words as well as the implied intentions of each speaker in the assigned exchanges.

Elizabeth
What does she say and how does she act?
What does she mean by her words and gestures?
How does she interpret what Darcy says and does?

Darcy
What does he say and how does he act?
What does he mean by his words and gestures?
How does he interpret what Elizabeth says and does?

Each group considers these questions for each line of dialogue. They must also evaluate each salient word in the narrator's comments: "Mr. Darcy with grave propriety requested to be allowed the honour of her hand" or "Elizabeth looked archly, and turned away" (26). The group must deduce from the sequence of comment and reply each character's intentions and the interpretations each must be making of the other's words and gestures as the conversation is created.

This exercise always produces exclamations of amusement and amazement: "I can't believe she's so blind!" "He *knows* the first sentence of the novel, and that's why he doesn't understand what she is saying!" The last exchange between Darcy and Elizabeth in the pianoforte scene can stand here as a characteristic instance of these moments that students can decode together in class:

> "I certainly have not the talent which some people possess," said Darcy, "of conversing easily with those I have never seen before. I cannot catch their tone of conversation, or appear interested in their concerns, as I often see done."
>
> "My fingers," says Elizabeth, "do not move over this instrument in the masterly manner which I see so many women's do. They have not the same force or rapidity, and do not produce the same expression. But then I have always supposed it to be my own fault—because I would not take the trouble of practising. It is not that I do not believe *my* fingers as capable as any other woman's of superior execution."
>
> Darcy smiled and said, "You are perfectly right. You have employed your time much better. No one admitted to the privilege of hearing you, can think any thing wanting. We neither of us perform to strangers."
>
> (175–76)

By patient close-reading, students can unravel the intentions of both speakers in every one of these assertions. They hear the mixture of defensiveness and self-importance in Darcy's claim that he has not the "talent which some people possess" to appear interested in other people at first meeting. They hear that Darcy believes himself too honest to learn the little insincerities of polite conversation, while he also claims to be somewhat shy.

Students recognize that what Elizabeth hears, however, is his protestation that he has no *talent* for easy conversation. Students understand intuitively her rejection of this idea, and her strategy in criticizing Darcy by weighing the balance of "talent" and effort in her piano playing. She implies that Darcy's failure as a comfortable conversationalist results from his not taking the trouble to practice; it is his own fault. Students know what she means, but he misses the analogy, replying to her literal comment on piano playing, not to the implied criticism of himself. Students realize how angry Elizabeth must be when Darcy smiles and praises Elizabeth for not practicing the piano and says that she has used the time much better. They see that his gallant (if contradictory) praise of her piano playing, and his affectionate claim of likeness between them, prove that he is oblivious to what she has just said.

When I ask students why Darcy doesn't notice Elizabeth's pointed criticism, they say that his failure is rooted in four feelings: his staunch good opinion of himself, his correct belief that almost every single woman in England would love to marry him, his incorrect belief that Elizabeth is "wishing, expecting" his addresses, and the feelings that "will not be repressed," his ardent love for Elizabeth (369, 189). Yet, as students point out, Elizabeth's prejudice keeps her from noticing the compliment to herself in Darcy's speech. She only perceives that his "abominable pride" prevents him from understanding her daring criticism of his behavior and even of his character. Some students may say that Darcy is able to hear a woman's self-criticism but cannot detect criticism of himself.

The epistemological problem of learning to know other people is a real one for college students, as for everyone else. Most of my students are young women, and the long-range plans of most include marriage. "Suppose," I say, "you are a nineteen-year-old woman who has just moved to a college. You are conscious as you meet men of trying to judge whether any one of them would be a person you would like to see again, whether you could love him, or consider marrying him. When you are meeting new people, on what basis do you judge them?" Resembling the Bennet sisters and Miss Lucas in this, many college women have the undeclared task of forming reliable judgments about men. At first, they must make these interpretations on the basis of what people say and do as strangers.

As my students begin — laughingly, sometimes hesitatingly — to describe their mental processes in judging a new acquaintance, it is possible to sort out their answers about first impressions into three clear categories. I write all on the board under these headings: *How he looks*, *How he acts*, and *What he says*. I pose another question: "Let us suppose that your first impressions are favorable and you begin an acquaintance with a previously unknown person. How do you confirm or test your first impressions?" Naturally and promptly, students start discussing their methods. "I talk with him and listen to what he says. I think about how he treats me. I check out his friends to see what kind of people they are. I get my friends to check him out." And later, "If I am really interested, I try to get invited to his home to meet his family. I bring him home to meet my parents."

Similar access to knowledge is available to Elizabeth Bennet, when, within the first pages of the novel, Darcy and Bingley enter the Meryton assembly ballroom, newcomers to the community. His height, handsome face, and distinguished bearing (and the report of his wealth) are all that strangers can tell about Darcy at first. *How he looks*, therefore, draws "great admiration" for the first half of the evening. Then, however, *how he acts* and *what he says* create a "disgust which turned the tide of his popularity." Darcy's impolite remark about Elizabeth, dramatized for the reader and overheard by Elizabeth ("She is tolerable; but not handsome enough to tempt *me*"), reveals him "to be proud, to be above his company, and above being pleased" (10, 12).

I point out that the novel almost immediately provides the characters and readers with other sources of knowledge beside first impressions, and these other sources tally with the students' own methods for confirming or denying first impressions. Just as students say they do, Elizabeth discusses her first impressions with friends who were present at the encounter and who provide two other vantage points from which to judge Darcy's manners: the cautionary view of Charlotte Lucas, and Jane's report that Miss Bingley described Darcy as "remarkably agreeable" among his close friends (19). Elizabeth and the reader soon also have other sources of information for forming a judgment of Darcy — *what he says* in many dramatized scenes, whom he has as friends, and *how he acts* in many other social situations. Yet Elizabeth's defensive stand against the arrogance she assumes exists in all wealthy people and her consistent interpretation of Darcy's manner as revealing that arrogance skew her judgment of his character. And, as students begin to point out, Darcy's behavior is truly open to Elizabeth's interpretation.

To understand Elizabeth's persistent errors in sizing up Darcy, the class might discuss her implied values. Elizabeth's morality for the first half of the book is similar to that of many American college students: she does not grant respect to people because of their prestige, wealth, or social class. Students find Elizabeth admirable because of her witty resistance to class-bound pomposity. But the value Elizabeth implicitly places on civility and kindness also appeals to many students. Her belief that people should be generous and respect one another's attempts at courtesy and conversation can be demonstrated in many early scenes — for instance, she disregards propriety and walks over the fields to visit Jane when she knows her sister is sick (32–33). Her dislike for Darcy after his initial rudeness to her is confirmed as she observes his cool, inattentive replies to Miss Bingley about his handwriting (47–48), his criticism of Bingley's "precipitance" (48–49), his haughty demeanor with Sir William Lucas (26), his transparent disdain for Mr. Collins (98), and his deliberate attempt to ignore Elizabeth on the Saturday at Netherfield when he feels himself to "be in some danger" (52). The attraction Elizabeth feels toward Wickham springs partly from her interpreting the warmth of his conversation as revealing care for others. We can discern a moral code in her judging people for being abrupt or responsive in conversation, or in her deploring Miss Bingley's equation of a person's worth with rank (94–95). It is a code that appeals to many students.

In the first proposal scene, Elizabeth's and Darcy's persistent misunderstandings of each other finally become apparent to them both. The dramatic epistemological moment occurs when Elizabeth, her passionate anger shining out despite her masterly effort to control complex syntax, triumphantly summarizes the history of her interpretation of Darcy's character:

> From the very beginning, from the first moment I may almost say, of my acquaintance with you, your manners impressing me with the fullest belief of your arrogance, your conceit, and your selfish disdain of the feelings of others, were such as to form that ground-work of disapprobation, on which succeeding events have built so immoveable

a dislike; and I had not known you a month before I felt that you were the last man in the world I could ever be prevailed on to marry. (193)

For my students, I elaborate on and diagram the architectural metaphor implicit in this statement. I argue that Elizabeth conceives of her opinion of Darcy as a constructed wall of evidence and interpretation. Pointing to the foundation stones in my drawing, I tell students that the numerous scenes they have examined in class — in which Elizabeth has construed Darcy's behavior as demonstrating arrogance, conceit, and selfish disdain for the feelings of others — have, she says, erected in her mind an entrenched structure of opinion, "a ground-work of disapprobation." On top of that, "succeeding events have built" an additional barrier to liking. Members of the class readily identify the "succeeding events" as what Elizabeth believes to be Darcy's unjust treatment of Wickham and his deliberate separation of Bingley from her sister Jane. I ask students if, when she refuses him in such ringing words and phrases as "had not known you a month . . . last man in the world I could ever be prevailed on to marry," Elizabeth could be hoping or expecting that Darcy will propose again later. They say it is impossible.

The challenge that Austen set for herself in this novel is plausibly to transform an intelligent woman who has uttered such a categorical refusal of a man's marriage proposal into a person who ardently loves that man and considers him as the one who suits her perfectly. How can a consistent and believable character totally change her mind? The issue of epistemology is thus not only a constant theme but the knot that ties the plot together. The task for students and teacher is to understand how Austen solves this central problem of her plot.

The first steps in Elizabeth's transformation, which Austen chronicles with painstaking exactitude, occur as Elizabeth reads and comes to understand Darcy's letter. As Austen traces these steps, she uses language that shows Elizabeth moving herself to a new vantage point in relation to events that she remembers so clearly that she can stand before them again and review, reinterpret, and recognize possible meanings of behavior:

[T]he affair . . . was capable of a turn which must make him entirely blameless throughout. . . .   (205)

She tried to recollect some instance of goodness [in Wickham]. . . . But no such recollection befriended her. She could see him instantly before her, . . . but she could remember no more substantial good than the general approbation of the neighbourhood. . . .

She perfectly remembered every thing that had passed in conversation between Wickham and herself. . . . Many of his expressions were still fresh in her memory. She was *now* struck with the impropriety

of such communications to a stranger. . . . She saw the in-
delicacy . . . , the inconsistency. . . . She remembered that he had
boasted. . . . She remembered also. . . .

How differently did every thing now appear. . . .   (206–07)

[Darcy's] actions were capable of a very different construction. . . .
                                                          (258)

Elizabeth's strenuous reading of Darcy's letter deconstructs her mistaken
interpretation of Wickham and her misjudgment about Darcy's separation
of Jane and Bingley. With these two events removed from the top of her
"immoveable . . . dislike," however, Elizabeth is still left with the "ground-
work of disapprobation" that she had constructed by observing Darcy
before she added resentment over those events to her opinion of him.
Her change of attitude is carefully qualified at this point: "His attachment
excited gratitude, his general character respect; but she could not approve
him; nor could she for a moment repent her refusal, or feel the slightest
inclination ever to see him again" (212). The drawing of the architec-
ture of Elizabeth's feelings helps clarify this qualified change of judgment
and enables students to see that she is *not* wishing that she had accepted
Darcy's proposal.

From this moment on in the novel, Austen examines the problem of knowing in a new way. In the first half of the book, she shows that different
people see things differently, that "knowing" is difficult because events and
behavior are themselves ambiguous, that externals do not always reveal
internal truth, and that one's own pride or prejudice may make one mis-
judge. But in the second half of the novel, Austen demonstrates that a person
who wants to understand rightly can come to a trustworthy way of knowing
things, events, and people. Achieving understanding may be time-consuming,
laborious, and personally painful; it may damage self-esteem. It demands
intellectual effort and may force one to relinquish cherished opinions of
oneself, one's family, and others. Yet the process leads to knowledge of what
is true and creates within the self a new capacity to love.

In class we work through the next stages in Elizabeth's change, which
involve two sources of new understanding, one internal and one external.
Elizabeth's change does not come simply from new experiences that overcome the effect of past experiences. Instead, she engages in mental and
emotional work, to review and reunderstand the past, her own mistakes,
and the events she lived through and helped create. A need for solitude,
a yearning for reflection, remembering, and reorganizing her memories — a
need caused by the humiliation of being forced to reinterpret the past —
emerge in Elizabeth. In solitude she is able to make the vigorous mental
effort that stimulates inner growth. Students often overlook passages that
describe this growth and usually miss the muted intensity of Austen's

vocabulary when it mixes feeling and thinking. One like this deserves to be read aloud:

> *Reflection* must be reserved for *solitary hours*; whenever she was *alone*, she gave way to it as *the greatest relief*; and not a day went by without a *solitary* walk in which she might indulge in all the *delight of unpleasant recollections.*
>
> Mr. Darcy's letter, she was in a fair way of soon *knowing by heart.* She *studied* every sentence: and her *feelings* towards its writer were at times widely different.   (212; emphasis added)

"Knowing by heart" includes studying, memorizing, and feeling. As Elizabeth studies every sentence of what she thinks of as "her letter" (209), she unconsciously commits its very phrasing to memory, so that each assertion is available to be consciously reconsidered in recollected context. She can ponder possible meanings of events in the past and decide which interpretation saves most of the evidence she remembers.

When I ask students to locate other instances in which they can see Elizabeth altering her mental construction of her world, they come up with numerous examples. Repeatedly in chapters between Darcy's letter and the visit to Pemberley, Austen gives evidence of Elizabeth in the process of changing her understanding. Such moments sometimes juxtapose Elizabeth's former understanding with her developing conception: "When she remembered the style of his address she was still full of indignation; but when she considered how unjustly she had condemned and upbraided him, her anger was turned against herself" (212). At other times, Austen shows Elizabeth using her new perceptions to illuminate familiar family scenes: "She felt anew the justice of Mr. Darcy's objections" (229). Sometimes, in contrasting new and old perspectives, Elizabeth sees her former position as an error and the later one as better informed: "She had even learnt to detect, in the very gentleness which had first delighted her, an affectation and a sameness to disgust and weary" (233). Describing her new view of Darcy to Wickham, Elizabeth makes clear that she comprehends that the shifts in her perception are the result of her own growth rather than a change in the truth: "When I said that he improved on acquaintance, I did not mean that either his mind or manners were in a state of improvement, but that from knowing him better, his disposition was better understood." It is in "knowing him better" that Elizabeth finds Darcy "improved." "In essentials, I believe, he is very much what he ever was" (234).

The funniest of the moments that reveal Elizabeth's awareness of her own internal change comes when she replies to Jane's attempt to exonerate both Darcy and Wickham. "This will not do," Elizabeth tells her sister. "There is but such a quantity of merit between them; just enough to make one good sort of man; and of late it has been shifting about pretty much. For my part,

I am inclined to believe it all Mr. Darcy's, but you shall do as you chuse" (225). Just as when, later, the river, trees, and lawns of Pemberley seem to be "taking different positions," so here, as the sisters talk in a bedroom at Longbourn, the merit seems to have been "shifting about pretty much" between the two men. Elizabeth's witticism reveals her comprehension that it is not merit that has been shifting about but her own point of view.

In reply to questions, students can tell moving stories about their own experiences of changing their minds. Have you ever completely misjudged a person at first meeting? What was it like to realize you were wrong? Have you ever made a misjudgment it took you months to correct? How did you correct it? Have you ever totally changed your mind about another person? The teacher can highlight the moments in each student's story that reveal inner turmoil, anguish, or effort, thus both providing vocabulary for stages of the process and recognition of the value of such growth.

The visit to Pemberley is an external experience that supplies Elizabeth with new evidence about Darcy's nature and past, enabling her to continue to deepen her knowledge of who he is. The visit also allows her to see him behave in a way that indicates he has attended to her reproofs.

The other main development in the plot that makes Elizabeth love Darcy is her coming to understand the full meaning of his rescue of Lydia. Elizabeth undergoes unfolding stages of disbelief, surprise, pain, wonder, and astonishment, each stage the result of her coming — incredulous and marveling — to see more of his love for her. Her feeling that such love is not probable, could not be, is gradually overcome by the certainty that "he had done it for her" (326). The magnitude of what he "had done" is measured in Edward Copeland's essay in this volume, by calculating the staggering amount of Darcy's money that was probably necessary to make Wickham marry Lydia; in Elizabeth Langland's essay, by examining the exact language Austen uses to discriminate the moral revulsion and personal anguish Darcy must have felt as he arranged the marriage; and in the essays by Susan Kneedler and Bruce Stovel, by interpreting the meanings of Elizabeth's unfolding surprise as she grasps what has happened.

As Elizabeth develops depth and complexity in her thinking, she taps a new level of herself as a passionate person. The capacity to love is created by the struggle to understand. Two passages from the novel that we read aloud in class explore the connection between thinking and feeling. The first occurs at the inn in Derbyshire when Elizabeth ponders the changes that have taken place in her own feelings during the time between receiving Darcy's letter and visiting Pemberley, and the changes that are now occurring as she attempts to read and interpret his altered behavior. With an almost laughable search for accurate language, Elizabeth works her way intellectually through an emotional vocabulary from "hate" to "love," pausing at a critical midpoint to produce and repeat a surprising word — "gratitude."

I read this passage aloud in order to highlight its modulated vocabulary of coming tó *know* what one *feels*:

> As for Elizabeth, her *thoughts* were at Pemberley this evening more than the last; and the evening, though as it passed it seemed long, was not long enough to determine her *feelings* towards *one* in that mansion; and she lay awake two whole hours, *endeavouring to make them out*. She certainly did not *hate* him. No; *hatred* had vanished long ago, and she had almost as long been *ashamed of ever feeling a dislike* against him, that could be so called. The *respect* created by the conviction of his valuable qualities, though at first *unwillingly admitted*, had for some time *ceased to be repugnant to her feelings*; and it was now heightened into *somewhat of a friendlier nature*, by the testimony so highly in his favour, and bringing forward his disposition in so amiable a light, which yesterday had produced. But above all, above *respect* and *esteem*, there was a *motive within her of good will* which could not be overlooked. It was *gratitude. — Gratitude*, not merely for *having once loved her*, but for *loving her still* well enough, to forgive all the petulance and acrimony of her manner in rejecting him, and all the unjust accusations accompanying her rejection. . . . Such a change in a man of so much pride, excited not only *astonishment* but *gratitude — for to love, ardent love*, it must be attributed; and . . . *its impression on her . . . could not be exactly defined.* She *respected*, she *esteemed*, she was *grateful* to him, she *felt a real interest in his welfare*; and she only *wanted to know* . . . how far it would be for the *happiness of both* that she should employ the *power*, which her *fancy* told her she still possessed, of bringing on the renewal of his addresses.   (265–66; most emphasis added)

The second passage wittily considers the two modes of falling in love that Elizabeth has tried during the novel — the blind leap of love at first sight and the slow development of love from the unromantic emotions of gratitude and respect:

> If gratitude and esteem are good foundations of affection, Elizabeth's change of sentiment will be neither improbable nor faulty. But if otherwise, if the regard springing from such sources is unreasonable or unnatural, in comparison of what is so often described as arising on a first interview with its object, and even before two words have been exchanged, nothing can be said in her defence, except that she had given somewhat of a trial to the latter method, in her partiality for Wickham, and that its ill-success might perhaps authorise her to seek the other less interesting mode of attachment.   (279)

The author herself may be heard in these sentences, wondering if we will find Elizabeth's "change of sentiment" either "improbable" or "faulty." If we think that love at "first interview" is more plausible, then nothing can be said in defense of this plot. Still, we did see both Elizabeth's and Lydia's experiments with love at first sight of Wickham. The novel teaches that a "less interesting mode of attachment" — *knowing* one's lover first — yields better results.

Why does this book reward student readers? The pleasure of romance is there, after all. But insights produced by looking at the theme of knowing also yield satisfactions to student readers and give deeper meaning to the romance. The novel celebrates a young woman's ability to change her mind and her feelings, and presents this ability as a sign of developing maturity. Its suggestions that inner growth is strenuous, painful, laborious, and worthwhile may encourage student readers to view their own struggles for inner growth with determination and hope. In locating the sources of deep passion in knowledge and in prosaic emotions like respect, esteem, and gratitude, *Pride and Prejudice* suggests that unless one knows oneself and truly knows the beloved, attachment is not real, enduring, or even truly love. For many student readers, these may be heartening and plausible correctives to the more "interesting mode of attachment" they encounter in popular culture. The novel celebrates the broadening of Elizabeth's morality from a rather superficial mode of interpreting the warmth of social conversations to an increased consciousness of socially responsible behavior, especially by elders in regard to younger people. Finally, its implicit and explicit exhortation to try "taking different positions" speaks to students as they journey through the emotional and intellectual changes of college, and supports their movement from simple, prejudiced, hasty, and judgmental thinking to more flexible, trustworthy, patient, self-aware, and accurate ways of knowing.

Appendix: Suggestions for Further Reading

As a sample of the abundant critical writing available on a particular approach to teaching, I include here an annotated bibliography of criticism examining the novel's central emphasis on epistemology, or the problem of knowing. All five of these works are mentioned in the "Materials" section of the volume; here I highlight their relevance to the construction of classroom discussion on the theme of knowing.

In his essay "Light and Bright and Sparkling," Reuben Brower points to Austen's "awareness that it is difficult to know any complex person," and he demonstrates the openness, in many early scenes of the novel, of Darcy's behavior to double interpretation. Brower illuminates Austen's "exquisite preparation" for Elizabeth's change of feeling by emphasizing the ambiguity of earlier scenes, explaining Elizabeth's erroneous interpretation of Darcy by the complexity of the novelist's presentation of him.

The inspiration for Howard Babb's book *Jane Austen's Novels: The Fabric of Dialogue* came to him in reading and rereading the pianoforte scene at Rosings and in scrupulously unraveling the depth and complexity of mutual misunderstanding in the conversation between Darcy and Elizabeth. For him the brilliance of the first half of the novel is that, in it, Austen "recreates the quality of our social experience, that sense we often have of the ambiguities inherent in behavior. She accomplishes this partly by engaging us . . . in making out a number of characters largely on the basis of what they say and do in public" (113). Babb's book, long out of print, influenced me as a beginning teacher of this novel, for his meticulous close readings of dialogue in *Pride and Prejudice* suggested not only how to read speech after speech of the novel's conversations but also how to translate those readings into questions that enable students to come up with the same insights about the difficulty that even intelligent people have interpreting each other's words and behavior reliably.

Alistair Duckworth's discussion, in *The Improvement of the Estate*, of the "perspectivist theme" in the novel reveals the way each character perceives and interprets events differently. Noting that "any number of scenes could illustrate" this point (116), Duckworth uses the reading of Mr. Collins's letter and the seven distinctive responses of the Bennet parents and daughters as an epitomizing instance of the novel's pattern (61–65). The letter evokes Mrs. Bennet's single-minded and undiscriminating eagerness to marry off all her daughters; Jane's imperceptive benevolence; Elizabeth's unique capacity to perceive, question, and speculate; Mr. Bennet's heartless relish of absurdity and his authoritative perceptiveness; Mary's pompous erudition and lack of practical experience; and Kitty's and Lydia's exclusive interest in officers (see Duckworth 117). The multiple responses to Mr. Collins's "olive branch" present a relatively static example of the novel's pattern of presenting multiple interpretations of single events, for the letter simply inspires each Bennet except Elizabeth to produce his or her own fixed idea. Only Elizabeth pauses over the letter to consider its meaning as a revelation of the writer's character. Her acuteness in pondering "something very pompous in his stile" and her deduction that he may not be "a sensible man" establish Elizabeth as the most intellectually flexible person in the family (64).

Two recent studies of *Pride and Prejudice* place epistemological issues at the center of the novel's concerns. In a brilliant essay, "An Epistemological Understanding of *Pride and Prejudice*: Humility and Objectivity," Martha Satz remarks that for "a reader alert to the problems of knowledge," the "disjunction" between "perception and interpretation" "leaps out from almost every page":

> At times, explicit epistemological discussions occur with grandeur, as when they are the stuff of reconciliation between Elizabeth and Darcy, but more often as trivia . . . in the most prosaic exchanges. Comments and discussion about knowledge and understanding, and the erratic and variable interpretations on which they rest, not only supply the central subject of the book but also constitute the warp and woof of its fabric.   (171–72)

Satz illustrates the insight that in this novel "almost any evidence can be given two contrary interpretations" and, in fact, that "an event, major or minor, is an occasion which in its interpretation exhibits the modes of perception of the characters." Satz mentions as instances of this pattern Miss Bingley, Mrs. Hurst, and their brother's differing interpretations of Elizabeth's three-mile walk across the countryside (32–33), Jane's and Elizabeth's opposed interpretations of Miss Bingley's letter about quitting Netherfield (134–37), and the paired opposing opinions of Jane and Elizabeth (14–15), and Bingley and Darcy (16), about the Meryton assembly ball.

Satz's essay goes beyond others on this topic in her acute location of a final irony of the book's attention to epistemology, which is that, contrary to the experience of every character in the novel, Austen confidently projects a view of all events and characters that certifies the truth as knowable and in fact *known* to the author. This insight explains the certainty of the narrator's claim that "every disposition of the ground was good" from the windows at Pemberley. The author's stance is characterized by Duckworth in terms that suggest his admiration: "that which is good and true resists the perversion of the individual viewpoint" (125). Satz, however, sees it as an epistemological problem: "[T]he author herself, by foisting on her reader, in spite of all the evidence to the contrary, a metaphysically and morally certified view of knowledge, projects a supreme arrogance about what is true, thereby contradicting the fabric of the entire novel" (183).

Tony Tanner places the problem of knowledge at the center of *Pride and Prejudice*. In his book *Jane Austen* he says the novel "is, most importantly, about prejudging and rejudging. It is a drama of recognition — re-cognition, that act by which the mind can look again at a thing and if necessary make revisions and amendments until it sees the thing as it really is" (105). He observes that "there is in the book a whole vocabulary connected with the process of decisions, opinions, conviction, stressing or suggesting how various and unstable are people's ideas, judgements, accounts and versions of situations and people." Unlike Satz, Tanner finds Austen's presentation of a world in which the truth is finally knowable to be heartening, for, if it highlights the problem of interpretation that constantly confronts the human consciousness, it also emphasizes the possibility of what he calls "salvation," because a person can "change his version of interpretation of things." I have developed my approach to teaching the novel partly out of my reading of these critics, for they have articulated what seems to me the deepest layer of the novel and the one most likely to engage the imagination of college student readers.

Surprise in *Pride and Prejudice*
Bruce Stovel

The students in literature courses have one great advantage over their
teachers: they are almost always first-time readers of the works to be studied.
They can be puzzled, stunned, disoriented, shocked — in a word, surprised —
as their instructors cannot. The students' ability to be surprised also offers
them some purchase upon the text, handholds that allow them to start climbing. *Pride and Prejudice* is especially suited to this kind of approach, since it
provides some of the finest moments of astonishment in all of literature; the
whole novel, for instance, is magically transformed toward the end when
Lydia Bennet, babbling on as she and her mother are wont to do, speaks an
apparently innocuous sentence: "However, I recollected afterwards, that if
he *had* been prevented going, the wedding need not be put off, for Mr. Darcy
might have done as well" (319). I argue here that the notion of surprise
illuminates both the structure and the theme of the novel, and in doing so
enables us to make use of our students' experience of having been surprised —
for, just like Elizabeth reading and rereading Darcy's letter, they will have
been jolted into new perceptions if they have responded fully to the novel.

The notion of surprise is closely connected to those of secrecy and silence:
the three form a single entity at the very heart of the notion of a plot. A
secret consists of information generally unknown yet understood by a select
few. A storyteller's plot is built around a secret, but the storyteller, while
continuing to narrate the tale, preserves silence until the time for divulging
the secret with greatest effect — the time for surprise — has come. Once all
the secrets have been revealed, we can no longer be surprised, and the plot
is over: the author relapses into literal silence. These ideas underlie the witty
title that Henry Fielding gives to book 1 of *Tom Jones*: "Containing as much
of the Birth of the Foundling as is necessary or proper to acquaint the Reader
with in the Beginning of this History." On the one hand, the author must
not give away the nub of the matter: a game of hide-and-seek is no fun if we
know the secret hiding places right away. On the other hand, the reader
must know a certain amount in order to play the game at all. Narration thus
proceeds by indirection — but also moves in a definite, foreknown direction.

A very young Jane Austen plays with these notions in "The Mystery: an
Unfinished Comedy," a squib she wrote at about age thirteen. The second
scene of this miniature drama pays homage to secrets and silence as overwhelmingly significant literary devices:

Scene the 2nd
A Parlour in HUMBUG's *House*
MRS HUMBUG & FANNY, *discovered at work.*

MRS HUM:) You understand me my Love?
FANNY) Perfectly ma'am. Pray continue your narration.

MRS HUM:)   Alas! it is nearly concluded, for I have nothing more to say
   on the Subject.
FANNY)   Ah! here's Daphne.
                    Enter DAPHNE
DAPHNE)   My dear Mrs. Humbug Howd'ye do? Oh! Fanny t'is all over.
FANNY)   Is it indeed!
MRS HUM:)   I'm very sorry to hear it.
FANNY)   Then t'was to no purpose that I . . .
DAPHNE)   None upon Earth.
MRS HUM:)   And what is to become of? . . .
DAPHNE)   Oh thats all settled. (*whispers MRS HUMBUG*)
FANNY)   And how is it determined?
DAPHNE)   I'll tell you. (*whispers FANNY*)
MRS HUM:)   And is he to? . . .
DAPHNE)   I'll tell you all I know of the matter. (*whispers
      MRS HUMBUG & FANNY*)
FANNY)   Well! now I know everything about it, I'll go away.
MRS HUM:)
            And so will I.   [*Exeunt*]
DAPHNE)   (*Minor Works* 56)

This set of ideas plays an important part in *Pride and Prejudice*, as we
can see in the comic playlet that is enacted in the opening paragraphs of
the novel. Mrs. Bennet pesters her husband to visit their new neighbor,
Mr. Bingley, so that Bingley will be able to marry one of their five daughters;
during successive days of badgering, Mr. Bennet replies with such masterful
indirection that Mrs. Bennet finally cries, "I am sick of Mr. Bingley," and
now the time has come for Mr. Bennet, the concealed author of this little
drama, to break his silence and reveal his secret: " 'I am sorry to hear *that*;
but why did not you tell me so before? If I had known as much this morning,
I certainly would not have called on him.' . . . The astonishment of the
ladies was just what he wished."

If Mr. Bennet contrives this little comedy, which might be called "The
Visit," for his own rather cruel amusement, for an audience of one, Austen
has constructed the whole novel on much the same principles, though for
a much larger audience and for a much more humane purpose. Students
will readily grasp the point: humbling as it may be, as readers we are all
in the same position as Mrs. Bennet, who goes on to declare that this reversal
of her expectations "was what she had expected all the while" (7). This
approach further emphasizes what many readers have noted: that although
the novel was written in three volumes, its plot falls into halves, divided
by the novel's central episode—Darcy's proposal, his letter the next morning,
and Elizabeth's ensuing reflections. Before this reversal and recognition,
Darcy and Elizabeth are separated by secrets; after the proposal scene and
the letter, which are in themselves secrets, the two characters are united

by secrets. Elizabeth reciprocates at Lambton and confesses to Darcy the secret of her sister's seduction by Wickham, and the lovers are united only after Elizabeth refuses to share with Lady Catherine the secret of her intentions — and, of course, her refusal to disclose her secret, in a lovely irony, itself discloses it to Darcy.

Similarly, the teasing dialogues between Darcy and Elizabeth in the first half of the novel (a form of pseudosilence in that speech serves to disguise meaning) is replaced during the second half, for the most part, by genuine silence: Darcy and Elizabeth are separated, and each now has the material, the opportunity, and the motive for introspection and moral change. Furthermore, the events that astonish Elizabeth in the first half of the novel are pseudosurprises for the reader: beginning with Wickham's nonappearance at the Bingleys' ball and climaxing in Darcy's proposal, each of these developments has been signaled in advance to us. Each is unpleasant, each is brought on by Elizabeth's own delusions, and each leaves Elizabeth with no understanding of why she has fallen into such embarrassing mistakes. Starting with Darcy's letter, however, which *is* a major surprise to us as well as Elizabeth, the second half of the novel contains a series of marvelous comic unfoldings: events that we could never have anticipated, that suddenly transform pain into pleasure, that cause the sober truth Elizabeth has vowed to respect to astonish her. She may tell herself that Darcy's love "could not in rational expectation survive such a blow" as Lydia's elopement with Wickham (311), but then the truth turns out to exceed such rational expectations.

To help students understand the novel's use of secrets, silence, and surprise, teachers should devote some class time to developing two even more fundamental ideas: that Elizabeth serves not only as the novel's heroine but as its narrative vantage point, and that Elizabeth is drawn to Darcy long before she realizes she is.

As for the first of these, Elizabeth prides herself on her discernment (208), on her ability to see the secrets that lie behind and explain the characters around her. Bingley, publicly anatomized by Elizabeth, confesses that "to be so easily seen through I am afraid is pitiful" (42). Elizabeth also has the intelligence necessary to keep a secret — unlike Lydia, who, without intending to do so, reveals that Darcy was at her wedding — and the self-discipline to keep sensitive facts to herself. Elizabeth is thus capable of deciding which secrets can be shared and which deserve silence: she tells Jane about Darcy's proposal and about one of the two secrets divulged in his letter — Wickham's misbehavior — but keeps from her the much more damaging one, that Darcy prevented Bingley from learning that Jane was in town the previous winter. Elizabeth can remain silent about her secrets; in the latter part of the novel she keeps many secrets from Jane: not only Darcy's interference with Bingley but his changed behavior at Pemberley; her own impulsive confiding in Darcy over Lydia's elopement; and her discovery, via Lydia and Mrs. Gardiner, that Darcy has arranged and paid for the marriage of Lydia and Wickham.

It is a measure of his perception that Darcy says in his long letter to Elizabeth, "I feel no doubt of your secrecy" (201) — just as she, though she may regret having immediately told Darcy the scandalous truth about Lydia's elopement, feels no doubt of his: "There were few people on whose secrecy she would have more confidently depended" (311).

Furthermore, Elizabeth's pride in her own discernment makes her a wonderfully sensitive gauge of surprise. Elizabeth tells Jane, just after her first encounter with Wickham, "I beg your pardon; — one knows exactly what to think" (86), and this assertion reflects her attitude: *she knows*. Because she has such precise expectations, she is capable of being utterly surprised, unlike, we might note, the novel's fools. Mrs. Bennet proves incapable of registering surprise. When she learns that Wickham and Lydia are to marry, she exclaims, "I knew how it would be" (306), and she says the very same words on learning of Bingley and Jane's engagement, adding, "I always said it must be so, at last. I was sure you could not be so beautiful for nothing!" (348). Elizabeth, unlike Mrs. Bennet and like Darcy, has the intelligence to take in unanticipated information and the humility to learn from it.

This first fundamental idea — Elizabeth as the narrative vantage point — leads naturally to the second: her unconscious, and ironic, attraction to Darcy. When Jane asks her at the novel's end how long she has loved Darcy, she replied, "It has been coming on so gradually, that I hardly know when it began" (373). It is one of the novel's finest ironies that Elizabeth falls consciously and deliberately in love with Darcy in the most proper way: only after she comes to understand and esteem his character and thus comes to be grateful for *his* clearly expressed regard for *her*. Nevertheless, Elizabeth is fascinated by Darcy from their first meeting onward, completely unaware of her hidden attraction to "*that* abominable Mr. Darcy": "to her he was only the man who made himself agreeable no where, and who had not thought her handsome enough to dance with" (144, 23). If she notices that he watches her closely at Netherfield, she assumes that his looks express disapproval, and decides, "She liked him too little to care for his approbation" (51). Yet she does like him a great deal and does want to win his approbation; she judges her family through his eyes as they expose themselves again and again, a sharing of his vision that is nicely symbolized much later when, standing before Darcy's portrait at Pemberley, she "fixed his eyes upon herself [and] thought of his regard with a deeper sentiment of gratitude than it had ever raised before" (251). But just as, before his proposal, Darcy struggles against his growing love for Elizabeth as something unworthy of himself, so Elizabeth is unwilling to admit her attraction: Darcy is the man she loves to hate, and hates to love. Like Beatrice in *Much Ado about Nothing*, Elizabeth goes out of her way to flirt with her Benedick, teasing Darcy, taunting him, quarreling with his statements and throwing his past words in his face, pointing out his character defects as well as his intellectual lapses, criticizing his treatment of his friends and his enemies, taking delight in vexing him. In short, Elizabeth falls in love both instinctively and deliberately; as a comic heroine, she embodies a harmonious concord of apparently incompatible opposites.

Once these two points have been articulated, students are in a position to consider the plot more closely and to define the novel's use of secrets, silence, and surprise. It seems to me that five secrets keep Darcy and Elizabeth apart during the first half of the novel: each secret is known by one of the central pair but not by the other. Darcy does not know that Jane Bennet, despite her placid demeanor, loves his friend Bingley. Elizabeth is ignorant of four crucial pieces of information: that Darcy had kept from Bingley the knowledge that Jane was in town; that Wickham is a detestable hypocrite; that Darcy is, against his will, increasingly in love with her; and that she herself is, against her will, increasingly fascinated with him. Elizabeth does know what Darcy does not: that Jane loves Bingley. Darcy clearly knows three of the four things that are hidden from Elizabeth — that he has kept Bingley ignorant of Jane's presence in London, that Wickham is far from being a victim of the Darcy family, and that he is in love with Elizabeth (if against his will, his reason, and his character [190]) — and he is, ironically, fully convinced of the fourth, of Elizabeth's love for him. He can see in her behavior to him what she cannot: "I believed you to be wishing, expecting my addresses," he tells her at the novel's end (369).

The proposal scene and its result, Darcy's letter, are thus pivotal. The proposal, itself a secret between them, reveals three of the five secrets: Jane's love for Bingley, Darcy's separation of Bingley from Jane, and Darcy's love for Elizabeth. Darcy's ensuing letter, also a secret between Elizabeth and Darcy, throws further light on all three of the secrets just revealed to Elizabeth. It is especially eloquent on the third secret, Darcy's love, for, despite its haughty opening and its cool tone, it is really a love letter — in its appeal to Elizabeth to join him in reaching a mutual understanding of their situation, in its painful efforts to be honest and precise, in its trust in her intelligence and ability to keep his confidence. Furthermore, the letter reveals a fourth secret, Wickham's past. By the time Elizabeth has read and absorbed the letter, only one of the five original secrets is unknown to her: her attraction to Darcy. That feeling will slowly become apparent to her as she moves in a series of steps, accelerated by her encounter with a transformed Darcy at Pemberley, from credence to respect to approval to esteem to gratitude to affection and, finally, the realization that "he was exactly the man, who, in disposition and talents, would most suit her" (312).

From the proposal and letter onward, then, Darcy and Elizabeth are united by their secret knowledge. This is even more evident when a new secret emerges in the second half of the novel: Wickham and Lydia have eloped and disappeared. The elopement has often been treated with disdain by critics; Tony Tanner considers that it presents us with "externalities . . . mere melodrama" (*Jane Austen* 120). The elopement in itself may have been melodramatic, but Austen carefully limits her presentation of it to its effects on the other characters, which are not. Elizabeth, motivated by impulses that she cannot explain and later regrets, spontaneously tells Darcy about the elopement right after reading Jane's letters announcing it: she is moved by her new trust in him and by his evident compassion at her equally evident suffering. By entrusting him with the secret of her sister's elopement with Wickham, she reciprocates the trust in her revealed by his disclosure to her of Wickham's intended elopement with *his* sister. Mutual confidences and mutual confidence have grown up together. Her disclosure allows Darcy to demonstrate his love for her: he secretly rescues Lydia and the Bennet family by arranging (and paying for) a marriage that guarantees that he will not only be allied to the Bennets but also have Wickham as a brother-in-law, if he proposes again to Elizabeth. Darcy's secret rescue of the Bennet family has further significance in the plot, since it is only when Elizabeth takes the initiative and thanks him for it that he finds himself able to ask for her hand a second time. But before that, Elizabeth guarantees Darcy's return to Longbourn by her refusal to divulge a secret — a refusal that is opaque to Lady Catherine but is a concealed confession to Darcy. Elizabeth carefully tells Lady Catherine only what Darcy already knows: that she is not engaged to him (356).

Discussing the importance of secrets in the novel can lead students to two further ideas. One is that the secrets that separate Elizabeth and Darcy in the first half are really pseudosecrets: the characters may be ignorant, but we are able to see the true state of affairs. Unlike the question of Tom Jones's parentage, which is a fact the author carefully conceals from all but the preternaturally acute reader, Austen has put us in a position to be in on these pseudosecrets. We know, of course, about Jane's love for Bingley, since Jane confides in Elizabeth and Elizabeth is the point-of-view character. We also can perceive, though we are not explicitly told, that Elizabeth is obtuse on each of the four remaining questions. She refuses to believe that Bingley has left Longbourn for good because she is convinced that he loves Jane and that "a young man so totally independent of every one" (120) will do just what he wants. She is correct on the first count, Bingley's love for Jane, but mistaken on the second, Bingley's independence. Similarly, Elizabeth can see clearly after reading Darcy's letter just how self-contradictory Wickham's posture of offended virtue has been. Despite Wickham's claim to Elizabeth that it is not for him to avoid Darcy (78), he does not attend the Bingley's ball, though he was invited along with the other officers (89). As for Darcy's growing love for Elizabeth, Austen leaves Elizabeth's viewpoint several times during the first third of the novel to give us direct glimpses of both his love and his struggle against it; and during her stay at Hunsford, later in the book, though we remain within Elizabeth's perspective, we can see increasingly clear signs that his struggle is going to be in vain. And, in fact, Darcy's growing love for her is further evidence to us of the fourth secret, that she is, ironically, attached to him, though without realizing it. Certainly Darcy's situation when he proposes is unlike that of her previous suitor, Mr. Collins, whose regard for her Elizabeth can dismiss as "quite imaginary" (112): Darcy has been responding to clear signals, even if Elizabeth did not intend to transmit them.

The second point about these secrets is that Darcy and Elizabeth cannot penetrate them because of their pride and prejudice. They are separated not so much by simple information as by a blindness to what is there to be seen; the gap is the result of moral failures on each side. Darcy cannot see Jane's love for Bingley because, hoping to arrange a marriage between Bingley and his sister, Georgiana, he does not want to. Similarly, Elizabeth does not want to recognize Darcy's power over Bingley, Darcy's moral superiority to Wickham, Darcy's evident admiration for her, or even her own feelings toward him, all for the same reason: to do so would be to lose her independence and her conviction of her own superiority. There is room for growth and change on each side. The final words regarding Bingley and Jane in Darcy's letter contain an unintended precision: "though the motives which governed me may to you very naturally appear insufficient, I have not yet learnt to condemn them" (199). Not yet, perhaps, but he will eventually. It takes more than five months, but, as Darcy explains to Elizabeth, "On the evening before my going to London, I made a confession to [Bingley], which I believe I ought to have made long ago" (370–71). In the same way, Elizabeth's understanding of her errors and their cause undergoes a long, slow change, culminating, perhaps, in her reaction to the news from Mrs. Gardiner that Darcy has secretly arranged the Lydia-Wickham match: "For herself she was humbled; but she was proud of him" (327). Elizabeth, like Darcy, has learned to condemn her earlier certainties.

Secrets presuppose silence. If students are thinking analytically about secrets in the novel, they will also be coming to understand its dramatic use of silence. The relationship of Elizabeth and Darcy during the first half of the novel consists largely of pseudosilence: Elizabeth may believe that Darcy is a man of silence and twit him repeatedly for being so, but actually their relationship during this section of the novel is a talkative one. This is nicely symbolized when Elizabeth finds herself dancing with Darcy at Netherfield: "she began to imagine that their silence was to last through the two dances, and at first was resolved not to break it; till suddenly fancying that it would be the greater punishment to her partner to oblige him to talk, she made some slight observation on the dance" (91). The key word is "fancying": Elizabeth grasps neither Darcy's devotion to her nor the complexity of her desire to punish him. The proposal scene and the letter put Elizabeth and Darcy into direct communication, and, as we have seen, this central episode is followed by a long period of genuine silence, introspection, and change on the part of each. Elizabeth has no interest in self-analysis in the first half of the novel: her attention is engaged by the mysterious events happening around her. The final sentence in Elizabeth's apostrophe to herself after reading Darcy's letter, "Till this moment, I never knew myself" (208), highlights the change in where her attention is directed.

In other words, Elizabeth begins the novel as someone determined to talk, because she knows exactly what to think: when she tells Jane about Darcy's letter, she admits, "And yet I meant to be uncommonly clever in taking so decided a dislike to him, without any reason. It is such a spur to one's genius, such an opening for wit to have a dislike of that kind" (225–26). Nevertheless, Darcy's proposal, his letter, and their ensuing separation force her to be silent, even with Jane, on some matters, and to understand the value of silence. Her first act in the plot is to entertain everyone with the story of what she has overheard Darcy say to Bingley about her (12); her decisive act of refusing to tell her story when Lady Catherine sweeps up in her chaise and four shows how much she has learned. Elizabeth has become more like Darcy during the course of their relationship, just as he has gained some of her liveliness and poise.

Secrets and silence are the conditions for surprise. Students who grasp this will be on the way to understanding their own surprises as readers of the novel; even introductory-level students can make the transition from autobiography to criticism, from reporting their responses to accounting for them. There are, it turns out, five major revelations within the first half of the novel, culminating in Darcy's proposal to Elizabeth, but these surprises are more apparent than real — events that catch Elizabeth, but not the novel's readers, unprepared. These shocks, all of them disturbing to Elizabeth, are brought on by her delusions. In the second half of the novel, however, beginning with Darcy's letter and culminating in Lady Catherine's descent upon Longbourn, there are another five surprises, but each of these is a genuinely astonishing turn of events that no one, neither Elizabeth nor the reader, could ever have predicted. Each of these surprises turns out to be pleasant and depends, paradoxically, on Elizabeth's new grasp of sober reality.

Elizabeth's first major unpleasant surprise occurs when Wickham does not attend the Bingleys' ball: "a doubt of his being present had never occurred to her" (89). An even more painful shock occurs when Charlotte Lucas tells Elizabeth that she has agreed to marry Mr. Collins:

> [T]hat Charlotte should encourage him, seemed almost as far from possibility as that she could encourage him herself, and her astonishment was consequently so great as to overcome at first the bounds of decorum, and she could not help crying out,
> "Engaged to Mr. Collins! my dear Charlotte, — impossible!"   (124)

Elizabeth's third surprise comes at about the same time. Bingley has indeed left Netherfield for good, though Elizabeth had been so certain it could not happen: "The idea of his returning no more Elizabeth treated with the utmost contempt" (120). Her fourth unpleasant surprise follows quickly and consists of another defection: Wickham leaves off his attention to Elizabeth and begins determinedly making himself agreeable to a Miss King, whose "most remarkable charm" is the sudden acquisition of £10,000 (149). Her fifth and greatest surprise comes when Darcy abruptly enters the drawing room at Hunsford, where she is sitting alone, and bursts out with the words, "In vain have I struggled" (189). Darcy's proposal is the culminating instance in a series of unsettling overtures on his part: she is so startled when he asks to dance with her at Netherfield that — an even greater surprise — she finds herself accepting his offer (90); she registers alarm at Hunsford when he draws his chair toward hers and says, "*You* cannot have a right to such very strong local attachment. *You* cannot have been always at Longbourn" (179). But his proposal caps all: "Elizabeth's astonishment was beyond expression. She stared, coloured, doubted, and was silent" (189).

Alert students will see that all these surprises are ironic ones: surprises to Elizabeth, but hardly to us. For instance, Wickham's tale to Elizabeth is preposterous: he intersperses his maligning of Darcy with claims such as "Till I can forget his father, I can never defy or expose *him*" (80). Similarly, we have heard Charlotte advocate an unromantic strategy for securing a husband. Elizabeth, however, does not believe that Charlotte means what she says, partly because she depends so much on Charlotte's intelligent friendship but also because Charlotte is *her* friend and no friend of hers could be simply crass. In much the same way, Elizabeth is more unprepared than we are for Bingley's desertion of Jane and for Wickham's defection in favor of Miss King (presumably once he discovers, as Mr. Collins knew so well, that Elizabeth is worth only £1,000 in the 4 percents [106]). And Darcy's proposal has been looming more and more as inevitable: an insistent flurry of hints while Elizabeth is at Hunsford shows us that he is a kettle about to reach the boiling point. In short, the greatest surprise of all to Elizabeth in the first half of the novel is an event that we expect. And, as we have seen, all these surprises to Elizabeth are disturbing and even humiliating. They all spring from her prejudices, her determination to think the best of herself and the worst of Darcy, but until she reads Darcy's letter, she chooses to ascribe these unanticipated events to the unsatisfying, undependable nature of reality itself. She tells Jane:

> The more I see of the world, the more am I dissatisfied with it; and every day confirms my belief of the inconsistency of all human characters, and of the little dependence that can be placed on the appearance of either merit or sense. I have met with two instances lately; one I will not mention [she is alluding to Bingley's desertion]; the other is Charlotte's marriage. It is unaccountable! in every view it is unaccountable! (135)

A great change occurs, however, with Darcy's letter to Elizabeth, the sequel to and even continuation of his proposal. The letter is, in effect, Darcy's proposal, part 2. It is a complete surprise to us as well as to Elizabeth. And unlike the earlier surprise, this one is pleasant for Elizabeth, if painful in its immediate effects, because it proves how much Darcy values her intelligence and moral sense, how much he wants her good opinion, how much he trusts her, how much he wants to continue to communicate with her. Not only the pivotal event in the novel's plot, Darcy's letter also gives us, in Elizabeth's changing reaction to it, a model of how the novel should be read and how its unfolding incidents are to be comprehended.

The letter is the first of five genuinely surprising events in the second half of the novel, each of which advances Darcy and Elizabeth's relationship. The second comes when Elizabeth finds herself at Pemberley, finds that the house is gracious, but not ostentatious, and finds, to her special astonishment, that his housekeeper Mrs. Reynolds insists that he is a kind master: she has "never had a cross word from him in [her] life, and [has] known him ever since he was four years old" (248). The crescendo in this series of surprises at Pemberley comes when Darcy himself steps out from behind his house, and the climax is the change in Darcy's manners. The third great unexpected occurrence is the news of Lydia and Wickham's elopement, though the surprise lies not so much in the elopement itself as in the change it makes in Darcy and Elizabeth's relationship. Five lines after Jane's second letter ends, Elizabeth runs to the door of the room and confronts—Darcy (276). And then something even more startling than the elopement happens: Elizabeth finds herself confiding in Darcy. This act is her response to, her reciprocation of, his letter. The fourth great surprise occurs when Lydia lets slip the astonishing fact that Mr. Darcy was present at her wedding (319); Elizabeth now induces her aunt to reveal all Darcy has secretly done to bring about Lydia's marriage, and his actions have a secret meaning of their own: "Her heart did whisper, that he had done it for her" (326). The fifth surprise is Lady Catherine's appearance at Longbourn. Lady Catherine, who loves to be of use, removes all Darcy's doubts about Elizabeth's feelings (381). Elizabeth is no longer self-deceived, and once she begins to see the world as it is, she finds that it far exceeds her expectations. Though, as she tells Wickham, "In essentials, . . . [Mr. Darcy] is very much what he ever was" (234), that true identity proves to be far better than she had ever imagined.

Concentrating on surprise in the novel offers the teacher larger advantages as well. To pay attention to secrets, silence, and surprise in *Pride and Prejudice* draws attention to Austen's qualities as a novelist: her work is distinctively ironic, subtle, and comic. The existence of secrets creates irony, since hidden information presupposes that there are a privileged, initiated few, those complicit and in the know, and a larger group of those who are ignorant. Similarly, silence, the means by which secrets are preserved, has always seemed—strangely enough—an important part of Austen's eloquence: Katherine Mansfield, pointing to this reticence or reserve, comments, "The truth is that every true admirer of the novels cherishes the happy thought that he alone — reading between the lines — has become the secret friend of their author" (302). The key words are "between the lines": without ever whispering rudely to her audience, like her characters in "The Mystery," Austen conveys an enormous amount that is never explicitly stated. And sudden surprise is a primary characteristic of literary comedy, just as it is the sine qua non of comic laughter in everyday life. What could be more surprising and more comic than the metamorphosis created when Lydia Bennet speaks seven words: "Mr. Darcy might have done as well"?

Teaching about the Marriage Plot

Pamela S. Bromberg

Since 1976, when I first developed the undergraduate course Women in Literature, the syllabus has begun with *Pride and Prejudice*. Almost all the texts I originally chose have long since been replaced, but, along with *Jane Eyre* and *A Room of One's Own*, *Pride and Prejudice* has remained because it seems essential. Once, a few years ago, I tried substituting *Mansfield Park* as an experiment; while the later novel highlights the self-division that Sandra M. Gilbert and Susan Gubar see as central in Austen and other nineteenth-century women writers, its analysis of marriage is more diffuse, and it does not dramatize epistemological issues in terms of the central character's growth into more complete understanding of self, other, and society. So I returned to *Pride and Prejudice* with renewed conviction.

Pride and Prejudice continues as the cornerstone of my Women in Literature course because it establishes the central novelistic marriage tradition with which all the other texts we read are in strenuous dialogue. The first half of the course looks at critical variations on Austen's classic marriage plot in works such as *Jane Eyre*, *A Doll House*, and Kate Chopin's *The Awakening*, and the second half examines more radical ruptures and divorces from it in twentieth-century literature. *Pride and Prejudice* furnishes a critique of the prevailing socioeconomic basis of marriage and its inscription in the sentimental novel while ultimately advocating a reformed version of marriage through the central courtship plot. Austen optimistically envisions Elizabeth and Darcy's marriage as a relationship fostering personal moral growth, self-discovery, and the mutual benefit of individuals, families, and the wider community. The later nineteenth-century works are all subversive texts representing marriage as an institution that confines, diminishes, and oppresses women. Only in the second half of the course, when we read such contemporary texts as Toni Morrison's *The Bluest Eye*, Paule Marshall's *Brown Girl, Brownstones*, and Margaret Drabble's *The Middle Ground*, do novelists move beyond the central marriage plot, in either its comic or its tragic variations, to narrate other kinds of stories and meanings for women's lives.

If *Pride and Prejudice* seems essential to the course in terms of feminist literary and social history, it is equally important as a text that speaks powerfully and directly to my students about their own emerging identities and values, especially about mediating among individual, family, and social interests in choosing friends and mates. Austen's formulation of ideal marriage as the culmination of a process of education about the self, the other, and the world furnishes a powerful metaphor for connecting reading and learning in academic classes with personal experience. Understanding the patriarchal institutions that shape characters' lives in Austen's novel also helps students perceive the ways in which gender defines their identities and life plots.

In my teaching of *Pride and Prejudice*, I emphasize the marriage debate, since marriage is the primary, in fact single, institution through which female protagonists in the nineteenth-century novel achieve identity. By juxtaposing the central plot of Darcy and Elizabeth's courtship with the counterplots that bring together Jane and Bingley, Charlotte Lucas and Mr. Collins, and Lydia and Wickham, Austen portrays both a realistic, critical view of the dominant marriage ideology and her own optimistic, idealistic revision. Austen's portrait of the unsatisfactory Bennet marriage and its impact on the Bennet daughters provides a sobering view of the long-term social costs of marriages that are not founded on mutual "respect, esteem, and confidence" (236; Austen may have adopted this formula from Henry Fielding in *Tom Jones* 6.1).

For the first reading assignment, I ask the students to think about how different characters in *Pride and Prejudice* perceive and define marriage and why people in this novel marry, about the makeup of the Bennet family, and about the theme of reading people, the processes we use to form judgments about strangers. Students keep a journal in which they write about the texts, their lives, and the intersection of the two. I encourage them to ask questions in their journals about texts and to reflect on points that catch their attention but not to summarize the plots. To help them get started on the journals, I suggest topics for the first couple of weeks. The second set of topics, on courtship and marriage, invites students to reflect on their own values and experiences.

The first class begins with close reading of chapter 1, emphasizing narrative tone and irony and the dramatic dialogue that Austen brackets with authorial commentary. We look at the economic metaphors and prevailing concept of the marriage market, in which female beauty, breeding, and "accomplishments" are exchanged for financial security and social status. For Mrs. Bennet such intangibles as character and intelligence do not matter when scheming on the disposition of "a single man of large fortune" to one of her beautiful daughters (3). The Bennet marriage, brilliantly dramatized through a brief exchange of wheedling and teasing, is exemplary of the moral and psychological cost of this materialistic definition of marriage.

It is essential at this point to give brief, informative lectures on the social and historical backgrounds to *Pride and Prejudice*. Students recognize the centrality of social class but do not understand the stratifications and the permeability of class barriers. Explanation of the entail leads naturally to awareness of some of the legal, economic, and social strictures on women. Students are often mildly shocked and disapproving as they realize that Mrs. Bennet and her daughters do no useful work. We discuss the absence of working women from the domain of the novel and the class privileges, then and now, associated with reading and writing.

Next, we explore the central epistemological issues in Darcy and Elizabeth's early encounters. Then we return to the problem of marriage, with a careful comparison of Elizabeth's idealistic and Charlotte Lucas's pragmatic views and decisions about wedlock. Charlotte is a critical character in my teaching of the novel, for she represents the limited options afforded a nineteenth-century woman who possesses intelligence and ambition but who lacks beauty, money, or high social status. Charlotte begins the novel as Elizabeth's "intimate friend." Unlike the tender-hearted Jane, Charlotte shares Elizabeth's clear-sighted interest in manners and character. Austen tells the reader that she is "a sensible, intelligent young woman" (18), and we see evidence of her keen observation of behavior and sound knowledge of psychology as she explains Darcy's apparent hauteur and then warns Elizabeth about the dangers of Jane's reserve with Bingley (21–22). Charlotte argues that Jane should take a more active role in showing her affection and encouraging Bingley's interest if she wants him to marry her. This turns out ultimately to be excellent advice, but Elizabeth rejects Charlotte's goal-oriented strategizing, arguing that Jane and Bingley need more time to understand each other's characters and see if they are really suited to each other. In response, Charlotte articulates a self-defensively cynical view of marital happiness as entirely "a matter of chance." She dismisses Elizabeth's belief in the importance of mutual knowledge and compatibility and concludes that "it is better to know as little as possible of the defects of the person with whom you are to pass your life." Elizabeth laughs at this philosophy but protests, "it is not sound. You know . . . that you would never act in this way yourself" (23).

Not long after, Elizabeth acts on her own idealistic vision of marriage as a union founded on love and compatibility by turning down Mr. Collins's proposal. Although marriage to Mr. Collins would keep Longbourn in the Bennet family and guarantee the future security of her mother and sisters, Elizabeth never gives the offer the slightest serious consideration. She has nothing but contempt for the conceited, pompous Mr. Collins, who is, in the narrator's words, "altogether a mixture of pride and obsequiousness, self-importance and humility" (70). The proposal itself reveals Mr. Collins's character and morals more fully than any of his previous behavior or dialogue. Although he twice makes obligatory mention of love, professing runaway "feelings" and "the violence of [his] affection" for Elizabeth, he returns each time, in the next sentence, to a businesslike exposition of his reasons for marrying or the anticipated financial arrangements (105, 106). Mr. Collins is far more eloquent on the subject of Lady Catherine than he is on his feelings for Elizabeth, whom he has known for less than a week. At the end of this scene, the reader shares Elizabeth's and Mr. Bennet's contempt for Mr. Collins's sublime stupidity. My students take Mrs. Bennet's dismay at her daughter's rejection of Mr. Collins's offer as yet another instance of *her* stupidity and inadequate appreciation of Elizabeth. Austen herself is so critical of Mrs. Bennet that it is difficult for readers to sympathize with her legitimate financial worries.

Yet when Charlotte Lucas maneuvers Mr. Collins into making the same offer to her a mere three days later and she accepts him "solely from the pure and disinterested desire of an establishment" (122), my students almost unanimously applaud her strategy and success. They recognize that Elizabeth, with her "lively, playful disposition," "fine eyes," and witty conversation is a heroine, reserved for better endings (12, 27). But, as they point out in class discussion and in journal entries, Charlotte at twenty-seven is nearly an old maid, who lacks the beauty and wealth that would have attracted suitors. Mr. Collins's offer is likely to be the only one, and Austen holds out no possibility of respectable work and independence for Charlotte as a single woman. Her only alternative is to remain at home, a dependent first on her parents and later on her brothers. My students admire Charlotte's capacity for effective action and sympathize with the predicament that leads her to marry a man for whom she feels no attraction or respect. Like her intimate friend Elizabeth, Charlotte is too intelligent to esteem or like Mr. Collins, and he is certainly not in love with her. But she is generally satisfied with the arrangement:

> Mr. Collins to be sure was neither sensible nor agreeable; his society was irksome, and his attachment to her must be imaginary. But still he would be her husband. —Without thinking highly either of men or of matrimony, marriage had always been her object; it was the only honourable provision for well-educated young women of small fortune, and however uncertain of giving happiness, must be their pleasantest preservative from want. (122–23)

Charlotte only worries that Elizabeth, "whose friendship she valued beyond that of any other person," will disapprove (123). Thus Charlotte projects all matters of conscience onto her friend and pleads with her, "I am not romantic you know. I never was. I ask only a comfortable home." Elizabeth does disapprove, judging that Charlotte has "sacrificed every better feeling to worldly advantage" (125).

At this point the class begins a vigorous debate about whether independence from her family and "worldly advantage" are worth Charlotte's lifelong alliance with a man whose character and intelligence she holds in contempt. Accusations that Charlotte is cold-bloodedly using Mr. Collins are usually defended with the observation that Mr. Collins is doing the same with her. Theirs is an alliance of mutual utility, if not mutual love, and therefore morally acceptable. Mr. Collins's smug self-absorption and patriarchal pride justify Charlotte's distaste at the same time that they effectively protect him from ever recognizing or suffering from it. Most of my students find the grounds of Elizabeth's moral condemnation of her friend too lofty and privileged. They argue, as Jane Bennet does, that Charlotte is merely being prudent, that she comes from a large family, lacks a fortune, and wants to establish her own life. Marrying Mr. Collins is her only chance at independence. Furthermore, she is acting in the best interest of her own family, who no longer have to worry about maintaining her as an old maid. Mine is occasionally the only voice in this debate joining Elizabeth's, who passionately replies to Jane: "You shall not, for the sake of one individual, change the meaning of principle and integrity, nor endeavour to persuade yourself or me, that selfishness is prudence, and insensibility of danger, security for happiness" (135–36).

The middle portion of the novel affords Elizabeth and the reader the opportunity to assess Charlotte's decision and Elizabeth's judgment of it when the latter pays an extended visit to Mr. and Mrs. Collins at Hunsford. Before she leaves Longbourn, however, Elizabeth reveals a certain lack of consistency in her moral standards when she defends Wickham's sudden interest in Miss King as prudent rather than mercenary (153). Elizabeth discovers that Charlotte enjoys her comfortable home and that she has managed to arrange her life so that she has a good deal of privacy. She encourages Mr. Collins to work in his garden and chooses the small back room for her own, since Mr. Collins is so fond of looking out the front windows at passing carriages. Charlotte's tactic of avoiding her husband reflects her characteristic practicality. At this point I concede that my students seem to be right. Charlotte remains "tolerably composed" now that she is married to Mr. Collins, and she is successful in ignoring him when he makes embarrassing remarks (122).

The "danger" that Elizabeth perceives in Charlotte's decision to act selfishly and marry a man whom she doesn't respect or love doesn't become apparent until later in the novel, and even then we have to look carefully to see it. The full implications of Charlotte's alliance begin to be clear when Mr. Bennet receives the letter in which Mr. Collins "condole[s]" with him about Lydia's elopement (296). His self-righteous condemnation of Lydia's behavior, his exaggerated and formulaic rhetoric, and his conventional morality demonstrate his lack of Christian charity and sympathy. But his smug self-congratulation for having avoided a contaminating alliance with the Bennet family that would have involved him "in all your sorrow and disgrace" reveal the vicious character that underlies his excessive concern for status and respectability (297). Charlotte, whom Mr. Collins pointedly includes in his "sympathy" and judgments, has gained an establishment but lost her voice to Mr. Collins. He has written, in her name, a harsh reproach to her best friend's father. The absorption of Charlotte's opinions and moral identity by her husband can be seen as the extension of patriarchal politics from the legal and economic spheres into the family.

Charlotte's marriage to Mr. Collins illuminates one of the novel's central arguments about the dangers to self, *and* to family and community, of marriages based solely on economic and social considerations rather than on mutual understanding, respect, and love. The Bennet marriage supplies a sustained exploration of this theme. He marries her beauty; she, his property. Austen tells us that her "weak understanding and illiberal mind, had very early in their marriage put an end to all real affection for her. Respect, esteem, and confidence had vanished for ever; and all his views of domestic happiness were overthrown." Mr. Bennet copes by withdrawing to his library and books and by amusing himself with "her ignorance and folly." He teases his wife as a way of maintaining his intellectual superiority and distancing himself from her concerns. He makes no effort at serious communication with her and abandons responsibility for the moral education of his younger daughters. The "impropriety" of his "behaviour as a husband" (236) and parental irresponsibility are made vividly evident through the counterplot of Lydia and Wickham's elopement. But, as Elizabeth so painfully discovers in Darcy's first proposal and letter, both she and Jane and Mr. Bennet have always been judged by the behavior of the rest of their family.

The same must inevitably hold true for Charlotte, who inescapably allies herself with Mr. Collins's character and values when she allies herself with his "establishment." Thus, toward the end of our reading of *Pride and Prejudice*, I ask the class to reconsider Charlotte's decision to marry Mr. Collins. Reexamination of Charlotte's choice within the novel's wider exploration of the interdependency of self and family leads students to recognize that for the elevation of material desire and self-interest over affection and esteem as the grounds for marriage, Charlotte must pay the price of promoting her husband's values and joining in his harm. Focus on the counterpointed plots of Mr. Collins's two proposals reveals the economic and social pressures on women of a profoundly gendered, stratified society. In a novel that celebrates its heroine's capacity for making a matrimonial choice informed by moral, psychological, and social knowledge, Charlotte provides a troubling reminder that such choice is available only to the fortunate few. It is interesting that of all the couples who are married by the novel's end, only Mr. and Mrs. Collins are specifically endowed with offspring. In the letter warning Elizabeth against marrying Darcy and counseling Mr. and Mrs. Bennet never to admit Lydia and Wickham "in your sight, or allow their names to be mentioned in your hearing," Mr. Collins then writes "about his dear Charlotte's situation, and his expectation of a young olive-branch" (364). When I point out this narrative detail, students often respond by imagining Charlotte and Mr. Collins as parents (and sexual partners!). They perceive that Charlotte is likely to be in a position comparable to Mr. Bennet's vis-à-vis his ill-matched spouse, but without Mr. Bennet's patriarchal power.

In keeping with this approach to the novel, we look carefully at the other marriage stories, or counterplots. Austen demonstrates that family and social problems devolve from materialistic marriages with both the Collinses and the Bennets. Lydia and Wickham illustrate the dangers of narcissistic eros and unprincipled greed — not only to themselves but, more important, to their families and victims. Lydia's elopement serves as a cautionary tale to parents and heroines on the importance of asserting parental responsibility and distinguishing between the appearance and the reality of goodness and on the dangers of romantic passion as the sole basis for marriage and of female desire in a society that requires a woman's sexual chastity as a condition for marriage. Lydia's plot narrowly misses the tragic trajectory of seduction and abandonment, an outcome that would exact a just penalty on the Bennets for their careless parenting but would unfairly spoil Jane's and Elizabeth's hopes. (Lydia's impulsiveness and egocentricity serve as interesting foils for Charlotte's cool pragmatism.)

I try to integrate this focus on the marriage debate with analysis of the ways in which all the characters, but principally Elizabeth and Darcy, arrive at knowledge, or false knowledge, of self and other. The two themes converge in Austen's conviction that good marriages are built on a foundation of mutual "respect, esteem, and confidence." Before leaving the novel, we note that the happy endings of Jane's and Elizabeth's courtship plots still leave the two sisters with thirty miles separating them; in Austen's novel women's friendships remain securely subordinated to the marriage axis.

My students almost all enjoy reading *Pride and Prejudice*. A love story with the happy ending of desire fulfilled and legitimized in marriage is, for many of them, the quintessential novel. They would like to tell the same kind of story about their own lives. They recognize their own families and friends in Austen's characters and identify powerfully with Elizabeth Bennet, admiring her wit, independence, self-regard, and capacity for growth. *Pride and Prejudice* supplies an imaginative arena in which students may rehearse their own struggles and strategies for accommodating individual will and romantic dream with social reality. I see my course Women in Literature as a way for women students to gain understanding of their own lives and choices through knowledge of the past and the vicarious experience of life imagined in literature. As Patricia Spacks observes, "The paradigms of fiction provide an opportunity for moral playfulness: cost-free experimentation" ("Novel" 185). Marriage continues to be for my students a central, if not *the* central, life choice. Reading *Pride and Prejudice* supplies them with an optimistic vision of mutuality, self-discovery, and happiness in marriage, and also with awareness of some of the social and economic factors that underlie their own romantic plots. Reading the novel helps them understand the stakes in their major life decisions — those involving work as well as love — and encourages them to believe that careful readings of texts and individuals will help them in achieving their goals.

Later in the course, we look back to Charlotte Lucas as the first of a series of intelligent, independent-minded women trapped in marriages of convenience to self-absorbed patriarchs. In Austen's world Charlotte enters marriage with her eyes nearly wide open and makes the best of an imperfect deal; in another century or so, she will be reborn as her rebellious counter-parts Edna Pontellier, in *The Awakening*, and Nora Helmer, in *A Doll House*. The rest of the course shows that marriage can also imprison and deaden women and, finally, that other plots can be written and lived.

Family Plots: *Pride and Prejudice* as a Novel about Parenting

Paula Bennett

While the conclusions of Jane Austen's novels inevitably conform to the conventions of the marriage plot, their substance is devoted to what happens
after the happy ending—namely, family life. Born second to last in a family
of eight siblings, Austen had far more direct experience with living in a
family than she seems to have had with romance, and her novels reflect
this imbalance. Austen's "marriages" are the stuff of fantasy, but her families
—peopled as they are with neglectful, narcissistic parents and willful, spoiled
children—are the very stuff of life. For the past six years, I have used *Pride
and Prejudice* as a required text in the course The Literature of Adolescence. Originally, I chose the novel because it was one of the few I knew that
dealt with adolescents in a large family unit. (Most novelists of adolescence
depict their protagonists either alone or, at most, with one sibling.) But in
reading the novel for its family perspective, I have been forced to reread
Austen herself.

The Bennet family in *Pride and Prejudice* is an intact, if dysfunctional,
family unit consisting of a mother, father, and five adolescent daughters:
Jane (22), Elizabeth (20), Mary (18?), Kitty (16), and Lydia (15).[1] In this
family, birth order is of strategic importance. As the first-born, Jane and
Elizabeth are by far the best off. In a manner typical of many older children
in dysfunctional families, they have gravitated naturally to the parental roles
their mother and father have abandoned, achieving early maturity as a
result. Their maturity has garnered them whatever positive attention their
father has to offer, and, equally important, it has spared them most of his
growing antipathy to his wife.

Like many eldest daughters, Jane has assumed the role of family caretaker.
Quiet, compliant, nurturant, and highly responsible, she is depicted as continually doing for others: taking their side, giving them emotional as well
as physical support. It is virtually impossible for Jane to think ill of anyone—
even those, like the Bingley sisters, who deliberately set out to do her harm.
In a family sorely in need of such a figure, she has become the ideal "mother"
—the one to whom the rest can turn for nurturance, the one who, for the
sake of others, always sits, as Virginia Woolf acidly comments, in the draft.

Elizabeth, in contrast, has put herself in her father's shoes, serving both
as his favorite daughter and his surrogate son. Intellectually, she is his only
equal in this family of women. She shares his wit, his irony, and, above
all, his impatience with the narcissistic follies and frivolities that define conventional female behavior for Mrs. Bennet and her younger daughters. Even
more than he—presumably because she has much more at stake—Elizabeth

struggles to keep the other Bennet women in line. It is Elizabeth who vehemently protests Lydia's excursion to Brighton with the Forsters, vainly urging on her father the paternal role of limit setter that, out of disgust at his wife's example, he has long refused to play. And it is Elizabeth who assesses all too accurately just how destructive his passive-aggressive rejection of this role is — not only to her sisters but also, potentially, to herself:

> If you, my dear father, will not take the trouble of checking [Lydia's] exuberant spirits, and of teaching her that her present pursuits are not to be the business of her life, she will soon be beyond the reach of amendment. Her character will be fixed, and she will, at sixteen, be the most determined flirt that ever made herself and her family ridiculous. (231)

Like her sister Jane, Elizabeth is attempting to fill the void improper parenting creates: to do for her sisters what her parents cannot do or refuse to do on their own. In the hierarchical schema Austen (like her culture) imposes on family life, however, it is the rule of the missing father that Elizabeth seeks to impose. No wonder Mr. Bennet is so quick to exempt his "Lizzy" from the general curse he lays on the other sex (5). She stands for the father (the limit setter, the upholder of principles) he himself declines to be.

Born first, Jane and Elizabeth have appropriated substance and responsibility for themselves by taking on the roles their parents cannot or will not play. Like many sibling pairs in similar situations, they have divided the work between them, each finding her own place, or position, with which to identify within the family system. Mary, Kitty, and, above all, Lydia are not so lucky. To understand the plight of the three youngest Bennets, one must look at both why and, chronologically speaking, where they were born. On the former subject, Austen is explicit. Each of these girls represents one more failed attempt to have a son who, by his very birth, would rescue the family from eventual economic ruin:

> When first Mr. Bennet had married, economy was held to be perfectly useless; for, of course, they were to have a son. This son was to join in cutting off the entail, as soon as he should be of age, and the widow and younger children would by that means be provided for. Five daughters successively entered the world, but yet the son was to come. (308)

The son does not come. And Mr. Bennet, husband to a wife he despises and five daughters whom he cannot possibly support, retires to his library, taking, faute de mieux, Elizabeth with him. Mary, Kitty, and Lydia are by order of birth left progressively further behind, Mary and Kitty to be ignored, Lydia, the youngest and the most completely abandoned, to become her mother's favorite instead. In a family in which good sense, insofar as it is available at all, is identified with the male parent, Lydia's is a bitter fate indeed.

With no alternative roles available to them, Mary and Kitty become surplus children in a family containing, in effect, no competent, full-fledged adults. Unwanted and untended, each struggles in her individual way to find some place in family life: Mary, by her pathetic attempts to educate herself; Kitty, by following her sister Lydia to the brink of disaster. But if we take the Bennets as a whole, it is Lydia on whom the family's dysfunctions come to rest. With her total and unremitting allegiance to her mother's narcissism and thoughtlessness and her rebelliousness toward a father who entirely neglects her because she is so much like the wife he loathes, Lydia becomes the family's problem child. Her ejection from the family at the end of the novel (into a chilling marriage with the worthless Wickham) is a classic example of scapegoating. After she is, in effect, sold to this improvident rascal by Darcy's payment of Wickham's considerable debts, her loss restores peace, tranquillity, wealth, and order to the Bennet line. Rescuing Lydia, the admirable Darcy cements his relationship to Elizabeth, making their storybook marriage possible. In other words, by sacrificing Lydia, the family rescues itself.

Reading *Pride and Prejudice* from a family perspective clarifies the bitter irony of Lydia's fate in a way that, perhaps, no other approach to the novel can. As an author of family life, Austen is often extraordinarily hard on failed family members—not just Lydia but, for example, Maria Bertram in *Mansfield Park* and Elizabeth Elliot in *Persuasion*. When viewed in the context of her family situation, however, Lydia's behavior, like that of many acting-out adolescents, is not without just cause, nor is Austen as unsympathetic as the harshness of the fate she hands out would seem to suggest:

> [Elizabeth] had never perceived, while the regiment was in Hertfordshire, that Lydia had any partiality for [Wickham], but she was convinced that Lydia had wanted only encouragement to attach herself to any body. Sometimes one officer, sometimes another had been her favourite, as their attentions raised them in her opinion. Her affections had been continually fluctuating, but never without an object. The mischief of neglect and mistaken indulgence towards such a girl.— Oh! how acutely did she now feel it.   (280)

As Austen makes clear, Lydia's hunger for attention, which is, in fact, a hunger for love, is as much a result of her father's neglect as it is of her mother's overindulgence. And on neither score is Lydia to blame. In refusing to set limits for his youngest daughter—indeed, in being indecently eager to have her out of the house altogether simply so that he can have "peace"—

Mr. Bennet has made Lydia's defection inevitable. Lydia is merely acting out where the source of the family problems lie: not in Mrs. Bennet's "foolishness," per se, but in her husband's passive-aggressive response to it:

> Had Elizabeth's opinion been all drawn from her own family, she could not have formed a very pleasing picture of conjugal felicity. . . . Her father, captivated by youth and beauty . . . had married a woman whose weak understanding and illiberal mind, had very early in their marriage put an end to all real affection for her. Respect, esteem, and confidence, had vanished for ever; and all his views of domestic happiness were overthrown. But Mr. Bennet was not of a disposition to seek comfort for the disappointment which his own imprudence had brought on, in any of those pleasures which too often console the unfortunate for their folly or their vice. He was fond of the country and of books; and from these tastes had arisen his principal enjoyments. To his wife he was very little otherwise indebted, than as her ignorance and folly had contributed to his amusement.   (236)

Unable to confront a wife who disgusts him, Mr. Bennet abandons not only her but their children as well. The only stable adult in the household, he nevertheless refuses to participate in its daily affairs. As Elizabeth informs the (appropriately) shocked Lady Catherine de Bourgh, the education of the Bennet children is left entirely to each child's own initiative and devices as a result:

> "No governess! How was that possible? Five daughters brought up at home without a governess! — I never heard of such a thing. Your mother must have been quite a slave to your education."
> Elizabeth could hardly help smiling, as she assured her that had not been the case.
> "Then, who taught you? who attended to you? Without a governess you must have been neglected."
> "Compared with some families, I believe we were; but such of us as wished to learn, never wanted the means. We were always encouraged to read, and had all the masters that were necessary. Those who chose to be idle, certainly might."   (164–65)

As her father's favorite, Elizabeth has flourished under such laissez-faire parenting, joining Mr. Bennet in the library, from which the others, perhaps excepting Jane, are excluded. But for Lydia — who was born at a point when, presumably, Mr. Bennet had given up on his family altogether — this method of child rearing must end in disaster. Since she is free to "choose" to be idle,

idle is precisely what she chooses to be. As Austen seems profoundly aware, from such arrangements problem children are bound to emerge.

While such a reading might seem perverse, I cannot help but view Lydia's fate as tragic—the wasting of a human life. Of the Bennet sisters, Lydia is, ironically, the closest in energy and perceptiveness to Elizabeth herself, a closeness Austen underscores in the very homophony of their names: Lydia and Lizzy. Like Elizabeth, Lydia dearly loves a laugh, and, like her older sister, she is susceptible to Wickham. More important, like Elizabeth, Lydia is a natural leader, albeit in the wrong direction. And like Elizabeth—indeed, more than Elizabeth—she knows her own mind and knows what she wants out of life: the status that being a married woman brings. When Lydia thrusts her ring in other people's faces and takes her place at the head of the line in front of big sister Jane, she is frankly acknowledging what her oldest sisters refuse to admit: that marriage is their only path to power. Blinded, perhaps, by their father's affection for them, Elizabeth and Jane want—or think they want—a man's love. Lydia, who has never known such affection, has her eye on the material and social advantages of this "love" instead. Judged by Lydia's aggressive candor, even Elizabeth seems tame. (After all, it takes visiting Pemberley to make Elizabeth value being "mistress" of it [246].) What, one wonders, would Lydia have been like had she been born first instead of last?

Such a question is specious, of course. *Pride and Prejudice* is fiction—not life. There are no options for Lydia to be anything beyond what her creator made her: a willful, headstrong, narcissistic, thoroughly ruined child. But Lydia is also a type readily found in life; and by shifting our perspective on Austen's novel away from Elizabeth's happy but highly improbable mating to Fitzwilliam Darcy to the Bennet family gestalt, we can see her tragedy more clearly. Like Austen's economic metaphors, Lydia's fate figures forth the "dark" side of marriage, which the novel's "sparkling" surface tends to obscure. Deconstructed, the novel is less about the triumph of love than about the miseries of marriage—and about the high price children pay for their parents' follies, inadequacies, and mistakes. As such, it is very much of a piece with other Austen novels, *Northanger Abbey*, *Mansfield Park*, and *Persuasion*, which also dwell subtextually on the dark side of family life. In these novels, the child who is ruined is the sacrifice the gods seem to demand for the heroine's happy ending.

Where, in fact, did Austen's sympathies lie? Since Austen is an ironist, there is no way to know. Despite their marriage plots and happy endings, Austen's novels do not achieve closure. In their family plots, too many ruined children are buried and too many disturbing questions are raised. But for our students, who come, largely, from homes that are dysfunctional, broken, or both, it is Austen's ability to raise these questions that makes her a singularly relevant author. While her endings are improbable, the lives and families she depicts are very much like our own.

NOTE

[1]While this essay does not present a systematic theoretical approach to the family, it obviously draws on research that presents the family as a system within which the behavior of individual family members evolves. Readers wishing further information concerning this approach to family life are referred to Nichols, *Family Therapy: Concepts and Methods.*

TEACHING ABOUT LANGUAGE

A Feminist and Formalist Approach
to Close Reading
Elizabeth Langland

Pride and Prejudice amply rewards close reading because it allows students to engage, on the level of style and technique, the novel's larger concerns. *Style* encompasses such elements as word choice, syntax, pace, passive versus active constructions, and use of nominalizations, while *technique* includes such matters as point of view or focalization and the means through which that focus is revealed: for example, omniscient narration, psychonarration, free indirect discourse. Jane Austen's style is distinctive, her technique innovative. In fact, most theoretical discussions of narrative technique date the effective appearance, in English literature, of free indirect discourse (also called narrated monologue) from Austen. Dorrit Cohn writes:

> It is not at all surprising then, that Jane Austen should have been one of the first writers to use narrated monologue frequently and extensively: for it is in her work . . . that the "divergent directions of Richardson and Fielding were first brought together. . . ." In her narrated monologues Austen seems precisely to cast the spirit of epistolary fiction into the mode of third-person narration. (113)

Margaret Doody, who has traced earlier uses of free indirect discourse in women's novels of the eighteenth century, sees it as an essential formal development to accompany a more authoritative female consciousness. Doody's is an important observation for *Pride and Prejudice*, and I detail how Austen solved some of the problems of female authority by negotiating between the inner life and a more objective view, in a style that makes the issues engaged more precise and eloquent.

I have chosen three exemplary passages for analysis; each works beautifully to demonstrate Austen's technical and stylistic resources, but those who teach this novel can locate many other, equally effective passages.

The famous opening lines to *Pride and Prejudice* continue to reward attention: "It is a truth universally acknowledged, that a single man in possession of a good fortune, must be in want of a wife." The key issue, marriage, is immediately introduced, as are the terms in which a good marriage is to be evaluated. This classic instance of irony can be explored through focalization: (1) Who narrates? an omniscient narrator outside the story; (2) Who sees? members of the community such as Mrs. Bennet and Sir William Lucas; and (3) What is seen? eligible single men and the desirability of securing them in marriages with portionless daughters. Austen signals the presence of irony and a shift in focus through the discrepancy between universally acknowledged truths and tacit local combats over eligible bachelors. Of course, Austen does not use the word *bachelor*; she chooses to describe this creature as a "single man," setting up a play between single and married, man and woman, husband and *wife*, the word that closes the sentence. The oppositions continue: the man who is "in possession" is also "in want"; ironically, his "good fortune" establishes a need or lack: the wife. And the sentence momentarily sets up an illogicality: "A single man in possession of a good fortune must be in want." The generous sibilants of *possession*, implying his ease secured by good fortune, give way to his *want*, a comparatively harsh, one-syllable word, closed off by the plosive t — a fitting center to the seven one-syllable words that conclude a sentence begun at a more leisurely pace and that generates a sense of narrative urgency ("must be in want of a wife"). *Want*, of course, denotes many things — a deficiency, a shortage, a lack; a state of destitution or penury; circumstances of hardship; the absence of something desired. The association of want with both monetary and emotional needs introduces the tension between money and love, between marriage as economic, social contract and marriage for affection, as personal fulfillment. Dorothy Van Ghent early identified this "clash and reconciliation of utility interests with interests that are nonutilitarian" in the language of *Pride and Prejudice* (102).

Thus initiated, this tension between the apparently superficial (money) and the apparently substantial (love or affection) cannot be simply resolved: monetary concerns are not entirely superficial, nor is love the exclusive issue of substance. The tension informs Darcy's pronouncement that the Bennets' uncle in Cheapside "must very materially lessen their chance of marrying men of any consideration in the world" (37). The pivotal words *materially* and *consideration* express both substance and surface. *Materially* connotes both "substantially" and "monetarily"; *consideration* connotes both "thoughtfulness," or reflection, and "consequence," or importance. This stylistic yoking anticipates a resolution that attempts to reconcile the two.

The novel's first sentence simultaneously reveals that in this society men "want" wives less than women, who have few other means of support, "want" husbands. At the same time, "wife" is identified, syntactically, as just another of a single man's prospective possessions, something to be acquired for status display, a point enhanced by Darcy's initial rejection of Elizabeth as "tolerable; but not handsome enough to tempt *me*" (12). Mr. Collins intensifies our sense of individual women as just so many interchangeable signifieds for the signifier "wife" when he moves with distressing ease from projecting Jane to Elizabeth to Charlotte Lucas in the role of Mrs. Collins. Of course, Mr. Collins is a fool, but pragmatic Charlotte advises that a woman had better "shew *more* affection than she feels" (22) or she will lose the opportunity of "fixing" a prospective husband (21). All single women are paradigmatically linked as prospective wives, just as all single men belong to the paradigm of prospective husbands. The novel seeks to disrupt these paradigmatic linkages by substituting the importance of the individual person over the generic "single man" and "wife."

One way Austen disrupts this signifying chain is by giving women authority and autonomy as desiring agents. Thus it is central that events be seen or focalized largely through Elizabeth's perspective. A second passage allows us to explore the use of focalization as it intersects with style and language:

> [1] The contents of this letter threw Elizabeth into a flutter of spirits, in which it was difficult to determine whether pleasure or pain bore the greatest share. [2] The vague and unsettled suspicions which uncertainty had produced of what Mr. Darcy might have been doing to forward her sister's match, which she had feared to encourage, as an exertion of goodness too great to be probable, and at the same time dreaded to be just, from the pain of obligation, were proved beyond their greatest extent to be true! [3] He had followed them purposely to town, he had taken on himself all the trouble and mortification attendant on such a research; in which supplication had been necessary to a woman whom he must abominate and despise, and where he was reduced to meet, frequently meet, reason with, persuade, and finally bribe, the man whom he always most wished to avoid, and whose very name it was punishment to him to pronounce. [4] He had done all this for a girl whom he could neither regard nor esteem. [5] Her heart did whisper, that he had done it for her. [6] But it was a hope shortly checked by other considerations, and she soon felt that even her vanity was insufficient, when required to depend on his affection for her, for a woman who had already refused him, as able to overcome a sentiment so natural as abhorrence against

relationship with Wickham. [7] Brother-in-law of Wickham! [8] Every kind of pride must revolt from the connection.   (326)

This passage blends consonant psychonarration (the omniscient narrator is present, although there is little discrepancy between the knowledge and values of the narrator and those of a character) with free indirect discourse (narrated monologue of the character) to achieve a subtle mix of diegesis and mimesis. The first two sentences describe Elizabeth's emotional state, from which we are still at some distance: the narrator's mediating role in representing Elizabeth's "flutter of spirits" is present also in the middle clause of the first sentence: "in which it was difficult to determine." The formal diction balances the informality of "flutter" and bids us to contemplate rather than to experience the tension between "pleasure" and "pain." Without immersing us in Elizabeth's own confusions, the narrator then invites us, in the second sentence, to experience her heroine's tension stylistically and formally rather than imitatively and empathically. That periodic sentence, whose main idea is "suspicions . . . were proved," puts pressure on two subordinate clauses interpolated between subject and verb: "which she had feared to encourage, as an exertion of goodness" and "at the same time dreaded to be just, from the pain of obligation." These dependent clauses, of course, develop the emotions of "pleasure" and "pain" introduced in the first sentence and make us experience Elizabeth's emotional conflict through stylistic tension. Austen's use of nominalizations ("suspicion," "exertion," "obligation"), a prominent feature of her style throughout, also enables her to render analytically rather than imitatively the chaotic emotions Elizabeth is experiencing. Thus we are persuaded that, as deeply as Elizabeth feels, she reasons as intensely.

At this point we are prepared for the movement into Elizabeth's consciousness through free indirect discourse; and, at the moment we make this change, the focus shifts from Elizabeth's feelings to Darcy's behavior. Because his actions are revealed through her description and assessment of them, we can appreciate what he has done only by first appreciating the quality of Elizabeth's mind: her judgment and insight. Thus she always authorizes our sense of his worthiness, and, in so authorizing, she acquires narrative authority. For example, Elizabeth emphasizes Darcy's "trouble" and "mortification," the physical difficulty and moral humbling he has endured; she focalizes this same complex effort in invoking a "woman whom he must abominate and despise." Austen is superb at subtle discriminations; whereas students may see "abominate" and "despise" as synonymous, in fact the former suggests that Mrs. Younge is morally despicable, the latter that she is personally despicable. That is, we may abominate the rogue who is actually somewhat appealing in person, and we may despise the sanctimonious individual whom we cannot fault morally. Students should note, too, that the somewhat awkward passive construction "in which supplication had been necessary" (as opposed to "he had to supplicate") mirrors and evokes Darcy's passive and suppliant position to this woman whom he dislikes personally and morally. Of course, the intensification of verbs — "reduced to meet, frequently meet," and so on — further underscores Darcy's effort as evaluated by Elizabeth, an effort encapsulated in the nominalization "punishment." We could rewrite the final clause of this sentence as "whose very name it was painful to him to pronounce" and discover in that seemingly small change how much each word is working to redeem any previous impressions we may have of Darcy's haughty and supercilious demeanor.

Subtly, in sentences 4 and 5, we return to consonant psychonarration as the narrator summarizes once more the state of Elizabeth's feelings and then returns us through free indirect discourse to Elizabeth's final assessment: "Brother-in-law of Wickham! Every kind of pride must revolt from the connection." Again, Elizabeth's assessment of Darcy insists on his extreme merit. It is not enough that his pride resist the relationship; his pride must "revolt from the connection."

Of course, at this point in their reading of the novel, students will be aware of proper and improper pride or vanity as central paradigms through which we both align and distinguish the characters. Thus, when we are told that even Elizabeth's "vanity was insufficient," that "every kind of pride must revolt," we put these words into a paradigmatic structure that begins with the novel's title. Darcy's "proud" behavior at the Meryton assembly wins Charlotte's defense: "His pride . . . does not offend *me* so much as pride often does, because there is an excuse for it. One cannot wonder that so very fine a young man, with family, fortune, everything in his favour, should think highly of himself. If I may so express it, he has a *right* to be proud." Elizabeth rebuts this assessment: "That is very true . . . and I could easily forgive *his* pride, if he had not mortified *mine*." At this point, Mary makes her pedantic distinction between pride and vanity: "A person may be proud without being vain. Pride relates more to our opinion of ourselves, vanity to what we would have others think of us" (20). Despite her pedantry, Mary is right to locate pride in one's self-assessment. Moreover, Elizabeth does not fault Darcy's right to think well of himself, only his corollary tendency to think ill of others. Darcy, of course, learns to distinguish the substantial from the inconsequential, to winnow the chaff of improper pride from the grain of proper pride so that he can admit in conclusion "how insufficient were all my pretensions to please a woman worthy of being pleased" (369), and Elizabeth can assure her father, "Indeed he has no improper pride" (376).

Distinguishing between the proper pride of Darcy or Elizabeth and the improper pride of Lady Catherine or Mr. Collins will prove less difficult to students than discerning what divides Darcy from Bingley on the issue of pride. Indeed, Bingley, too, has no improper pride, but he also lacks proper pride: the capacity for correct judgment and discrimination that allows one to assess a desirable course of conduct and pursue it. The classic discussion between Bingley and Darcy illuminates the problems stemming from insufficient pride. Darcy exposes Bingley's so-called "humility" as "only carelessness of opinion" and "sometimes an indirect boast" (48). And Bingley proves himself to be careless of his own opinion, deferring to Darcy's even when Bingley is in a superior position to judge, as in matters of Jane's affections and merits. The events of the novel proleptically justify Darcy's criticism of Bingley's "humility" and his own assertion that "vanity is a weakness indeed. But pride — where there is a real superiority of mind, pride will be always under good regulation" (57). Not only does Bingley fail to direct his own affairs of the heart, but, once married — with Darcy's permission — he still falls prey to prolonged visits from Lydia and Wickham and musters the resolution only "to *talk* of giving them a hint to be gone" (387).

This linking of pride with "real superiority of mind" should help readers appreciate the novel's privileging of thought over action as a major way Austen establishes a balance between male and female characters. Elizabeth may not be able to *act* as Darcy does in redeeming Lydia, but, as we have seen, her mind is fully equal to his, and she assesses the quality of his actions. Although Elizabeth asserts that "from [Darcy's] judgment, information, and knowledge of the world, she must have received benefit of greater importance" (312), nonetheless, because Austen focalizes the story through Elizabeth in psychonarration and free indirect discourse, we experience her mind as superior.

Because of her mastery of free indirect discourse, it may surprise readers to discover that Austen employs a distanced omniscient view in the second proposal scene and that narrative authority supersedes identification. This will be our final passage to consider. Austen has been criticized for her proposal scenes because they do not represent passion directly, and her choice of technique has often been interpreted as a failure of ability. I suggest instead that Austen has earned the authority she claims in conclusion and that she deliberately distances us from her protagonists to maintain her focus on the proper balance of reason and passion in a good marriage. Any direct representation must focus on the emotion to which the characters are given over. Only the narrator can remind us, as she does, that Darcy and Elizabeth's relationship achieves a balance between reason and passion and culminates a period of growth — a "material" change "since the period to which he alluded," resulting in Elizabeth's pleased reception of Darcy's "present assurances."

The proposal scene follows:

> [1] Elizabeth feeling all the more than common awkwardness and anxiety of his situation, now forced herself to speak; and immediately, though not very fluently, gave him to understand, that her sentiments had undergone so material a change, since the period to which he

alluded, as to make her receive with gratitude and pleasure, his present assurances. [2] The happiness which this reply produced, was such as he had probably never felt before; and he expressed himself on the occasion as sensibly and as warmly as a man violently in love can be supposed to do. [3] Had Elizabeth been able to encounter his eye, she might have seen how well the expression of heart-felt delight, diffused over his face, became him; but, though she could not look, she could listen, and he told her of feelings, which, in proving of what importance she was to him, made his affection every moment more valuable.

(366)

The compound-complex structure of the first sentence is formal and somewhat awkward, a syntax that mirrors the complexities and anxieties of Elizabeth's feelings. Elizabeth, never at a loss for words previously, must now force herself to speak, and that "not very fluently." A substitution of "made herself speak" for "forced herself to speak," while not changing the surface meaning of the sentence, substantially weakens our sense of the power of Elizabeth's feelings. The formality of the language in words like *sentiments*, *gratitude*, and *assurance* and of the syntax — "gave him to understand," "as to make her receive" — plays off against the turbulence of Elizabeth's emotions and maintains that balance for which Austen always strives, the balance between reason and emotion.

The second sentence continues the restraints on the representation of passion — "probably never felt," "as sensibly and as warmly as a man violently in love," "can be supposed to do." In addition, the omniscient narrator employs the hackneyed phrase "violently in love," reminding us of Mr. Collins's earlier proposal to Elizabeth and his assurance in the "most animated language of the violence of [his] affection" (106) and the earlier discussion between Elizabeth and Mrs. Gardiner by which we can measure Elizabeth's growth in understanding and discrimination. Elizabeth expostulates to her aunt: "It does not often happen that the interference of friends will persuade a young man of independent fortune [Bingley] to think no more of a girl [Jane], whom he was violently in love with only a few days before." And Mrs. Gardiner corrects Elizabeth: "But that expression of 'violently in love' is so hackneyed, so doubtful, so indefinite, that it gives me very little idea. It is as often applied to feelings which arise from an half-hour's acquaintance, as to a real, strong attachment. Pray, how *violent* was Mr. Bingley's love?" Elizabeth is thus forced into a process of careful discrimination in which we also participate: "I never saw a more promising inclination" (140–41). Violent love thus becomes amenable to reasonable assessment.

Other stylistic choices emphasize this balance as well as the balance achieved between Darcy and Elizabeth, supporting a union of equals, not the more traditional dominant husband, submissive wife. We can note, for example, that in the three sentences that make up the proposal scene, the first takes Elizabeth as subject ("Elizabeth . . . forced herself to speak . . . and gave him to understand"); the second, Darcy ("he had . . . never felt . . . and he expressed himself"), while the third continually shifts subject and object, capturing the mutuality that informs the relationship ("but, though *she* could not look, *she* could listen, and *he* told *her*," etc.). Observant students may argue that the syntactic balance of male-female is jeopardized by a disparity between male and female behavior: the properly ardent male, the properly submissive woman. The usually voluble Elizabeth is silenced in the last sentence; her eyes, which won Darcy's interest initially, are downcast. He speaks, she listens; he looks at her, she looks at nothing. But if the balance is momentarily endangered, Austen's representation of the married couple reasserts it in depicting Georgiana's alarm at Elizabeth's "lively, sportive, manner of talking to [Darcy]" and the younger sister's discovery that "a woman may take liberties with her husband" (387–88).

This reading closes off the novel's meaning very tidily: a balance of reason and emotion, male and female. The novel achieves, in short, a hermeneutic closure. But some perceptive students will notice that the action of what Roland Barthes calls the symbolic code — the code of antithesis — was set in motion with the initial destabilizing oppositions we identified: substance-surface, possession-want, money-affection. And it cannot be arrested even in this culminating moment. Darcy's "affection" is "valuable" just as Elizabeth's "sentiments" have undergone a "material" change. Monetary diction informs the discourse of the heart and resists assimilation and subordination. It is part of what makes Austen's novel ideologically and historically specific.

The Duets of *Pride and Prejudice*

Marylea Meyersohn

Students discover early that action in Austen novels is largely carried by speech, especially in *Pride and Prejudice*. Of the many speech events that compose the plot of the novel—the exquisitely boring postures of Mr. Collins, the rantings of Mrs. Bennet, the pomposities of Lady Catherine, the lies of Wickham—the speech duets that bring Elizabeth Bennet and Fitzwilliam Darcy together, after first driving them apart, constitute the heart of the novel.

The pleasures to readers of conversation in *Pride and Prejudice* derive not so much from the single sentences that the characters utter as from the dialogues, the speech acts of talkers and listeners who jointly construct social reality, especially those sequences between heroine and hero. In these dialogues, Elizabeth Bennet exchanges life in modest economic circumstances for life at the top and is herself, as a marriageable young woman, the unit of exchange, as Claude Lévi-Strauss might call it. She exchanges and is exchanged through conversations with Darcy that are the duets of *Pride and Prejudice*. When I teach the novel, I discuss those duets rendered directly by Austen, not summarized or described, as, for example, when Austen writes about a conversation between Elizabeth and Jane, "All was acknowledged, and half the night spent in conversation" (374).

The Elizabeth-Darcy duets represent the linguistic equality of the speakers as a paradigm of the possibilities of equality of women and men. We are offered, in their duets, speeches equal in length and in vocabulary, a glimpse of what Jürgen Habermas has called "the ideal speech situation," which requires a "symmetrical distribution of chances to select and employ speech acts. All participants must have the same chance to initiate and perpetuate discourse, to put forward, call into question, and give reasons for or against statements, explanations, interpretations, and justifications" (*Communication* xvii).

The importance of the male-female duet in *Pride and Prejudice* is best seen in the mishaps that beset it, as the heroine and hero subvert the form by a systematic violation of the rules of talk, or of what H. P. Grice has called "the cooperative principle of conversation" (42). The violation (Grice's word is "flouting") of that principle is both the source of irony and the framework for the chief linguistic pleasure of the novel—the stichomythic release of aggression between heroine and hero. In *Pride and Prejudice* the duets that go wrong, that Habermas might term "systematically distorted communication," are part of the vision of courtship as contest.

Duets dominate the narrative events of *Pride and Prejudice*, and they carry the moral purpose of the book: the establishment of a rational, unconstrained consensus between a woman and a man. Elizabeth and Darcy are partners in talk; they must talk, and they must achieve consensus through talk. How they arrive at an understanding begins with their use of language. They know the rules of talk, of who gets to talk next, of turn taking and of silences, since duets, like all speech acts, are rule-governed. (Indeed, Elizabeth reproaches Darcy for not observing those rules: "One must speak a little, you know. It would look odd to be entirely silent for half an hour together" [91].) They know "how conversation works, how it is organized, how topics are introduced and changed, how to interrupt, ask questions, give or evade answers, and maintain or disrupt the flow" (Stubbs 7). And they understand the necessity for "phatic communion," the shared sense of the social function of speech to unite speakers in camaraderie. Elizabeth and Darcy know in effect what a well-formed duet should be, just as they know what the rules of the dance should be, but, for our delight, they violate that knowledge, she for her purposes, he for his.

There are two lengthy unsuccessful duets and one lengthy successful duet in *Pride and Prejudice*. All are prepared for — by short volleys, or uncomfortable silences, or the foregrounding of the value of conversation itself. At the very beginning, before any conversations have taken place between the antagonists, there is considerable discussion about Darcy as conversationalist. He has been overheard to call Elizabeth merely "tolerable" to look at (12); he has sat by Mrs. Long for half an hour without opening his mouth. Jane quotes Bingley about Darcy's conversational habits with those he knows very little; and, indeed, Darcy does not talk to Elizabeth without first listening to her conversation with others. She counters, wonderfully, by pointing out her linguistic prowess in what he has overheard (24). The preparations, therefore, for their engagement in duets create an erotic suspense, since there is so much energy given to their getting to it. These skirmishes occur before Elizabeth and Darcy are joined in battle. Other listeners and other speakers, Bingley and his sisters, enter and leave the dialogues; they make us long to hear Elizabeth and Darcy alone. One skirmish in the drawing room at Netherfield — the conversation about being too nice about rules without regard to friendship and affection (49–50) — seems a paradigmatic male-female argument in which the rule of law (male) is opposed to the rule of caring (female), an ancient debate that has a modern echo in Carol Gilligan's work *In a Different Voice*. Each begins the exchange with the words "To yield," which neither will do. Later, her impertinence bewitches him, and he attempts to ward off a duet by withdrawing from talk; "he scarcely spoke ten words to her through the whole of Saturday, and though they were at one time left by themselves for half an hour, he adhered most conscientiously to his book, and would not even look at her" (60).

These earlier linguistic preparations culminate in the unsuccessful duet at the Netherfield ball (91–94), where Elizabeth is "resolved against any sort of conversation" with Darcy (89) but finds herself standing opposite him in the dance. "They stood for some time without speaking a word; and [Elizabeth] began to imagine that their silence was to last through the two dances, and at first was resolved not to break it; till suddenly fancying that it would be the greater punishment to her partner to oblige him to talk, she made some slight observation on the dance" (91). Here the flouting of the cooperative principle of conversation, by the forcing of talk or by the withholding of it, becomes an erotic component of their relationship.

The second unsuccessful duet and the great linguistic encounter of the novel — Darcy's proposal to Elizabeth at Hunsford — is also preceded by a skirmish, at the Collinses' parsonage, and by the chorus of other voices, Lady Catherine's, Colonel Fitzwilliam's, the Collinses'. The presence of these other characters heightens our desire for Elizabeth and Darcy to be alone. As in the earlier passage, the dialogue is threatened, before it begins, by the possibility of "sinking into total silence" (177). Darcy comes often to the parsonage, "frequently [sitting] there ten minutes together without opening his lips" (180) and going away without engaging in any talk at all. Again, at Hunsford, Elizabeth breaks the silence, as at the Netherfield ball. Perhaps she is doing what women traditionally do in conversation with men, introducing topics for them to develop or abandon, but her effort is counterbalanced by Darcy's introducing topics too, since she was "now determined to leave the trouble of finding a subject to him. He took the hint and soon began" (178). Here is an indication of their linguistic equality and of their resistance to conventional linguistic roles. However, when the duet begins (189), it is not a duet at all. Darcy's long monologue, narrated in indirect discourse, effectively silences Elizabeth, relegating her to the position of audience, as she notes when she finally speaks. The duet that follows Elizabeth's flouting "the established mode" of expressing "a sense of obligation" (190) enables the two to understand each other's true feelings for the first time in the novel. So violent are the emotions of this scene that the next communication requires the distance of a letter. Darcy's textual solo, however, is just as much a voice in his letter to Elizabeth as in his spoken discourse, since the "printed voice," as Eric Griffiths calls it, still forces the reader, Elizabeth, like the readers of the novel, into the active role of imaginative hearer and creator of the speaking other. Darcy's solo voice brings us to the center of the novel, to Elizabeth's magnificent solo of discovery: "Till this moment, I never knew myself" (208).

The successful duet — the second proposal — is snatched out of silence by Elizabeth's "desperate resolution" to speak (365), to break what had appeared to be "an embargo on every subject" (257). Elizabeth and Darcy are finally alone, a state difficult to achieve in the light of the decorums of courtship, but while her courage is high, she "resolves" to speak, an act reminding us of her "resolve" not to speak to him at the Netherfield ball. She thanks him for helping the Bennet family; he demurs and then offers what is in effect the marriage proposal — that he did it all for her. The duet ceases until Austen has described his expressions of love and her gratitude and pleasure. The duet then resumes. They are two equal speakers, who have achieved an ideal of discourse. They retell the story of what happened, and, most important, they criticize themselves, she for her abominable "*frankness,*" he for his unmannerly behavior. He tells her that her reproof of him at the first proposal — "had you behaved in a more gentleman-like manner" — shall never be forgotten; her words "tortured" him (367). The emphasis is on speech. Her words have cured him, although she disclaims knowing the power of her voice. "I was certainly far from expecting them to make so strong an impression. I had not the smallest idea of their being ever felt in such a way" (368). Perhaps. We believe Elizabeth, that she did not think that her words would matter to a person of his rank, but indeed she chose the only words that could have had an impact. Then it is his turn: Did his words have an effect on her? She explains what the effect of his letter's words has been, to remove her prejudices against him. They agree to acknowledge the power of their words; they recognize that they have misused language. They achieve, in Habermas's terms, an "ideal speech situation." In fact, they begin to sound more and more like each other, as equals who talk together for any length of time will do. Perhaps Darcy talks a bit too much at the end of the scene, outdoes her in castigating himself, claiming that he was spoiled by his parents (369); and she represses certain words, since he "had yet to learn to be laught at, and it was rather too early to begin" (371). Still, the well-made duet achieved at the conclusion of the novel represents an equality in speech that remains for most readers a metaphor for marriage as partnership.

Even irony itself in this supremely ironic novel seems threatened by the ideal duet form, however impudently Elizabeth describes how she came to love Darcy ("my first seeing his beautiful grounds at Pemberley" [373]). The duet form (marriage) overtakes all. The male-female duet manages to mute the ironic thrust of the novel by establishing the duet as the approved form of rational speech. Here perhaps is a feminist dilemma of *Pride and Prejudice*: that the ironies of the male-female struggle, the core of the novel, are silenced by anti-ironic tendencies toward creating a discourse in which Elizabeth and Darcy are equal speakers. There is at the end of *Pride and Prejudice* a "suitably close resemblance between the idiolects of two strong-minded, intelligent, and essentially well-mannered characters whose disputes are conducted on even terms and whose eventual rapprochement is entirely credible" (Burrows, *Computation* 83). Ah, yes.

The New Romance in *Pride and Prejudice*

Susan Kneedler

Austen's undergraduate and professional readers have trouble with *Pride and Prejudice* for different reasons. After reading volume 1 (the first twenty-three chapters), students often exclaim, "There's no plot!" but lament by the end that the construction is only too formulaic. Most literary critics, however, historically declared that there were no politics, though now the majority insists that the politics are aggressively conservative. My responses to these objections reflect my belief that Austen opens up the question of power in human relations, a move that is not only implicitly sociological but revolutionary. With classes, I answer that, yes, this novel is difficult, for its action is more psychological than physical. But the emotional complexity of the plot can also refute the still-fashionable refrain about Austen's "limits" — what Raymond Williams calls "a settled and remarkably confident way of seeing and judging" with a "remarkable unity of tone" (*English Novel* 21, 22), a perspective replicated most recently in D. A. Miller's claim that "Austen's attitude" wields a stifling "authority."[1] The view that Austen's narrative voice constricts rather than explores ignores the obvious structural point that her narrator continually turns over interpretative authority to her readers.

After the assembly at which Mr. Darcy insults Elizabeth Bennet by refusing to dance with her, Mrs. Bennet chats blithely about Mr. Bingley's partners: "and the two fifth with Jane again, and the two sixth with Lizzy, and the Boulanger — " until her husband cuts her off (13).[2] But Mrs. Bennet's recital reveals a fact told nowhere else: that immediately after Mr. Darcy's affront, Charles Bingley hurries over, if not to console Elizabeth, then at least to ensure that she has a partner for the next dances. The narrator, trusting that readers will examine even seemingly irrelevant details, directs us only by strategically placing the news near, but not on, the subtly dramatic interruption. I ask my students to read *Pride and Prejudice* twice, and their first reward is to discover that the narrative, far from exerting a dogmatic tyranny, entrancingly invites us to investigate for ourselves.

Charles Bingley's attitudes about sexual politics may be discerned from his courtesy to Elizabeth not only at the ball but at Netherfield when Jane is ill (35, 40, 42). But this man is bedeviled by a "great natural modesty" and "diffidence" that amount to insecurity (199, 350); he is readily convinced that Jane cares nothing for him. Like Jane Bennet, Mr. Bingley may at first seem an "innocent"; for a generation, these lovers have been underestimated as flat, "very simple people" (Mudrick 106). Yet Mr. Bingley's ability to be "unaffectedly modest" (371) looks weak only if one believes that men should be as cocksure as Mr. Collins. Mr. Bingley's appeal lies in his vulnerability and his attempts to use his power in a kind and creative way. The peculiar gratification of "the unaffected cordiality with which" Mr. Bingley greets Elizabeth in Lambton (261) is surpassed only by the "great cordiality" with which Elizabeth and Mr. Bingley "shook hands" at the prospect of becoming sister and brother (347). Getting to know Mr. Bingley is one of the many post-narrative fantasies we are invited to entertain for Elizabeth and is one means by which *Pride and Prejudice* imagines new-fashioned forms of manhood.

The figure of Charles Bingley reassures students that, to Austen, reform does not demand reflexively blaming men, for they may be hurt by courtship systems too. His sisters' malevolence in turn shows that no simpleminded defense of females as genetically "nicer" than males will suffice as feminism or will solve the problem of competition among women. When Elizabeth has athletically walked three miles (mostly over wet fields) to nurse her sister, Caroline's and Louisa's ejaculations of outrage — "Her hair so untidy, so blowsy!" (36) and "She really looked almost wild" (35) — twist her motives from sisterly concern to an implicitly sexual looseness. Caroline Bingley's affection for her own sister extends only to the "danger of hating each other for the rest of our lives, for a whole day's tête-à-tête between two women can never end without a quarrel" (30). Miss Bingley's antipathy for other women, little disguised by the gooey repetition of "My dearest friend" in her letter to Jane (116, 117), is ably summarized — as Mr. Darcy obliquely points out — in her own words: she is "one of those young ladies who seek to recommend themselves to the other sex, by undervaluing their own" (40).

Elizabeth's violation of what makes women, in Mrs. Bennet's words, "fit to be seen" allows her to protect the person in the world dearest to her. The simplicity with which Elizabeth replies to Mrs. Bennet, "I shall be very fit to see Jane — which is all I want," succinctly contrasts those to whom a spotless petticoat is everything with her own feeling that Jane's welfare matters incomparably more (32). When "at five o'clock [Caroline Bingley and Louisa Hurst] retired to dress, and at half past six Elizabeth was summoned to dinner" (35), nothing in the tone of a straight-faced narrator conveys her mirth, until we recall how Henry Tilney tells Catherine Morland that "half an hour [to dress for dinner] at Northanger must be enough" (*Northanger Abbey* 195). But if the Bingley sisters' inordinate concern with dress reduces women's power, strength will be given by neither platitudes nor patriarchs.

Elizabeth's sisterhood for Jane reverses the earlier motif of heroine as mere recipient of peripheral characters' devotion. But *Pride and Prejudice* also warns us that crude formulas can manipulate ideals of womanly loyalty for opposite ends. In the midst of Elizabeth's uncertainty about Mr. Darcy's affection, a "close . . . confederacy" of women "crowd[s] round" the two eldest Bennet sisters, frustrating Elizabeth's hopes that her beloved will sit near her. One young woman unwittingly exposes her own aims: "on the gentlemen's approaching, [she] moved closer to [Elizabeth] than ever," whispering, "The men shan't come and part us, I am determined. We want none of them; do we?" (341). Like *Northanger Abbey*'s Isabella Thorpe, the flirtatious young speaker tries to attract men by clenching onto women. Her feigned solidarity with women and her actual affiliation with men lights up a continuing problem feminist readers have had with Austen's novels.[3] Both male and female characters' boasts of their principles — including absolute support for women — are always fake. We cannot establish Austen's politics by extracting one line from its context, because *Pride and Prejudice* is committed to skepticism of easy pronouncements and to making us compare professions with conduct. Students eagerly volunteer that we, who have long followed the intricacies of Elizabeth's relation to Jane, have no need for aphorisms from anonymous characters about loyalty among women. But more enlightening is the revelation that Mr. Bennet, whom most students seize as the alternative to twisted ambition, is the apotheosis of it. Mr. Bennet's pedestrian presumption that greed and stock rivalry motivate Elizabeth's engagement — "you may have more fine clothes and fine carriages than Jane" (376) — reveals the would-be sage as a fool.

Austen's critique of existing dogma starts by locating our enterprise not in "truth" but among "truths universally acknowledged" — in other words, in culture, in how we think. And the novel immediately sets about dismantling prejudices in favor of the "philosopher" whose raison d'être is the malice with which he ridicules women (236). Mr. Bennet's disdain — with which most students sympathize — for what he sees as womanly trivia about meeting Mr. Bingley is immediately belied by his actions: "Mr. Bennet was among the earliest of those who waited on Mr. Bingley. He had always intended to visit him" (6). By later admitting that Mr. Darcy "is the kind of man, indeed, to whom I should never dare refuse any thing which he condescended to ask" (376), Mr. Bennet implicates himself in the very systems of acquisitiveness and social climbing that he professes to despise. Lacking the just pride and integrity with which Elizabeth refused Mr. Darcy at Hunsford, Mr. Bennet does not even say, "I must talk to Elizabeth before I consent." Students are consoled for their disillusionment over Mr. Bennet by Austen's justice in distributing good and evil, talent and waste — in fact, the full range of human qualities — among women and men. Henry Tilney's still-visionary faith that "in every power of which taste is the foundation, excellence is pretty fairly divided between the sexes" (*Northanger Abbey* 28) reveals Austen's own fairness and exposes gender divisions as needlessly limiting.

Critics' difficulties with Austen's method have been equaled by their attacks on her subject. The standard view can be summed up in Williams's objection to "the precise social world of Jane Austen" (*English Novel* 12) as "very precisely selective," in which "most actual people are simply not seen" (24). But what Williams turns out to mean by "the actual country people" is men: "landowners, tenant farmers, dealers, craftsmen and labourers" are categories not usually defined as including women (100). Williams goes so far as to argue that Austen's subject "is not personal relationships, in the abstracted sense of an observed psychological process," but, "rather, personal *conduct*" (18). Because women's lives have traditionally been considered "social" rather than political or even psychological, the radically feminist politics and psychology of *Pride and Prejudice* have been disregarded. When readers have considered the politics of *Pride and Prejudice*, they have traced streams of thought outside the novel instead of focusing on how the plot itself takes up questions of institutionalized power and value. By reducing Austen to the ideas and "great events" of her day, traditional readers portrayed her as evading the real world of Napoleonic strife by creating a safe, domestic, conservative enclave; now, in a more liberal reading, some critics depict her as mimicking a new orthodoxy about women begun by acknowledged feminists like Mary Wollstonecraft. Austen is usually dubbed simultaneously subversive and reactionary, while seen by only a few as progressive.[4]

At the end of *Pride and Prejudice*, Elizabeth Bennet has a moving reunion with her sister Jane in which she reveals that she is engaged to Mr. Darcy, convinces Jane that she does indeed love him, and then tells all that he has done for their sister Lydia. The narrator says, "All was acknowledged, and half the night spent in conversation" (374). Commentators have tended to ignore this scene, as they ignore Elizabeth's amity with Jane as a central movement of the plot. The omission of this turning point suggests that in many readers' "selective" interpretations of Austen's stories, the importance of relations between women is "simply not seen." Yet *Pride and Prejudice* is filled with moments stressing the value of Elizabeth's connection with Jane. After the Meryton assembly, Elizabeth's principal reaction is that she "felt Jane's pleasure" (12), and she will as distinctly feel Jane's pain when her sister reads Caroline Bingley's message that the rest of the party has joined Mr. Bingley in London. Elizabeth is the only viewer who can see Jane's distress, and we glimpse their intimacy when the "glance from Jane invited [Elizabeth] to follow her up stairs." The narrator informs us that Elizabeth's "anxiety" about Jane has been so great that it "drew off her attention even from Wickham" (116). That "even" becomes a jest about hierarchies that rank lovers as dearer than sisters, for George Wickham never comes close to engaging from Elizabeth the concern that she feels for Jane.

When Elizabeth casts up at Mr. Darcy the "other provocations" (besides his rudeness to her) that justify the "incivility" with which she refused his offer of marriage, she defends first not Mr. Wickham but Miss Bennet (190). Though Mr. Darcy may feel that ruining Mr. Wickham's prospects is a far more serious charge than that of separating Mr. Bingley from Jane (196), Elizabeth accuses Mr. Darcy of reducing Mr. Wickham to "comparative poverty" merely as an afterthought (192). Her more urgent outrage emerges immediately when she indignantly demands, "[D]o you think that any consideration would tempt me to accept the man, who has been the means of ruining, perhaps for ever, the happiness of a most beloved sister?" (190). Perhaps Mr. Darcy has not before imagined such union among women.

Yet toward the end he shows an appreciation of what he could but dimly feel before, by recalling to Elizabeth the "good in [her] affectionate behaviour to Jane, while she was ill at Netherfield" (380). Mr. Darcy may have learned more from Mr. Bingley than we have recognized. It was this friend who, in response to his own sisters' censure, first announces that Elizabeth's muddy walk to Netherfield "shews an affection for her sister that is very pleasing" (36).

Although Mr. Darcy, like many students, concludes that Jane cares little for his friend but would marry him anyway, Jane's "rectitude and delicacy" would make her "do any thing rather than marry without affection" (128, 373). My students are eventually persuaded of Jane's extraordinary integrity by grappling with her achievement in reaching the age of twenty-two without ever having "even fancied herself in love before" (227). So strong is Jane's sense of self that she can receive Mr. Bingley, on his return, with a manner "equally free from any symptom of resentment, or any unnecessary complaisance" (335). Small wonder that Mr. Darcy is at a loss to estimate Jane rightly, for all his vaunted "impartial[ity]" (197), because he has never met anyone like her. Even Elizabeth must grow into a full appreciation of Jane's "sweetness and disinterestedness" and her "delicate sense of honour" (134, 320).

At Lambton, Elizabeth's loyalty to her older sister had been so great that even in the midst of the excitement in her newfound acquaintance with Mr. Darcy, she has room for Jane: "In seeing Bingley, her thoughts naturally flew to her sister; and oh! how ardently did she long to know, whether any of his were directed in a like manner" (262). The emotion of this moment qualifies it as a climax, though one often overlooked by readers, as Elizabeth spends a whole page trying to read Charles Bingley's mind. Elizabeth's involvement in the vicissitudes of Jane's story removes her own experience from the limited realm of the "heroine," safely lodged at the center of the universe, beyond compare. But, more, the challenge will be for Elizabeth to find a romantic love that is as strong as her love for Jane. The novelty of that hope is the focus of volume 3.

Students, like many critics, question the point of the last volume (the final 19 chapters) of *Pride and Prejudice* because they already know who will "get" whom. Many feminist scholars portray Austen's happy unions as either sexist, sellouts, or parodies.[5] But critics' declared dissatisfaction with marriage as a narrative resolution is never reconciled with unexamined prejudices against single women, against "genteel poverty and spinsterhood" (Newman 705).[6] A number of critics themselves reiterate the tired news that Austen was a "spinster," a term that Austen's books never once invoke and that hardly defends singleness as a liberating option.[7] The twin assumptions that neither single nor married women can be powerful, useful, or happy leads to a deadlier myth: the curiously perverse axiom that suicide is woman's only "life-affirming" choice. In fact, the art — particularly Kate Chopin's *The*

Awakening — and the authors — Virginia Woolf and Sylvia Plath — in vogue during the last few decades have often been seen as glorifying death as the only way out for women in an inexorably unjust culture. By implication, simply surviving, let alone coping, becomes synonymous with compromising. The last third of *Pride and Prejudice*, however, imagines an alternative: far from smothering under a shroud of "the marriage plot," Elizabeth Bennet works out a new institution of love based on a new conception of self.[8]

After the crisis of Elizabeth's initial embarrassment at Mr. Darcy's unexpected arrival at Pemberley, including her "amaze[ment] at the alteration in his manner" (251–52), Elizabeth and her aunt and uncle the Gardiners "were again surprised, and Elizabeth's astonishment was quite equal to what it had been at first, by the sight of Mr. Darcy approaching them." Elizabeth's second surprise is that "he really intended to meet them." The encounter here between Elizabeth and Mr. Darcy encapsulates the recurring action of this final volume; Elizabeth continually assumes that Mr. Darcy will "strike into some other path," but whenever the "turning" that obscures him fades away, he always turns up, "and at no great distance" — in fact, "immediately before" her (254). Every time that "her thoughts were all fixed on that one spot . . . whichever it might be, where Mr. Darcy then was" (253), she finds that he is on an errand expressly to see or to help her.

In the woods of Pemberley, Elizabeth is far from imagining that Mr. Darcy is on such a quest. In fact, she begins an alternating pattern of distancing herself from him — fancying that her friendly praise "might be mischievously construed" (254) — yet nevertheless bewildering herself with his mystery: "Why is he so altered? . . . It cannot be for *me*, it cannot be for *my* sake." Always the stunning answer is that her "reproofs at Hunsford [did] work such a change as this," because "it is [not] impossible that he should still love" her (255). Mr. Darcy himself later explains why he does not "avoid her as his greatest enemy" (265), by distinguishing between hatred and anger: he could never hate her, and even his anger "soon began to take a proper direction" (369) — at himself. Through an affecting contrast, Austen honors this man's exceptionally receptive resilience. Elizabeth's response to the events at Hunsford had been an inability to "feel the slightest inclination ever to see him again" (212); Mr. Darcy, however, not only wishes to continue as Elizabeth's friend but hopes that his sister, Georgiana, may come to know her as well (256).

The trope of Elizabeth's shock will be picked up when she is home at Longbourn, looking out the window to see Mr. Darcy riding up to the house with Mr. Bingley. The narrator explains, "Her astonishment at his coming . . . was almost equal to what she had known on first witnessing his altered behaviour in Derbyshire" (334). Elizabeth's surprise is great because she has felt that the disgrace of Lydia's elopement would destroy Mr. Darcy's affection. But we also learn that although Mr. Darcy continues to astound, the shock is lessening and is now only "almost equal" to what she had felt before. The stupefaction Elizabeth experiences here, like that created by Mr. Darcy's behavior at Pemberley, reflects the conventional belief that men cannot be loyal and deeply attached lovers. Mr. Darcy's arrival at Longbourn enlarges Elizabeth's expectations of men's capacity to love. One measure is that when he returns yet again, after Lady Catherine de Bourgh has stormed through Longbourn vowing to separate her from Mr. Darcy, Elizabeth now only "half expect[s]" him not to come (365).

Back in Lambton, Elizabeth had begun to rely on Mr. Darcy's affection, or on her own "power, which her fancy told her she still possessed, of bringing on the renewal of his addresses" (266). But that confidence is shattered by the news of Lydia Bennet's elopement. For readers swept by a growing excitement at Elizabeth's discovery of Fitzwilliam Darcy's "impossible" power "still [to] love me" (255), the turning point at the lodgings is a careful frustration of our hopes, a transformation of exhilaration to anguish. Elizabeth mistakenly, and conventionally, reads Mr. Darcy's "earnest meditation" about how to find Mr. Wickham as a sign that "her power was sinking" (278). The inadequacy of Elizabeth's equation of love with "power" is suggested by a sudden shift in tone. From the pathos of "she could neither wonder nor condemn," the narrator unexpectedly swells into sentimental clichés: "but the belief of his self-conquest brought nothing consolatory to her bosom, afforded no palliation of her distress." "Of course not," respond students, who readily see that women's self-sacrifice is silly. Elizabeth realizes only "now, when all love must be vain," that she "could have loved him" (278); yet she, at least as much as Mr. Darcy, must let go of such traditional, and false, visions of sexual relations.

At issue are assumptions about the selfishness and instability of men's love. When Elizabeth discovers that Mr. Darcy had been at Lydia's wedding, "conjectures as to the meaning of it, rapid and wild, hurried into her brain," but they "seemed most improbable" (320). However, what she considers her most farfetched fancies will be "proved beyond their greatest extent to be true!" (326). Elizabeth's inability to conceive that Mr. Darcy could cherish a concern for her as "ardent" as hers for Jane culminates when we learn that while her new respect for Mr. Darcy is fervent, it still does not do him justice. "Elizabeth was now most heartily sorry" that she had not concealed the elopement from "all those who were not immediately on the spot" (311). By designating Mr. Darcy as just another bystander, Elizabeth would, in her yearning for secrecy, negate her unreflecting confidence — her disclosure of how fully she has accepted his revelations about Mr. Wickham — and deprive herself of Mr. Darcy's delicately underspoken comfort. But Elizabeth's regrets are hilariously inappropriate because the joyful truth is that Lydia's problems never would have been solved had Elizabeth not confided in Mr. Darcy. Only he knew how to find Mr. Wickham.

Elizabeth's doubts about the possibility of allegiance from Fitzwilliam Darcy are hardly a private matter. Neither Austen's culture nor our own has traditionally demanded much of men as lovers. William Collins's spleen when Elizabeth refuses him reflects the customary churlishness of the disappointed suitor. Mr. Darcy's own first movement toward Elizabeth embodies the sexist view that he is a good catch who has only to choose and be accepted, that no matter how he has insulted any woman, she will be happy either to dance with or marry him whenever he can force himself to ask. The novel does not support such conventional views. Most students have been raised on the interwoven notions of women's craving for men and men's indifference to women, a trope misnamed "the battle of the sexes" and a heritage that *Pride and Prejudice* explicitly invokes in its opening torture scenes in which Mr. Bennet baits Mrs. Bennet. Readers continue to adore Mr. Bennet's bitter humor on a first reading and only later learn to reevaluate "that continual breach of conjugal obligation and decorum which . . . was so highly reprehensible" (236). *Pride and Prejudice* offers a vision of love in which women and men may care about each other with a passionate tenderness at least equal to that felt by strongly united sisters: the other person's well-being is simply and immediately crucial. Mr. Darcy's concern for Elizabeth is so great, so sublimely disinterested, that, whether or not she loves him, he wants to make her happy and never claim the credit.

At stake is how we recognize romance. What are the signs in others that we respond to as allure, and what are the alterations in ourselves that we identify as passion? What *Pride and Prejudice* offers to Elizabeth Bennet through Fitzwilliam Darcy is a sexuality that casts away usual power relations with their traditional alternatives of confrontation and capitulation, when men sweep women off their feet but both sides nurse an underlying narcissism as their truly dominant passion. The traditional proposal Mr. Darcy made at Hunsford betrays a masturbatory fixation with his own desires and sacrifices; however, his avowal of love in the lanes near Longbourn portrays a generous focus on Elizabeth Bennet, foretelling a relation of listening reciprocity. Mr. Darcy's reform is convincing because it is based on a goodness and generosity that Elizabeth had never credited him with, and it is moving because it is unimaginable according to cultural ideas of men's capacity and feelings. The sexual politics of the relation between Elizabeth Bennet and Fitzwilliam Darcy locates erotic pleasure in kindnesses that any person can show another. To women Austen offers a vision in which nothing about men's honest devotion is too good to be true—a prophecy that women need not settle for less. In a final volume made up almost exclusively of characters' astonishment at how others' actions surpass or betray their expectations, the delicately crocheted chain of Elizabeth's surprises carefully builds excitement over reunions that we are asked to celebrate because they change our ideas about what love, even marriage, can mean.

Yet as Elizabeth discovers Mr. Darcy's affection, she must explore her own—in a process that protects the integrity and disinterestedness of her attachment: "She respected, she esteemed, she was grateful to him, she felt

a real interest in his welfare" (266). Her effort to "make [her feelings] out,"
as she "lay awake two whole hours" (265), is a comic reversal of an earlier
moment when, with "something like regret" (246), she had toyed with envy
about the position as "mistress of Pemberley" (245). Now, as Elizabeth inves-
tigates her new tenderness for Mr. Darcy, we can delight in how she stretches
out the process of committing herself. Respect, esteem, gratitude, and an
interest in his welfare all add up to love. Such feelings are the origin of
love based on knowledge, and, *Pride and Prejudice* shows, nothing else
is love.

But Elizabeth's discerning standards for heterosexual affection display a
revolution of self as well as of eros. Even at the height of her suspense about
Mr. Darcy, Elizabeth asserts the worth of her own life, gloriously declaring
to herself, "[I]f he is satisfied with only regretting me, when he might have
obtained my affections and hand, I shall soon cease to regret him at all"
(361). Such faith that if need be she can outlive her affection for Fitzwilliam
Darcy is based on the new idea that he will be unworthy if he cannot
continue to love. The value for her own future, separate from her connection
to a man, and her resolve to judge his rather than her own worth by his
performance intensify our suspense over the test: Can Mr. Darcy justify her
affection? The fulfillment of that quest comes in a love scene that readers
have long depreciated as an anticlimax.[9]

The veil over this love scene, the famous line about what Elizabeth
"gave [Mr. Darcy] to understand" that substitutes the narrator's voice for
Elizabeth's words, has often been called an intrusion. In class, I point
out how the veil, the narrator's descriptive details "covering" Elizabeth's
"actual" reply, connects us to the action as effectively as it distances us.
This fulfillment challenges readers to explore the problem of what constitutes fictional action and, in turn, action outside books as well. Rather
than repeat predictable scenes of tenderness, the narrator acknowledges
merrily that we already know what Elizabeth wants to say, because we
have been waiting many pages for this opening. Students soon figure
out that what is piquant about our fascination with the fulfillment is the
distance between our sense of its importance and how little Elizabeth really
can say. The myth is that something momentous happens beneath the veil
and that Austen skips it, thereby depriving us of some ideal climax, of
beautiful poetry — passages designed to enflame. But when Elizabeth "immediately, though not very fluently, [gives Mr. Darcy] to understand" that
she loves him, the seeming defect, the lack of fluency, vanishes because Mr.
Darcy probably "understand[s]" "immediately" (366). So Elizabeth has been
as fluent as she could wish. We must laugh both about the reversal of inar-
ticulateness to eloquence — for the awkwardness merely accentuates Elizabeth's affection — as well as about our own absurd wish to hear a few stam-
mered syllables.

When the fulfillment scene surprises us by refusing to recite word by word, gasp by gasp, throb by throb, the avowals of love between Austen's lovers, it alters our relation to the action of the book and makes possible a different sort of thrill. When students try to define the demands that this climax makes, they see that our imaginations must work not just as would-be heroines, vicarious protagonists lost in Austen's creation, but as readers. Students appreciate that reading offers pleasures beyond the pretense that we are the main character. By reminding us that we are engrossed in a book, fictions invented by someone else, *Pride and Prejudice* teaches us that we are always connected to what is outside us through imaginative structures. When the novel demands a more active imaginative participation, it suggests how even our sense of our own lives is composed of conventions or fantasies we inherit or invent. Austen's narration of the fulfillment scene is not an interruption or a telling instead of a showing but an alternate subject: the reader's conscious relation to our own adventures. Veiling the fulfillment changes it from an exemplar to be imitated the way Mr. Collins steals phrases for his recitals, into a process, something that must be imagined to be felt or held. We are invited to enjoy our own visionary power.

When asked, by the very conventions of comic climaxes, to tell breathless readers what dreams matter, what hopes are worth reaching, Austen's response is to remind us of our own separateness, of our own relation to the action through what we can envision. She reminds us of ourselves by including us — to our surprise. As readers we are also authors, and Austen shows that we must make up our own lives without locking ourselves into the deadly permanence of fixed structure or asking for easy and established answers. The novel's commitment to the challenges our lives pose is the reason that Elizabeth Bennet at first has trouble replying to her beloved: she "now forced herself to speak" after first feeling "too much embarrassed to say a word" and only stutters out a reply because of her concern for Mr. Darcy's undeserved suspense. Even our clearest moments, when we are sure of our feelings and of what we want to do, are fraught with the difficulties of acting when the instant is here. But that joyfully unconventional "awkwardness" does yet more, for it points out the inherent discordance when people — who have come to love each other fully without each other's knowing — avow their affection for the first time.

Austen's enchanting principle that "pictures of perfection make me sick and wicked" (23 Mar. 1817) can describe not only heroines but their plots and culminations. *Pride and Prejudice*, by choosing not to establish conventions for the perfectly fulfilling words that will make readers feel inferior, makes us look for fulfillment in some place other than an ending. We find it in our discovery that life fulfills itself less through dramatic moments than through the "years of happiness" that Elizabeth, in an "instant" of wretchedness, fears can never make amends for "moments" of embarrassment (337). The aesthetics of Austen's ending teach that if this reunion is the best time of all, a climax of joy never to be equaled, then an injustice is implied to the very future of intensified affection and deepening intimacy that this period celebrates and makes possible. This book's preference for the charm of that quotidian hereafter explains why Elizabeth, at first, "rather *knew* . . . than *felt* herself" to be happy (372); moreover, it is why "the season of courtship" is untraditionally deprived of "much of its pleasure" — pointing us ahead toward "all the comfort and elegance of their family party at Pemberley" (384). Elizabeth's new harmony with Mr. Darcy is no more than the beginning of the life before them. Austen claims such contented bliss, not for our moments of triumph and surprise but for the long future and the everyday. And the political dimension of that unfulfilling fulfillment alters the possibilities for women.

Elizabeth Bennet does not occupy the traditional position of divine princess at the pivot of the universe. *Pride and Prejudice*'s feminist originality lies partly in envisioning women achieving happiness without idealizing climactic moments or eclipsing the rest of the novel. The "postheroic" qualities of Austen's leading characters and plots enable her to offer happiness without falling into the conservatism of "just deserts." Susan Morgan's percipience that "the endings are presented not just as fortuitous, but as virtually a joke" (*In the Meantime* 16) and that they "need not be understood in moral terms at all" (17) points to how what I call the "hinged" quality of Austen's veiled fulfillments in general, and this one in particular, disrupts a connection between effort and reward. The ending of *Pride and Prejudice*, by smoothing the climax into the ongoingness of living, avoids implying that experience is lived only individually, unconnected to context, or that the meritorious naturally "succeed," whereas the poor deserve their fates. The narrative works against the self-destructive habit of undervaluing daily efforts in favor of spectacular achievements, pinnacles that paradoxically but inevitably project a future as anticlimax. Students, raised on jargon about how they can be whatever they want to be, find a more liberating politics in the unconventional climax that begins Elizabeth and Mr. Darcy's life together. But apart from a general psychological innovation, the veiled declarations and the ending work against deceptive, regressive visions of marriage as metamorphosis, with woman incarnated anew. "Whether married or single" (152), Elizabeth is a single person. When Elizabeth marries, Mr. Collins and Mrs. Bennet will think her more important than before, will believe that she has transformed her life. However, by making the fulfillment scene rush past, Austen presents affection as a joy but never portrays marriage as the defining act, let alone success, of Elizabeth's life.

Pride and Prejudice is a pivotal moment in our feminist heritage, an achievement whose power has in many senses been lost, as we have so often lost women's history and work. This novel offers an iconoclastic representation of women and men. Austen is a creative political thinker in her own right, but her politics must be located through attention to the relationships among her characters, between those characters and their narrator, and between narrator and reader, before we try to place her in extratextual heritages or contexts. Rather than look for politics by turning away from the text to events outside the novel, we need at last to accept that the book's explicit concerns are themselves political. *Pride and Prejudice* does more than teach us about the debates of Austen's day; it can guide us among the many urgent issues of identity and gender with which we continue to struggle. In an age when we have learned to see the battle of the sexes as one aspect of the abuse that women have been taught to label as "love," the answer is not to throw out romance altogether. *Pride and Prejudice*'s moving prophecy is that we may also make Elizabeth Bennet's demand that Fitzwilliam Darcy become worthy of her love.

At Pemberley, Elizabeth makes possible her unexpected reunion with Mr. Darcy because, as she and the Gardiners walk away from the house, she "turned back to look again," just as, a few moments before, she had "returned to [the portrait of Mr. Darcy]" and quite intimately "fixed his eyes upon herself" (251, 250). This turning back, the looking again, images how one can sometimes go forward to meet one's life by revolving back rather than by walking away, by rethinking rather than by seizing conclusions. Elizabeth is willing to protract her visit to ponder her discoveries, to look and wonder without the blinders of her own acceptance of old romantic convention. Seeing for herself, she can know herself, and know Mr. Darcy anew. Even then, the novel dramatizes the shatteringly funny difference between exploring in the abstract and in the flesh. Out of "shame" Elizabeth "instinctively turned away" from Mr. Darcy when he arrived (252, 251), just as she had "turned away" from him at the gates of Rosings after the debacle of his boorish proposal (195). But Mr. Darcy can now do his half. By "recovering himself," by "advanc[ing] towards the party, and [speaking] to Elizabeth," he can show that he deserves her new regard, both in terms of its new vision and its new interest (251). That movement toward Elizabeth means that soon, during Elizabeth's emergency in Lambton, Fitzwilliam Darcy will arrive precisely when he is needed. He has equaled such felicitous timeliness at least twice before. His convenient arrival at Pemberley occurred because, unlike *Mansfield Park*'s Henry Crawford, Mr. Darcy devotes himself to his duties toward his tenants through the "business with his steward" that brings him home a day early (256). And his general benevolence, his refusal to fall into the pattern of "the wild young men now-a-days, who think of nothing but themselves" (249), extends to the attentive care with which he "joined [Georgiana] unexpectedly a day or two before the intended elopement [with Mr. Wickham]" (202). In Lambton, Mr. Darcy is available to Elizabeth at the crucial juncture purely because he tries to be with her as often as possible. That effort explains why, "as [Elizabeth] reached the door, it was opened . . . and Mr. Darcy appeared" (276).

NOTES

[1]Williams discusses "that cool and controlled observation which is the basis of her narrative method; that highly distanced management . . . which need not become either open manipulation or participation and personal involvement" (*English Novel* 22). D. A. Miller sees in Austen's narrative rhetoric "a complete, confident mastery of what it has to say," "precise, authoritative, self-generating," and he concludes that it implies, I can write this way but you can't. Austen's fiction, he says, is marked by a "cold heart" and a "snippy" manner ("Attitude"). A few critics have been sensitive to the scope and variety of Austen's narrative voices. Booth details how the opening of *Northanger Abbey* "demands a play of mind over almost every phrase" (*Rhetoric of Irony* 129). Tave shows that "the same passages and words can be returned to . . . and each time they present more meaning as the angle of return varies" (xi). Morgan demonstrates that Austen offers "speculative resolutions to the general issue of how we perceive" (*In the Meantime* 5).

[2]Morgan (in *In the Meantime*) was, to my knowledge, the first scholar who regularly referred to Austen's male characters with the title "Mr." I do the same partly because the novels usually do — except when they are being familiar — and because I feel that such chumminess is normally the prerogative of narrators rather than of critics. Premature informality is an explicit issue in *Sense and Sensibility*, *Mansfield Park*, and *Emma* and is even touched on in *Pride and Prejudice* itself, which looks with concern at Miss Bingley's rapid and insincere singling out of Jane Bennet. This book also takes up the careless freedoms of Lydia Bennet, who cavalierly mentions "Clarke's library" (30) and, later, describes a frolic in which she and her pals "Pen" Harrington, Kitty Bennet, Mrs. Philips, and Colonel and Mrs. Forster induce "Chamberlayne" to masquerade as a woman in order to fool a group of men that includes "Denny, and Wickham, and Pratt" (221). To discern that Austen does not simplistically equate openheartedness with folly, one has only to think of the "easiness, openness, ductility of [Mr. Bingley's] temper" (16) and of how Mr. Darcy learns to reject his own "fastidious" "reserve" (11, 16, 171) in favor of a more "general complaisance" (263). Yet, even so, Mr. Darcy resumes "in [Elizabeth's] mother's presence" his former quiet distance (335). The point is for readers as well as characters to choose, and I wish to grant Austen's creations more dignity than has been customary.

After according such respect to Fitzwilliam Darcy, what can one do for Elizabeth Bennet? Despite the fact that the novel hardly ever includes characters' full names, I sometimes put them in as a way of evening out the difference in resonance between "Mr." and "Miss" and of looking at characters' roles as directly as possible. But I take particular pleasure in giving Elizabeth Bennet her last name. I suspect that the critical custom of taking it for granted, of using only her given name even on a first mention — let alone that of abbreviating it to "Lizzy" — may have helped diminish the stature of one of English literature's originals, contributing to the popular fallacy that *Pride and Prejudice* details the Bennet family's struggle to marry off its children rather than its actual story of a revolutionary leading figure's efforts to understand her adventures.

I bring up these problems of address because I know that in the classroom they allow teachers and students to explore issues of personal territory or integrity, inspiring conversation about what deference we grant one another by our choice of names and titles. When do we assume that a fictional character is due a respectful sensitivity to boundaries? How can we make sense of differences in custom and yet live up to our own political principles?

³J. P. Brown makes a similar point in her excellent discussion of the traditional feminist disparagement of Austen: "Doesn't the success of the passage depend rather on our seeing that the 'girl' is a coquette and that Elizabeth, who is now maturely engaged by Darcy's presence in both mind and body, is beyond the vulgarity of such power games?" ("Feminist Depreciation" 311).

⁴Some of the writers who have questioned Austen's feminism are Moers (157), Gilbert and Gubar (154), Monaghan ("Position of Women" 109–10), Butler (*Romantics* 98), and J. Miller (33, 35). Readers who paint Austen as conservative include Duckworth (34), Butler (*Jane Austen* 165), Lovell ("Jane Austen and the Gentry"), Monaghan ("Introduction" 6), and Sales (30).

Critics who present Austen as simultaneously subversive and conservative include Newton, who remarks, "[W]hile I was finding subversive power in Jane Austen [I thought] this can't be! I must be going mad!" (xvii). Ultimately, though, Newton contends that in Austen "the rebellion itself works in the interests of tradition" (79). Newman quotes the Marxist Feminist Literature Collective as commenting that Austen's novels contain "a subversive dimension of which she herself was unaware," yet she argues that Austen "is both reactionary and revolutionary" (707, 706). According to L. Smith, Austen is "pre-feminist," because "her dissatisfaction does not cause an open break with her society." "Female protest is latent rather than overt" (24–25). Poovey adds that "Jane Austen's fundamental ideological position was conservative; her political sympathies were generally Tory," though her novels do not "support so strict a delineation of her sympathies," for they sometimes favor "individualism" (181). C. L. Johnson discusses Austen as one of the "moderately progressive novelists" who "smuggle in their social criticism, as well as the mildest of reformist projects, through various means of indirection" (xxiii–xxiv). Johnson contends that "In *Pride and Prejudice* alone Austen consents to conservative myths, but only in order to possess them and to ameliorate them from within" (93).

Readers who explore the progressivism of Austen's novels include Morgan (*In the Meantime*; "Why There's No Sex"; *Sisters in Time*); Polhemus (*Comic Faith*; *Erotic Faith*); and Evans. Kirkham emphasizes Austen's connections to earlier Enlightenment feminism, particularly Wollstonecraft (*Jane Austen*).

⁵For Gilbert and Gubar, Austen's plots offer a "story as sexist as the taming of the shrew" (155). Their view, widely influential, has been that "dramatizing the necessity of female submission for female survival, Austen's story is especially flattering to male readers because it describes the taming not just of any woman but specifically of a rebellious, imaginative girl who is amorously mastered by a sensible man" (154). Butler claims that "the distinctive turns of [Austen's] plots . . . rebuke individualistic female initiatives, and imply that the consummation of a woman's life lies in marriage to a commanding man" (*Romantics* 98).

On Austen's unions as sellouts, see, for example, Newton, who argues that Elizabeth Bennet "dwindles by degrees into a wife" (55–56).

Newman asserts that "Austen's parodic conclusions measure the distance between novelistic conventions with their culturally coded sentiments and the social realities of patriarchal power" (708). This perspective was originally marked out by Gilbert and Gubar's sense of "duplicity in the 'happy endings' of Austen's novels in which she brings her couples to the brink of bliss in such haste, or with such unlikely coincidences, or with such sarcasm that the entire message seems undercut" (169).

[6]J. Miller speaks of the "clever and imaginative young women in Jane Austen's novels . . . who might . . . have . . . made a life for themselves without a husband. Yet if that had happened to Elizabeth, say, in *Pride and Prejudice*, we would have regarded the novel as a tragic one, and so would Jane Austen" (36). Aside from positing a strange split between Austen's aesthetic principles and her own life, such a fear of singleness does an injustice both to the complexity of Elizabeth's story and to its politics.

[7]Only Austen's most dim-witted figures use even the term "old maid": the Lucas boys, Lydia Bennet (122, 221), and *Emma*'s Harriet Smith (84, 85).

[8]D. A. Miller has argued that Austen's novels are limited by their conformity to "the marriage plot" ("Attitude").

[9]See Mudrick 59, 179; Donovan 123–27; Odmark 102; and Litvak 351–52.

Talking about Talking

Juliet McMaster

In my experience of teaching I include *being* taught, and I was taught *Pride and Prejudice* at school, twice, by different teachers: at the university as an undergraduate and again as a graduate. I have taught the work myself to high school students, to undergraduates, and to graduates. And I have gone on giving papers on it to my peers in the profession whenever opportunity arises, and hearing papers too. That is, I go on teaching and being taught *Pride and Prejudice*, and I haven't come to an end of it yet.

My intimate knowledge of Austen's novel, and the layering of different readings at different phases of my life, have never blunted the pure joy that certain passages always afforded me. Even when I was a schoolgirl with inky fingers, finding my way through a dog-eared school copy, there were moments in my reading when I was inclined to stand up and cheer, rejoicing in language so perfectly matched to character and action, phrases and sentences so clean, exact, inspired. Which moments? They are the ones that make us laugh, but with a laughter raised to the level of keen intellectual delight. I expect we all have our favorites. Mine include Mr. Bennet in the midst of the family uproar over Mr. Collins's proposal, articulating the "unhappy alternative" that faces Elizabeth: "From this day you must be a stranger to one of your parents. —Your mother will never see you again if you do *not* marry Mr. Collins, and I will never see you again if you *do*" (112); Elizabeth confiding her love for Darcy to Jane: "Why, I must confess, that I love him better than I do Bingley. I am afraid you will be angry" (373); Mr. Bennet again, after he has given consent to Elizabeth's marriage: "If any young men come for Mary or Kitty, send them in, for I am quite at leisure" (377). Oh, yes, even then I registered such moments as light, bright, sparkling, witty, brilliant. The achieve of, the mastery of the thing! —I would have said, if I had known my Hopkins in those days.

When I teach *Pride and Prejudice* to first-time readers, my initial object is to put them into the way of experiencing this keen delight for themselves. For that, it might be argued, all they need is a copy of the book. Granted. But as a teacher I choose to dwell on the delight, to focus on it and on what causes it, so that as a class we may savor it together. And that means reading it together — or at least reading a part that will serve as a focus for the exact and witty use of language.

Jane Austen wrote for audiences that commonly experienced their novels as read aloud in a group (Michaelson 65), and it makes sense to try to duplicate some part of that experience in a modern classroom. When the published volumes of *Pride and Prejudice* first came to hand, the Austen family "set fairly at it, and read half the first vol[ume]" to their guest, Miss Benn. Jane Austen had high standards for the performance. In the

second reading she objected to her "mother's too rapid way of getting on:
. . . though she perfectly understands the characters herself, she cannot
speak as they ought" (29 Jan. 1813, 4 Feb. 1813). In an interesting passage
in *Mansfield Park*, Henry Crawford and Edmund discuss the important
subject of reading aloud and lament "the too common neglect of the qualification, the total inattention to it, in the ordinary school system" (339).
Clearly Austen expected a reader to be able to read dramatically, as Henry
Crawford does, and to differentiate in delivery between the voices of different characters.

By way of reversing the too common neglect of the art of reading aloud,
and so of affording my students the opportunity to experience aurally the
fine verbal distinctions in the text, I arrange a reading of the climactic verbal
battle between Elizabeth and Lady Catherine. And to do justice to the
drama of the passage — one of those that are almost exclusively dialogue,
with scarcely even a "said she" to interrupt the characters' speeches — I assign
roles in advance, and even allow time for rehearsal if possible. The text
has already given directions about delivery. In an earlier scene at Rosings,
Lady Catherine has told Elizabeth, "Upon my word, . . . you give your
opinion very decidedly for so young a person" (165–66) — a piquant inti-
mation of what she has yet to discover of the woman who will become her
niece-in-law. And of Lady Catherine herself we have heard that "whatever
she said, was spoken in so authoritative a tone, as marked her self-importance"
(162). If it is my happy fortune to read Lady Catherine myself, I give it
all I've got. My model is Edith Evans's immortal Lady Bracknell in the movie
of *The Importance of Being Earnest*. Lady Bracknell questions, in a voice
trembling with indignation, "A *hhanndd*-bag??" In much the same tone
Lady Catherine can demand, "Are the shades of Pemberley to be thus
polluted?" (357).

A dramatic reading makes audible and vivid the extraordinary verbal
felicities of the exchange. Elizabeth, wielding her finely pointed lance, becomes the St. George to Lady Catherine's dragon, and we can appreciate
and applaud her dexterity in the face of her adversary's cumbersome weight
of authority. "My character has ever been celebrated for its sincerity and
frankness," rumbles Lady Catherine. "I do not pretend to possess equal
frankness with your ladyship," Elizabeth neatly parries. "*You* may ask
questions, which *I* shall not choose to answer" (353, 354).

Through a dramatic reading the students come to focus on the issue of
style in speech and delivery that is so constantly of import to the characters
themselves. Because Elizabeth, Darcy, and the rest are all in some measure
critics of one anothers' discourse, they require the reader to become one
too. Just as Mr. Bennet and Elizabeth, in her similar role as "a studier of
character" (42), provoke a high degree of awareness of character from the
reader, so the commentary on style in speech and writing makes us
connoisseurs of language and delivery. Elizabeth, Mary, and their father

settle down to a regular piece of practical criticism over Mr. Collins's first letter: "There is something very pompous in his stile. . . . Can he be a sensible man, sir?" "No, my dear; I think not," replies Mr. Bennet, and adds words in his own style that reveal his virtues and limitations as fully as Mr. Collins's letter had displayed *his* (64). We know these characters by what they say and by the way they say it, and also by how much they say and what they choose to leave unsaid. Thus the strategy of dramatic reading and subsequent discussion develops student awareness of the characters' use of language as the essential means of characterization. By exploring the various modes of discourse with my students, I induce them to be critics too.

Elizabeth's two suitors are matched and contrasted in various ways — for instance, in their neatly balanced sins of pride on the one hand and servility on the other. In the realm of discourse, one says too little, the other too much; one tends to blame, the other's vocation is praise. Of Darcy, in contrast with the sanguine Bingley, we hear early that "the manner in which they spoke of the Meryton assembly was sufficiently characteristic. Bingley had never met with pleasanter people or prettier girls in his life. . . . Darcy, on the contrary, had seen a collection of people in whom there was little beauty and no fashion" (16). Darcy's niggardliness of speech is an ongoing concern. He gives offense by his stately taciturnity at the assembly, and at the Netherfield ball Elizabeth has to extract conversation from him by reminding him, "It is *your* turn to say something now, Mr. Darcy" (91). At Rosings, he is contrasted with the genial and forthcoming Colonel Fitzwilliam, who "entered into conversation directly with the readiness and ease of a well-bred man, and talked very pleasantly" (171). By now Darcy has recognized and can articulate his failing: "I certainly have not the talent . . . of conversing easily" (175); but he does not yet choose to correct it. Only at Pemberley has he learned to take the necessary pains to enter into conversation directly, like his well-bred cousin. His housekeeper testifies, "Some people call him proud; but . . . it is only because he does not rattle away like other young men" (249). *Now* the implied contrast is with the facile volubility of Wickham, and it is to Darcy's advantage.

Mr. Collins is an important figure in the patterning of discourse in the novel: he is a compulsive talker and writer with a strong (if misguided) sense of the different modes of rhetoric and of their conventions. His speeches and letters function as unconscious parodies of whatever genre he is currently operating in; like other parodies they show a high consciousness of the order and conventions of a form. (In England the thank-you letter has even been given the name of "a Collins.") He has mastered the art of compliment (at least well enough to satisfy Lady Catherine's exacting standards) and has developed an aesthetics of flattery that includes the sophisticated principle of *ars celare artem* (the "art to conceal art"): he makes his calculatedly "elegant compliments" unobtrusive by giving them, he thinks, "as unstudied an air as possible" (68). When it comes to a more demanding genre, the proposal of marriage, he again shows a strong sense of rule and precedent: "[H]e set about it in a very orderly manner, with all the observances which he supposed a regular part of the business" (104). He proceeds according to a mental checklist, enumerating his "reasons for marrying," one, two, and three, dealing with the financial arrangements, and congratulating himself for arriving safely at the end of his list: "And now nothing remains for me but to assure you in the most animated language of the violence of my affection" (105–06). (The word must here serve as substitute for the thing, since it's clear that the violence of Mr. Collins's affection is a purely verbal entity.) Moreover, he assumes that his interlocutor observes a similar set of rules, so that her refusal carries no more weight of reality than his own declaration of love. Her refusal must be "merely words of course" (108).

Although Elizabeth claims on this occasion to be "a rational creature speaking the truth from her heart" (109), she is more like Mr. Collins in her use of language than she would like to admit. The informed student can relish the irony of her claiming, "I am not one of those young ladies . . . who are so daring as to risk their happiness on the chance of being asked a second time" (107), when that is precisely what she does in the case of Darcy's proposal. And the same student can follow up on her characteristic use of language as "merely words of course." For language is both more and less than a means for a rational creature to speak the truth from her heart. For Elizabeth it is a medium for play and wit as much as for direct communication. She too is a parodist — a more conscious one than Mr. Collins — of modes of discourse, with a developed sense of the conventions that belong to each mode. Her parody of ballroom conversation (in the manner of Henry Tilney, in *Northanger Abbey*, who is another expert on language among Austen's characters) when she is dancing with Darcy prompts him to ask, "Do you talk by rule then, while you are dancing?" (91).

Polite conversation on the dance floor is not the only mode she parodies. She has an amused sense, for instance, of the rhetoric of love — "that pure and elevating passion," as she calls it, with deliberate linguistic inflation. She knows that she can't be in love with Wickham by her own down-to-earth feelings and expressions. Far from denouncing Miss King, her rival in his affections, she notes of herself, "I cannot find out that I hate her at all, or that I am in the least unwilling to think her a very good sort of girl. There can be no love in all this" (150). She has inherited her father's distanced and cerebral attitude toward the tendency of lovers to "rant and storm" (377). And she can humorously suggest that a lover's effusions are a kind of catharsis, the vent for emotion and so its cure: "[O]ne good sonnet will starve it entirely away" (45). Even when called on to make a serious response to a proposal, Elizabeth shows herself, like Mr. Collins, highly conscious of the rules pertaining to the appropriate discourse. "In such cases as this, it is, I believe, the established mode to express a sense of obligation for the sentiments avowed" (190). On this occasion, however, though explicitly aware of the convention, she proceeds to infringe it.

Darcy is even more astute in observing Elizabeth's habits of discourse than she is in observing his. He comments at Rosings, "I have had the pleasure of your acquaintance long enough to know, that you find great enjoyment in occasionally professing opinions which in fact are not your own" (174). What he has registered is her use of language as play, cut loose from its utilitarian function as an expression of fact; and he finds it a "pleasure" indeed, and highly attractive. He may be referring to her earlier conversation during the dance at Netherfield:

> "I have always seen a great similarity in the turn of our minds [she tells him, clearly making this up as she goes along]. —We are each of an unsocial, taciturn disposition, unwilling to speak, unless we can expect to say something that will amaze the whole room, and be handed down to posterity with all the eclat of a proverb."
>
> "This is no very striking resemblance of your own character, I am sure," said he. "How near it may be to *mine*, I cannot pretend to say. —*You* think it a faithful portrait undoubtedly."
>
> "I must not decide on my own performance."   (91)

Darcy is quite right in his rather prosy judgment of Elizabeth's playful sally. It is far from being either a measured statement of fact or a striking resemblance to reality. It is, rather, what she calls it: a "performance." And herein lie both Elizabeth's fault and her attraction. She uses language creatively, and she is apt to stray from the strict path of truth in the process. Her "prejudice" against Darcy, so prominent in theme and plot, is largely a verbal matter: she has convinced herself by her own lively but ill-founded witticisms. "I meant to be uncommonly clever in taking so decided a dislike to him, without any reason," she admits. "It is such a spur to one's genius, such an opening for wit to have a dislike of that kind" (225–26). To follow through with my students the sincerity (or otherwise) of her pronouncements is to discover with them that Elizabeth *talked* herself into prejudice.

To Lady Catherine, Elizabeth disavows "frankness," the expression of truths not usually expressed: "I do not pretend to possess equal frankness with your ladyship." But not much later she is almost apologizing to Darcy for being *too* frank: "Yes, you know enough of my *frankness*. . . . After abusing you so abominably to your face, I could have no scruple in abusing you to all your relations" (367). Since Elizabeth uses language for effect as well as for direct expression, one accepts her overt statements at one's peril, at the end of the novel as well as at the beginning. "You must learn some of my philosophy. Think only of the past as its remembrance gives you pleasure," she tells Darcy breezily, when they are safely at accord.

"I cannot give you credit for any philosophy of the kind," he responds staunchly; and he is right (368–69). Elizabeth is at linguistic play again.

Elizabeth's use of language can give a focus for classroom discussion of the feminist issue of whether Austen has "tamed" her heroine, cut away her vitality to fit her into the procrustean patriarchal bed (C. O. Brown 460). It is true that Darcy's letter (the most sustained attempt in the novel at achieving a measured expression of reality, with personal bias and linguistic seductions reduced to the minimum) shakes Elizabeth profoundly and makes her regret her verbal vivacities. But she has not given up her playful speech habits, only reined them in, moving one step nearer to a happy medium between an exact but unimaginative rendering of fact and the fanciful repartee of old. Her response to Jane's question about how long she has loved Darcy — "I believe I must date it from my first seeing his beautiful grounds at Pemberley" (373) — is delightful for its combination of truth and invention. The cynics who argue that marriage in Austen's novels is only a matter of economics read it straight; Jane Bennet, who begs Elizabeth to be serious, hears it as play. We (my students and I, after pursuing Elizabeth's evolution in discourse) are privileged to read it both ways.

Alerted to characterization through modes of discourse, students proceed to find for themselves the wealth of detail on who says what in which way. They learn to recognize ideolects: Mary's "observations of thread-bare morality" (60), Lady Catherine's confirmed habit of "dictating to others" (163), Mr. Collins's obsession for "testifying his respect" (101), Mrs. Bennet's compulsive querulousness and self-contradiction. "I told you in the library, you know," she reminds Elizabeth, "that I should never speak to you again, and you will find me as good as my word" (113). (Elizabeth must have felt that her threat sounded tantalizingly like a promise!) But in either case her words, like Mr. Collins's, are "merely words of course." All these are eager talkers, for whom speech is an activity pleasurable in itself, quite apart from its use as a vehicle for expression.

The characters can be arranged, for purposes of discussion, in a scale according to the relation their words bear to reality. Mr. Collins, the "merely words of course" man, would be at one end of the scale. Although he tells no deliberate lies, language for him is a realm to be developed for its own sake; he believes in the reality of his verbal constructs without feeling the need to measure them against what other people call fact. His bad dancing is a neat reminder of his not being at home in the ordinary physical realm of human engagements: on the dance floor, where other characters in Austen's novels often find perfect self-expression (Tave 1), he is "awkward and solemn, apologising instead of attending, and often moving wrong without being aware of it" (90). Mr. Bennet, for all his superior wit and intelligence, belongs on the scale close to Mr. Collins, for he too can substitute words for reality and live comfortably in that realm, avowing his preference for Wickham among his sons-in-law. Before her reform, Elizabeth is like her father, often using language as separate from the earnest business of life; Lady Catherine, who rejoices in her frankness, believes in a closer relation between language and experience. In fact, as dictator she strives for a causal connection between her edicts and the shape of the world, as when she "determine[s] what weather they were to have on the morrow" (166) or sallies forth among the poor and the discontented to "scold them into harmony and plenty" (169). Darcy, the moral norm in this respect — although his literal-mindedness makes him rather a heavy — is the character whose language most nearly expresses the truth. He has no small talk, but when he needs to express himself, he acts under strong compulsion; there is a direct relation between his feelings and his words. "In vain have I struggled. . . . My feelings will not be repressed," he begins his proposal (189). He goes on to tell Elizabeth rather more than she is glad to hear of his feelings about her family. And his letter, of which he declares, "my character required it to be written and read" (196), is another verbal structure that receives close reading and full critical examination within the text, both on its first reading and in the subsequent, relatively tranquil discussion about it between the writer and the addressee. Darcy admits that though he believed he was calm and reasonable when he composed it, "I am since convinced that it was written in a dreadful bitterness of spirit" (368). The best-laid plans for objective expression give way to subjectivity and the irresistible seductions of style. *Le style, c'est l'homme même*, Jane Austen would agree. (She would, at least, in *Pride and Prejudice. Mansfield Park*, which sides with Fanny's principle against Mary Crawford's style, is another matter.)

It's my endeavor in teaching *Pride and Prejudice* to put my students in touch with the characters' words and their characteristic manner of using them. Reading aloud is a step on the way to such consummation, and full study and discussion follow. In a series of guest lectures on *Pride and Prejudice* that I was invited to give in a high school, I assigned an oral exercise in mimicry. The students each selected a character and composed and delivered their own speech or letter in the person of that character. Darcy's new incarnation ingeniously chose to write the letter — mentioned though not given in full in the novel — in which he announces to Lady Catherine his engagement. The new Miss Bingley indited her own letter to Georgiana Darcy from Netherfield, properly fulsome on the charms and affection of dear Charles, appropriately bitchy on the outrageous behavior of members of the egregious Bennet family, particularly Miss Eliza of the speciously bright eyes. It was a pleasure to watch these teenagers, like chameleons, taking on some coloring from the verdant patterns of Austen's text and learning to recognize the diverse styles in discourse by mimicking them. This was one way of helping them to become even better readers of the novel than the author's mother, able not only perfectly to understand the characters but to "speak as they ought."

CONTRIBUTORS AND SURVEY PARTICIPANTS

The instructors responding to the Modern Language Association's survey on teaching *Pride and Prejudice* have informed and shaped this collection. I am grateful for their generosity and their perceptive comments on teaching the novel. The contributors to the volume have written essays reflecting their commitment both to students and to the novel. Without their work, there would be no book. To them, my thanks.

Brenda K. Ameter
Indiana State University

Harriet Avery
Jane Austen Society of North America

Linda Bamber
Tufts University

Paula Bennett
Southern Illinois University

Jerry Bernhard
Emmanuel College

Pamela S. Bromberg
Simmons College

Julia Prewitt Brown
Boston University

Anne Burley
Towson State University

Virginia Coe
Cabrillo College

Edward Copeland
Pomona College

Patricia Craddock
University of Florida

Marcia McClintock Folsom
Wheelock College

Susan Fraiman
University of Virginia

Dorothy Gonson
Newton South High School

Gloria Sybil Gross
California State University

Jocelyn Harris
Harvard University

Helen Heineman
Framingham State College

Joseph Heininger
Saint Olaf College

Kathleen Hickock
Iowa State University

Carrie Kaplan
Saint Michael's College

Deborah Kaplan
George Mason University

Laurie Kaplan
Goucher College

Catherine Kenney
Mundelein College

Susan Kneedler
Ohio State University

Gene Koppel
University of Arizona

Elizabeth Langland
University of Florida

Jane Langton
Lincoln, MA

David M. Larson
Cleveland State University

Deirdre Lashgari
California State Polytechnic University

Alan Lin
University of California, Santa Barbara

Darrell Mansell
Dartmouth College

Mary Mason
Emmanuel College

John McAleer
Boston College

Fleming McClelland
Northeast Louisiana University

Karen McGuire
Pasadena City College

Juliet McMaster
University of Alberta

Marylea Meyersohn
City College of New York

Helena Michie
Brandeis University

Kenneth L. Moler
University of Nebraska

Anne Waldron Neumann
Ohio State University

Ruth Perry
Massachusetts Institute of Technology

Paul Pickrel
Smith College

Richard H. Rupp
Appalachian State University

Ruth Saxon
Mills College

William R. Siebenschuh
Case Western Reserve University

Elton E. Smith
University of South Florida

Johanna M. Smith
University of Texas, Arlington

Maaja A. Stewart
Tulane University

Bruce Stovel
University of Alberta

Barbara W. Swords
Elmhurst College

James Thompson
University of North Carolina,
   Chapel Hill

Ian Watt
Stanford University

Barbara Welch
Westfield State College

Judith Wilt
Boston College

Cynthia Griffin Wolfe
Massachusetts Institute of
   Technology

Susan J. Wolfson
Rutgers University

WORKS CITED AND CONSULTED

Adams, Samuel, and Sarah Adams. *The Complete Servant*. London, 1825.

Auerbach, Nina. *Communities of Women: An Idea in Fiction*. Cambridge: Harvard UP, 1978.

———. "Jane Austen and Romantic Imprisonment." Monaghan, *Social Context* 9–27.

Austen, Caroline. *My Aunt Jane Austen: A Memoir*. New York: Jane Austen Soc., 1952.

———. *Reminiscences of Caroline Austen*. New York: Jane Austen Soc., 1986.

Austen, Henry. "Biographical Notice." *Northanger Abbey* and *Persuasion*. London: 1818. Rev. ed. 1832. New York: Penguin, 1965. 29–34.

Austen, Jane. *Emma*. Ed. R. W. Chapman. 3rd ed. London: Oxford UP, 1932, 1965.

———. *Jane Austen: Selected Letters 1796–1817*. Ed. R. W. Chapman. Oxford: Oxford UP, 1955. Rpt., with introd. by Marilyn Butler, 1985.

———. *Jane Austen's Letters to Her Sister Cassandra and Others*. Ed. R. W. Chapman. 2nd ed. London: Oxford UP, 1952.

———. *Mansfield Park*. Ed. R. W. Chapman. 3rd ed. New York: Oxford UP, 1932, 1966.

———. *Minor Works*. Ed. R. W. Chapman. Oxford: Oxford UP, 1954. Rev. ed. 1963.

———. *Northanger Abbey* and *Persuasion*. Ed. R. W. Chapman. 3rd ed. Oxford: Oxford UP, 1933. Rev. ed. 1965.

———. *Pride and Prejudice*. Afterword by Joann Morse. New York: Signet, 1961.

———. *Pride and Prejudice*. Ed. Donald J. Gray. Norton Critical ed. New York: Norton, 1966.

———. *Pride and Prejudice*. Ed. R. W. Chapman. 1932, 1967. London: Oxford UP, 1976.

———. *Pride and Prejudice*. Introduction by Mark Schorer. Riverside ed. Boston: Houghton, 1956.

———. *Pride and Prejudice*. Introduction by Tony Tanner. Harmondsworth, Eng.: Penguin, 1972.

———. *Sense and Sensibility*. Ed. R. W. Chapman. 3rd ed. New York: Oxford UP, 1933, 1967.

Austen-Leigh, J. E. *A Memoir of Jane Austen*. London: 1865, 1870, 1871; Oxford: Clarendon, 1926. Rpt. in *Persuasion*. New York: Penguin, 1965.

Austen-Leigh, William, and Richard Arthur Austen. *Jane Austen: Her Life and Letters—A Family Record*. New York: Dutton, 1913.

Austin, J. L. *How to Do Things with Words*. London: Oxford UP, 1962.

Babb, Howard. *Jane Austen's Novels: The Fabric of Dialogue*. Columbus: Ohio State UP, 1962.

Bennet, Elizabeth. *Emily; or, The Wife's First Error* [and] *Beauty and Ugliness; or, The Father's Prayer and the Mother's Prophesy.* 2 tales. 4 vols. London, 1819.

Booth, Wayne C. *The Rhetoric of Fiction.* Chicago: U of Chicago P, 1961.

———. *A Rhetoric of Irony.* Chicago: U of Chicago P, 1974.

Brower, Reuben A. "The Controlling Hand: Jane Austen and *Pride and Prejudice*." *Scrutiny* 13 (1945–46): 99–111.

———. " 'Light and Bright and Sparkling': Irony and Fiction in *Pride and Prejudice*." *The Fields of Light.* Oxford: Oxford UP, 1951. Rpt. in Watt 62–75.

Brown, Carole O. "Dwindling into a Wife: A Jane Austen Heroine Grows Up." *International Journal of Women's Studies* 5.5 (1982): 460–69.

Brown, Julia Prewitt. "The Feminist Depreciation of Jane Austen: A Polemical Reading." *Novel* 23 (1990): 303–13.

———. *Jane Austen's Novels: Social Change and Literary Form.* Cambridge: Harvard UP, 1979.

———. *A Reader's Guide to the Nineteenth-Century English Novel.* New York: Macmillan, 1985.

Brownstein, Rachel M. *Becoming a Heroine: Reading about Women in Novels.* London: Viking, 1982.

Bruce, Anthony. *The Purchase System in the British Army, 1660–1871.* London: Royal Historical Soc., 1980.

Brunton, Mary. *Self-Control. A Novel.* 3 vols. Edinburgh, 1811.

Burke, Henry G. "Seeking Jane in Foreign Tongues." *Persuasions* 7 (1985): 17–20.

Burlin, Katrin R. " 'Pictures of Perfection' at Pemberley: Art in *Pride and Prejudice*." Todd, *Jane Austen* 155–67.

Burney, Frances. *Cecilia; or, Memoirs of an Heiress.* Ed. Peter Sabor and Margaret Anne Doody. Oxford: Oxford UP, 1988.

———. *Evelina; or, A Young Lady's Entrance into the World.* Ed. Edward A. Bloom. Oxford: Clarendon–Oxford UP, 1968.

———. *The Wanderer; or, Female Difficulties.* Winchester: Pandora, 1988.

Burrows, J. F. *Computation into Criticism: A Study of Jane Austen's Novels and an Experiment in Method.* London: Oxford UP, 1987.

———. "A Measure of Excellence: Modes of Comparison in *Pride and Prejudice*." *Sydney Studies in English* 5 (1979–80): 38–59.

Butler, Marilyn. *Jane Austen and the War of Ideas.* London: Oxford UP, 1975.

———. *Romantics, Rebels, and Reactionaries: English Literature and Its Background 1760–1830.* New York: Oxford UP, 1982.

Caldor, Jenni. *Women and Marriage in Victorian Fiction.* New York: Oxford UP, 1976.

Cecil, Lord David. *A Portrait of Jane Austen.* New York: Hill, 1978.

Chapman, R. W. *Jane Austen: Facts and Problems.* London: Oxford UP, 1948.

Charlton, Mary. *The Wife and the Mistress.* 4 vols. London, 1802.

Cohn, Dorrit. *Transparent Minds: Narrative Modes for Presenting Consciousness in Fiction.* Princeton: Princeton UP, 1978.

Copeland, Edward. "Jane Austen and the Consumer Revolution." Grey, Litz, and Southam 77–92.

———. "What's a Competence? Jane Austen, Her Sister Novelists, and the 5%'s." *Modern Language Studies* 14 (1979): 161–68.

Craik, W. A. *Jane Austen in Her Time*. London: Nelson, 1969.

Donovan, Robert Alan. "The Mind of Jane Austen." Weinsheimer 109–27.

Doody, Margaret Anne. "George Eliot and the Eighteenth Century Novel." *Nineteenth Century Fiction* 35 (1980): 260–91.

———. "Jane Austen's Reading." Grey, Litz, and Southam 347–63.

Duckworth, Alistair M. *The Improvement of the Estate: A Study of Jane Austen's Novels*. Baltimore: Johns Hopkins UP, 1971.

Duffy, Joseph. "Criticism, 1814–1870." Grey, Litz, and Southam 93–101.

Evans, Mary. *Jane Austen and the State*. New York: Tavistock, 1987.

Farrer, Reginald. "Jane Austen, *ob*. July 18, 1817." *Quarterly Review* 228 (1917): 1–30.

Fergus, Jan. *Jane Austen: A Literary Life*. New York: St. Martin's, 1991.

———. *Jane Austen and the Didactic Novel*. Totowa: Barnes, 1983.

Fielding, Henry. *The History of Tom Jones, a Foundling*. 1749. Ed. Sheridan Baker. New York: Norton, 1973.

Forster, E. M. *Howards End*. New York: Random, 1921.

George, Mary D. *English Social Life in the Eighteenth Century*. London: Sheldon, 1923.

Gilbert, Sandra M., and Susan Gubar. *The Madwoman in the Attic: The Woman Writer and the Nineteenth Century Literary Imagination*. New Haven: Yale UP, 1979.

Gilligan, Carol. *In a Different Voice: Psychological Theory and Women's Development*. Cambridge: Harvard UP, 1982.

Gilson, David. *A Bibliography of Jane Austen*. Oxford: Oxford UP, 1982.

———. "Editions and Publishing History." Grey, Litz, and Southam 135–39.

Gisborne, Thomas. *An Inquiry into the Duties of the Female Sex*. 4th ed. London, 1799.

Glover, Michael. *Wellington's Army in the Peninsula, 1808–1814*. London: David, 1972.

Gooneratne, Yasmine. *Jane Austen*. Cambridge: Cambridge UP, 1970.

Greene, Donald J. "Jane Austen and the Peerage." *PMLA* 68 (1953): 1017–31.

———. "The Myth of Limitation." Weinsheimer 142–75.

Grey, J. David, A. Walton Litz, and Brian Southam, eds. *The Jane Austen Companion*. New York: Macmillan, 1986.

Grice, H. P. "Logic and Conversation." *Syntax and Semantics*. Ed. Peter Cole and Jerry L. Morgan. Vol. 3. New York: Academic, 1975. 41–58.

Griffiths, Eric. *The Printed Voice of Victorian Poetry*. London: Oxford UP, 1989.

Habermas, Jürgen. *Communication and the Evolution of Society*. Trans. Thomas McCarthy. Boston: Beacon, 1979.

———. "On Systematically Distorted Communication." *Inquiry* 13 (1970): 205–18.

Halperin, John. *Jane Austen: Bicentennial Essays*. Cambridge: Cambridge UP, 1975.

———. *The Life of Jane Austen*. Baltimore: Johns Hopkins UP,1984.

Harding, D. W. "Regulated Hatred: An Aspect of the Work of Jane Austen." Watt 166–79.

Harris, Jocelyn. *Jane Austen's Art of Memory*. Cambridge: Cambridge UP, 1989.

Heilbrun, Carolyn G. *Writing a Woman's Life*. New York: Norton, 1988.

Helm, W. H. *Jane Austen and Her Country-House Comedy*. New York: Lane, 1910.

Hennelly, Mark M., Jr. "*Pride and Prejudice*: The Eyes Have It." Todd, *Jane Austen* 187–207.

Holbrook, David. "What Was Mr. Darcy Worth?" *Cambridge Review* 105 (1984): 219–21.

Honan, Park. *Jane Austen: Her Life*. London: Athlone, 1986; New York: St. Martin's, 1987.

Howard, Lord William. *Selections from the Household Books of the Lord William Howard of Naworth Castle*. Durham, 1878.

Jameson, Fredric. *The Political Unconscious: Narrative as a Socially Symbolic Act*. Ithaca: Cornell UP, 1981.

Jenkins, Elizabeth. *Jane Austen: A Biography*. London: Gollancz, 1938.

Johnson, Claudia L. *Jane Austen: Women, Politics, and the Novel*. Chicago: U of Chicago P, 1988.

Johnson, Samuel. "Alexander Pope." *Lives of the English Poets*. Vol. 2. London: Dent, 1925. 143–243. 2 vols.

Kaplan, Deborah. *Jane Austen among Women*. Baltimore: Johns Hopkins UP, 1992.

Kirkham, Margaret. "Jane Austen and Contemporary Feminism." Grey, Litz, and Southam 154–59.

———. *Jane Austen, Feminism, and Fiction*. Totowa: Barnes, 1983.

Lanser, Susan. "No Connections Subsequent: Jane Austen's World of Sisterhood." *The Sister Bond: A Feminist View of a Timeless Connection*. Ed. Toni McNaron. New York: Pergamon, 1985. 51–65.

Lascelles, Mary. *Jane Austen and Her Art*. Oxford: Clarendon–Oxford UP, 1939.

Laski, Marghanita. *Jane Austen and Her World*. New York: Viking, 1969.

Leavis, F. R. *The Great Tradition: George Eliot, Henry James, Joseph Conrad*. New York: Steward, 1948.

Leavis, Q. D. "A Critical Theory of Jane Austen's Writings." *Scrutiny* 10 (1941–42): 61–67; 12 (1944–45): 104–19. Rpt. in Austen, *Pride and Prejudice* (ed. Gray), 293–305.

Le Faye, Deirdre. *Jane Austen: A Family Record*. London: British Library, 1989.

Lefroy, Anna Austen. *Jane Austen's Sanditon: A Continuation by Her Niece Together with "Reminiscences of Aunt Jane."* Ed. Mary Gaither Marshall. Chicago: Chiron, 1983.

Liddell, Robert. *The Novels of Jane Austen*. London: Longman, 1963.

Litvak, Joseph. "The Infection of Acting: Theatricals and Theatricality in *Mansfield Park*." *ELH* 53 (1986): 331–55.

Litz, A. Walton. "Criticism, 1940–1983." Grey, Litz, and Southam 110–17.

——. *Jane Austen: A Study of Her Artistic Development.* New York: Oxford UP, 1965.

——. "Plot Summaries." Grey, Litz, and Southam 333–41.

Lovell, Terry. *Consuming Fiction.* London: Verso, 1987.

——. "Jane Austen and the Gentry: A Study in Literature and Ideology." *Sociology of Literature: Applied Studies* 26 Apr. 1978: 15–37.

Luckcock, James. *Hints for Practical Economy.* Birmingham, 1834.

Mansell, Darrel. *The Novels of Jane Austen: An Interpretation.* New York: Barnes, 1973.

Mansfield, Katherine. *Novels and Novelists.* Ed. J. Middleton Murry. London: 1930; Boston: Beacon, 1959.

Marishall, Jean. *A Series of Letters.* 2 vols. Edinburgh, 1789.

Mathews, Mary. "Jane Austen: *Pride and Prejudice*." *Social Education* 42 (1978): 346–48.

McKendrick, Neil, et al. *The Birth of a Consumer Society.* London: Europa, 1982.

McMaster, Juliet. *Jane Austen's Achievement.* London: Macmillan, 1976.

Michaelson, Patricia Howell. "Reading *Pride and Prejudice*." *Eighteenth-Century Fiction* 3.1 (1990): 65–76.

Miller, D. A. "Austen's Attitude." Austen's Manner, spec. sess., MLA Convention. San Francisco, 29 Dec. 1991.

——. *Narrative and Its Discontents: Problems of Closure in the Traditional Novel.* Princeton: Princeton UP, 1981.

Miller, Jane. *Women Writing about Men.* London: Virago, 1986.

Modert, Jo, ed. *Jane Austen's Manuscript Letters in Facsimile.* Carbondale: Southern Illinois UP, 1990.

Moers, Ellen. *Literary Women.* New York: Doubleday, 1976.

Moler, Kenneth L. " 'The Balm of Sisterly Consolation': *Pride and Prejudice* and *Sir Charles Grandison*." *Notes and Queries* 30 (1983): 216–17.

——. *Jane Austen's Art of Allusion.* Lincoln: U of Nebraska P, 1968, 1977.

——. Pride and Prejudice: *A Study in Artistic Economy.* Boston: Twayne, 1988.

Monaghan, David, ed. Introduction. *Jane Austen in a Social Context.* Totowa: Barnes, 1981.

——. "Jane Austen and the Position of Women." Monaghan, *Social Context* 105–21.

——. *Jane Austen: Structure and Social Vision.* London: Macmillan, 1980.

Mooneyham, Laura G. *Romance, Language, and Education in Jane Austen's Novels.* New York: St. Martin's, 1988.

Morgan, Susan. *In the Meantime: Character and Perception in Jane Austen's Fiction.* Chicago: U of Chicago P, 1980.

——. *Sisters in Time: Imagining Gender in Nineteenth Century British Fiction.* Oxford: Oxford UP, 1989.

———. "Why There's No Sex in Jane Austen's Fiction." *Studies in the Novel* 19 (1987): 346–56.

Morse, Joann. Afterword. *Pride and Prejudice*. New York: Signet, 1961. 327–32.

Mudrick, Marvin. *Jane Austen: Irony as Defense and Discovery*. Princeton: Princeton UP, 1952.

Nardin, Jane. "Jane Austen and the Problems of Leisure." Monaghan, *Social Context* 122–42.

———. *Those Elegant Decorums: The Concept of Propriety in Jane Austen's Novels*. New York: State U of New York P, 1973.

Neale, R. S. "Class and Class Consciousness in Early Nineteenth Century England: Three Classes or Five?" *History and Class: Essential Readings in Theory and Interpretation*. Ed. Neale. Oxford: Blackwell, 1983. 143–64.

Newman, Karen. "Can This Marriage Be Saved: Jane Austen Makes Sense of an Ending." *ELH* 50 (1983): 692–710.

Newton, Judith Lowder. *Women, Power, and Subversion: Social Strategies in British Fiction, 1778–1860*. Athens: U of Georgia P, 1981.

Nichols, Michael P. *Family Therapy: Concepts and Methods*. New York: Gardner, 1984.

Nicolson, Harold. Address. *Collected Reports of the Jane Austen Society: 1949–1965*. Introd. Elizabeth Jenkins. London: Dawson, 1967. 94–103.

———. *Good Behaviour: Being a Study of Certain Types of Civility*. London: Constable, 1955.

Nicolson, Nigel. "Jane Austen and the English Class System." *Southwest Review* 70.2 (1985): 173–76.

Odmark, John. *An Understanding of Jane Austen's Novels: Character, Value, and Ironic Perspective*. Oxford: Blackwell, 1981.

Parsons, Eliza. *The Castle of Wolfenbach*. 1793. Ed. Devendra P. Varma. London: Folio, 1968.

Perkin, Harold. *The Origins of Modern English Society: 1780–1880*. London: Routledge, 1969.

Perry, Ruth. "Interrupted Friendships in Jane Austen's *Emma*." *Tulsa Studies in Women's Literature* 5.2 (1986): 185–202.

Petersen, Per Serritslev, ed. "On the First Sentence of *Pride and Prejudice*: A Critical Discussion of the Theory and Practice of Literary Interpretation." Spec. issue of *Dolphin* (Feb. 1979): 5–101.

Polhemus, Robert M. *Comic Faith: The Great Tradition from Austen to Joyce*. Chicago: U of Chicago P, 1980.

———. *Erotic Faith: Being in Love from Austen to Lawrence*. Chicago: U of Chicago P, 1980.

Poovey, Mary. *The Proper Lady and the Woman Writer: Ideology as Style in the Works of Mary Wollstonecraft, Mary Shelley, and Jane Austen*. Women in Culture and Society. Chicago: U of Chicago P, 1984.

Radcliffe, Ann. *The Mysteries of Udolpho*. 1794. Oxford: Oxford UP, 1970.

Rich, Adrienne. "Compulsory Heterosexuality and Lesbian Existence." 1980. *Blood, Bread, and Poetry: Selected Prose, 1979–1985.* New York: Norton, 1986. 23–75.

Richardson, Samuel. *The History of Sir Charles Grandison.* 1753–54. Ed. and introd. Jocelyn Harris. 3 parts. New York: Oxford UP, 1972, 1986.

Roberts, Warren. *Jane Austen and the French Revolution.* New York: St. Martin's, 1979.

Robinson, Lillian. "Why Marry Mr. Collins?" *Sex, Class and Culture.* Bloomington: Indiana UP, 1978. 178–99.

Robinson, Maria Elizabeth. *The Shrine of Bertha: A Novel in a Series of Letters.* 2 vols. London, 1794.

Roche, Regina Maria. *The Children of the Abbey: A Tale.* 1798. 2nd American ed. 2 vols. New York, 1805.

Roth, Barry. *An Annotated Bibliography of Jane Austen Studies, 1973–1983.* Charlottesville: UP of Virginia, 1985.

———. "Confessions of a Jane Austen Teacher." *Focus* 5 (1978): 25–29.

Roth, Barry, and Joel Weinsheimer. *An Annotated Bibliography of Jane Austen Studies, 1952–1972.* Charlottesville: UP of Virginia, 1973.

Sales, Roger. *English Literature in History, 1780–1830: Pastoral and Politics.* New York: St. Martin's, 1983.

Satz, Martha. "An Epistemological Understanding of *Pride and Prejudice*: Humility and Objectivity." Todd, *Jane Austen* 171–86.

Schorer, Mark. Introduction. *Pride and Prejudice.* Riverside ed. Boston: Houghton, 1956. v–xxi.

———. "Pride Unprejudiced." *Kenyon Review* 18 (1956): 72–91.

Sheridan, Frances. *Memoirs of Miss Sidney Bidulph.* 3 vols. London, 1761.

Smith, Adam. *Theory of Moral Sentiments.* London: Strahan, 1790.

Smith, Leroy W. *Jane Austen and the Drama of Women.* New York: St. Martin's, 1983.

Southam, Brian C. "Criticism, 1870–1940." Grey, Litz, and Southam 102–09.

———. *Jane Austen's Literary Manuscripts.* London: Oxford UP, 1964.

———. *Jane Austen: The Critical Heritage.* London: Routledge; New York: Barnes, 1968.

———. "Janeites and Anti-Janeites." Grey, Litz, and Southam 237–43.

Spacks, Patricia Meyer. *The Female Imagination: A Literary and Psychological Investigation of Women's Writing.* New York: Knopf, 1975.

———. "Female Resources: Epistles, Plot, and Power." *Persuasions* 9 (1987): 88–98.

———. "The Novel as Ethical Paradigm." *Novel* 21 (1988): 181–88.

Spring, David. "Interpreters of Jane Austen's Social World: Literary Critics and Historians." Todd, *Jane Austen* 53–72.

Stewart, Garrett. "Teaching Prose Fiction: Some 'Instructive' Styles." *College English* 37 (1975–76): 373–401.

Stone, Lawrence. *The Family, Sex and Marriage: England, 1500–1800.* London: Weidenfeld, 1977.

Stubbs, Michael. *Discourse Analysis: The Sociolinguistic Analysis of Natural Language*. Chicago: U of Chicago P, 1983.

Sulloway, Alison G. *Jane Austen and the Province of Womanhood*. Philadelphia: U of Pennsylvania P, 1989.

Tanner, Tony. Introduction. *Pride and Prejudice*. Harmondsworth, Eng.: Penguin, 1972.

———. *Jane Austen*. Cambridge: Harvard UP, 1986.

———. "Knowledge and Opinion: *Pride and Prejudice*." *Jane Austen* 103–41.

Tave, Stuart. *Some Words of Jane Austen*. Chicago: U of Chicago P, 1973.

Thompson, James. *Between Self and World: The Novels of Jane Austen*. University Park: Pennsylvania State UP, 1988.

———. "Jane Austen's Clothing: Things, Property, and Materialism in Her Novels." *Studies in Eighteenth-Century Culture* 13 (1984): 217–31.

Todd, Janet, ed. *Jane Austen: New Perspectives*. New Series 3. New York: Holmes, 1983.

———. *Women's Friendship in Literature*. New York: Columbia UP, 1980.

Treitel, G. H. "Legal Puzzles in Jane Austen's Works." Annual General Meeting of the Jane Austen Society. 1986.

Trilling, Lionel. "Why We Read Jane Austen." *TLS* 5 Mar. 1976: 250–52.

Trusler, John. *The Economist*. London, 1774.

Van Ghent, Dorothy. *The English Novel: Form and Function*. New York: Holt, 1953.

Wagner, Anthony. *English Genealogy*. Oxford: Oxford UP, 1972.

Wallace, Robert K. *Jane Austen and Mozart: Classical Equilibrium in Fiction and Music*. Athens: U of Georgia P, 1983.

Watt, Ian. *Jane Austen: A Collection of Critical Essays*. Englewood Cliffs: Prentice, 1963.

Weinsheimer, Joel, ed. *Jane Austen Today*. Athens: U of Georgia P, 1975.

White, Edward M. "Freedom Is Restraint: The Pedagogical Problem of Jane Austen." *San Jose Studies* 2 (1976): 84–90.

Williams, Raymond. *The Country and the City*. New York: Oxford UP, 1973.

———. *The English Novel from Dickens to Lawrence*. London: Hogarth, 1984.

Wollstonecraft, Mary. *Collected Letters*. Ed. Ralph M. Wardle. Ithaca: Cornell UP, 1979.

———. *A Vindication of the Rights of Woman*. *English Romantic Poetry and Prose*. Ed. Russell Noyes. Oxford: Oxford UP, 1956.

———. *A Vindication of the Rights of Woman*. New York: Knopf, 1992.

———. *The Wrongs of Woman*. Ed. Gary Kelly. Oxford: Oxford UP, 1976.

Woolf, Virginia. *A Room of One's Own*. London: Hogarth, 1929.

Wright, Andrew. "Dramatizations of the Novels." Grey, Litz, and Southam 120–30.

INDEX